The Compilation of Romans

The Compilation of Romans

Paul's Four Letters for the Romans

YOSEOP RA

WIPF & STOCK · Eugene, Oregon

THE COMPILATION OF ROMANS
Paul's Four Letters for the Romans

Copyright © 2025 Yoseop Ra. All rights reserved. Except for brief quotations in critical publications or reviews, no part of this book may be reproduced in any manner without prior written permission from the publisher. Write: Permissions, Wipf and Stock Publishers, 199 W. 8th Ave., Suite 3, Eugene, OR 97401.

Wipf & Stock
An Imprint of Wipf and Stock Publishers
199 W. 8th Ave., Suite 3
Eugene, OR 97401

www.wipfandstock.com

PAPERBACK ISBN: 979-8-3852-3927-6
HARDCOVER ISBN: 979-8-3852-3928-3
EBOOK ISBN: 979-8-3852-3929-0

VERSION NUMBER 02/21/25

Unless otherwise noted, Scripture quotations contained herein are from the HOLY BIBLE, NEW INTERNATIONAL VERSION® Copyright © 1973, 1978, 1984 by International Bible Society. Used by permission of Zondervan Publishing House. All rights reserved. The "NIV" and "New International Version" trademarks are registered in the United States Patent and Trademark Office by International Bible Society. Use of either trademark requires the permission of International Bible Society.

Dedicated to
my wife, Kyoungeun,
with thanks in God.

Contents

Preface | ix

Prologue | 1

I   Rom(A) | 30

II Rom(B) | 81

III Rom(C) | 136

IV Rom(D) | 191

Epilogue | 234

Bibliography | 239

Scripture Index | 241

Preface

PAUL IS THE MOST important figure in the formation of Christianity. Having identified Jesus as Christ, he developed an understanding of Christianity. In this respect, he can be said to be the founder of Christianity. Among his epistles, Romans has received the most attention because it has been considered a doctrinal book that formed the basic instructions of Christianity. In addition, the relationship between Christ and the Law has been written in the most developed form. Therefore, in order to understand Paul's faith and thoughts, it is essential to deal with the letters sent to the Roman church.

Interest in Romans did not arise suddenly to me. This goes back to 1989 when I was pursuing a Th.M. degree in New Testament at the Princeton Theological Seminary. I was given an assignment to study the structure of Romans and submit it. I was quite embarrassed because it was beyond my ability to analyze properly. Afterwards, I gave up taking the Romans class and stopped paying attention to Romans. However, I realized that Romans was no longer something that could be avoided in order to know the nature of Christianity.

Having received the doctorate from the Joint PhD Program of the University of Denver and the Iliff School of Theology in 1997, I have written several books on Paul's epistles in Korean. First of all, *Galatians: The Gospel of the Cross,* was published in 1999. Afterwards, in 2018, *Paul's Six Letters for the Corinthians* and *Paul's Four Letters for the Romans* were presented to the Korean theologians. I then revealed the process by which Paul's thoughts were developed in a book titled *The Formation of Paul's Theology*. This was improved hermeneutically, translated into English, and published with the title *Paul, the Founder of Christianity* in the United States in 2021. However, in order to further solidify the process of Paul's theology, it was necessary to inform Western theologians of my research on the compilation of Romans. Accordingly, I developed hermeneutically and translated what I had written in Korean into English and published it under the title *The Compilation of Romans*. With this, I would like to conclude my exploration of the essence of faith presented by Paul. What I studied was sufficient to reveal my own views on the beginning and development of Christianity to the New Testament scholars of world.

It is necessary to reconstruct the circumstances in which Romans was written. If this task is overlooked, Romans will end up being a doctrinal document. However, if we can separate the four letters compiled into Romans and find out the circumstances in which each letter was written, the purpose of Paul writing them will be revealed. Only then will Romans be reborn as a text full of life. Since this book was written for this very purpose, it requires careful study and critique.

As reflected in Romans, it is clear that Paul had a grand plan when he sent the first letter to the Roman church. A missionary trip to Spain had been planned to preach the gospel, which was considered the western end of the world at that time. Paul asked the members of the Roman church, which he had not founded, for financial support to complete the mission to Spain; however, the Romans did not seem to be pleased with his request. Accordingly, he continued to send letters in order to achieve his goal, probably four letters in total. They appear to have been compiled into the present form of Romans.

The claim that Paul sent four letters to the Roman church is absolutely new to the Pauline scholars. It was possible for me as a follow-up to the discovery that 1 Corinthians and 2 Corinthians each consisted of three letters. Redaction-critical and the composition-critical approaches will show that Romans can be divided into four letters. Having considered the theological developments reflected in the four letters, the sequence of Paul's letters to the Roman church will be revealed. This will show how Paul developed the theological thoughts over time.

In this book, a theological interpretation of each verse of Romans is not the main concern. Rather, I will focus on distinguishing the four letters compiled into the present form of Romans and then discuss the position of each verse in the context in which each letter was written. Accordingly, the interpretations of previous scholars will rarely be cited. The process how Paul developed the theological thought will be pursued in his relationship with the Romans. As a result, it will be shown how

PREFACE

Romans was formed as time went by. My study is expected to be a refreshing shock to many scholars.

Some additional explanations are necessary. When referring to the biblical text in this book, the abbreviation will not be used in the case of Romans. The scriptural reference indicated only by numbers refers to the text of Romans. For other books, the abbreviation and numbers will be indicated. As I noted beforehand, we will not find much of the opinions of other scholars. Accordingly, the bibliography will be organized in a minimal form. Rather, footnotes will appear in a developed form.

Many people contributed to the publication of this book. First, I would like to thank Dr. Taeyeon Cho for mentioning the possibility that Romans consists of three letters. His advice made me take another look at Romans. I thank to Dr. Daniel S. Kim DDS and his wife Stella H. Cheon Kim for providing financial funds, so that this book can be published in the United States. I dedicate this book to my wife, Kyoungeun, who devoted her life to me in God.

October 27, 2024
Yoseop Ra

Prologue

THE PROLOGUE WILL COVER directions for reading this book. As a result, readers will understand more easily in advance what I am trying to demonstrate in this book. Anyway, in the prologue, I would like to show that the letter Romans was formed through a more complicated process than readers generally think. In its present form, Romans appears to be a composite of four short letters. Accordingly, I want to lead readers in pursuing what Paul originally wanted to say in each letter to the Romans, the members of the Roman church.

The letter Romans consists of a total of sixteen chapters. In its present form, Romans is a long letter, along with 1 Corinthians and 2 Corinthians. As in the case of 1 Corinthians and 2 Corinthians, the flow of content is interrupted in many places in Romans. This suggests that just as 1 Corinthians and 2 Corinthians each consisted of at least three short letters, Romans is possibly composed of four short letters. In addition, having considered the circumstances at the time of writing in the mid-first century CE, such a long letter on papyrus or parchment was not realistic. This kind of factor makes it possible to access to Romans from a fragmentary perspective.

The prologue will consist of four parts. First, the fragmentary theories presented by scholars regarding the compilation of Romans will be introduced. Although they are not as much as generally expected, I will show the possibility of a different interpretation by introducing a couple of views on the compilation of Romans. Second, methodology will be discussed. A redaction-critical analysis of Romans will be discussed, as well as a composition-critical one. In addition, the history of ideas will be studied. This will serve to place related texts in terms of theme according to their chronological order. Third, critical analysis of each text will be conducted in order to separate literary layers embedded in the present form of Romans. Ultimately, this work will reveal the principles on which Romans was compiled. Fourth, a summary description of each letter will be presented. This will show the main content or character of each letter. Then, the prologue will complete its mission to make readers anticipate my interpretation of Romans.

1. FRAGMENTARY ANALYSIS

Critical scholars have often questioned the unity of Romans. First of all, this was supported by the fact that it was considerably longer than the letters of the time. Of course, the letter may have been long; however, the more important matter is that the flow of content is frequently interrupted. This has led scholars to claim that Romans is a collection of at least two letters. However, we will reach the conclusion that it is a composite of several letters.

First of all, there are many scholars who argue for the unity of Romans. Most scholars regard Romans as a coherent letter and argue for its integrity because each text has its proper role in its current location.[1] The theory of the compilation of Romans did not gain much force, even among the critical scholars. Most Christians think that its compilation downgrades the authority of the Bible. In addition, they avoid dealing with it because distinguishing the editorial work is too complicated an issue. Nevertheless, it cannot be overlooked that the flow of content is often interrupted when reading Romans carefully. As a result, since doubts arise about the unity of Romans, the fragmentary theory is bound to be raised for its compilation.

The view that Romans consists of two or more letters has often been suggested. According to Brown, very few scholars argue that the two letters were combined to form Romans; however, he does not discuss in detail how the two letters are combined.[2] There is a view that chapter 16 was added later. It is, however, to be noted that the editorial job is found between 16:1–16 and 16:17–20 because they reflect different genres of writing. While the former consists of friendly greetings, the latter is a reprimand. The latter is difficult to view as following part of the former which consists of warm greetings supposed to have been written in the first letter sent to the Roman church. The fact that friendly greetings

---

1. Cf. Fitzmyer, *Romans*, 55–67; and Beker, *Paul*, 60–61, 94.
2. Brown, *Introduction*, 560, 575–76.

reappear in 16:21-24 indicates the interruption of 16:17-20 in between surrounding texts. Accordingly, it is necessary to consider that chapter 16 is a combination of at least two letters written in different period.

Some scholars have suggested that chapters 9-11 were probably added later.[3] This has received the most support because the relationship between the Law and faith, which was dominantly mentioned in chapters 1-8, is relatively dealt with little in chapters 9-11. Rather, issues between Jews and gentiles are dominantly treated. This implies that Paul was in a different situation when he wrote chapters 9-11 than when he wrote chapters 1-8. In addition, the fact that Paul strengthened the apologetics in chapters 9-11 makes readers think that this was written after he had faced a certain critique from the Romans. Moreover, chapters 9-11 are considered to be an appropriate length to compose a letter. For instance, in case of Philemon and Galatians, which show unity among Paul's authentic letters, each show an appropriate amount of personal and public letter each. The details described above show the possibility that chapters 9-11 originated from a different letter than the letter to which chapters 1-8 belonged.

Having based on the foregoing discussion, various opinions have been presented in connection with the compilation of Romans.[4] It can be said that Romans is composed of at least three short letters so far. However, when we analyze texts not covered above, other possibilities will emerge regarding the compilation of Romans. This requires more careful research as it shows a more complex aspect than what has been presented so far. This is difficult because it requires relying on internal evidence without external one. Conclusively, I would like to argue that Romans is a composite of four short letters.

My argument presupposes that the editor used all the main texts of letters Paul sent to the Romans. However, there seems to have been only one exception. This is the beginning of a letter that consists of the sender, the recipient, and greetings. It seems that the editor did not need all four. It is possible that only one of the four was used and the other three were

---

3. Cf. Bultmann, *Theology*, 132; and Dodd, *Romans*, 148-49. For the discussion the integrity of Romans, refer to Sanday and Headlam, *Romans*, lxxxiv-xcviii.

4. A few scholars even isolate 1:1-15 and 15:14—16:23 and then study the remaining texts only. This view is based on a logical difference between the question of visiting Rome and that of visiting Jerusalem. Cf. Barth, *Romans*, 6-11; Kinoshita, "Romans," 258-77; and Schmithals, *Römerbrief*, 210. However, this is not a problem at all, since Paul had plans to visit both cities. Accordingly, this view has not received much support.

deleted because they are redundant. In any case, a critical analysis will be conducted on the texts currently included in Romans.

The historical background is important for the study of the compilation of Romans. Although there is little external evidence for this, it can be said that Romans had been compiled before it was included in the New Testament in the mid-second century CE. It should be noted that as several letters were compiled into Romans, it was no longer possible to trace the relationship that Paul had with the Roman church at the time of each letter. However, if the compiling process of Romans is revealed, it will be possible to restore the history that Paul had with the Romans.

In summary, the compilation of Romans should be noted. This should be studied based on the fragmentary theory. Although very few critical scholars have engaged in this study, their attempts to search for the formation of Romans should continue to uncover historical situations on the basis of literary approach. Without this study, the process of change in the theological teachings that Paul shared with the Romans would not be completed.

2. CRITICAL METHODS

A methodology is inevitably needed to distinguish the letters compiled into Romans. Scholars often present different interpretations depending on the methodology that they used; however, I will mainly apply a literary approach to Romans. This not only reveals the fact that Romans was compiled as a literary work but also allows each letter to be distinguished according to the order of being written. Finally, this provides a theoretic foundation for revealing the process of how Paul developed the theological thoughts in the relationship with the Romans as time went by.

First, redaction criticism will be used to distinguish texts of each letter from the current form of Romans. This is possible when we recognize the differences that appear among texts. For instance, a thematic change occurs between 1:9–17 and 1:18–23. While the former focuses on Paul's intention to visit Rome and righteousness by faith in God, the latter mentions God's wrath to the unrighteous. Rather than a smooth connection between the two, a sudden break is detected in the flow of topic. The difference implies the possibility that they originated from different letters written at different stages. Without doubt, there are many of these cases in Romans. Then, we will see how they were combined by an editor at the time of compiling Romans. Redaction criticism originally began based on comparisons among the Synoptic Gospels; however, when this is applied to Romans, it can lead to similar results. Thus, the redaction-critical approach is considered effective in studying various differences embedded in the texts of Romans.

Subsequently, composition criticism will be used to connect texts distinguished by the redaction-critical approach. This is useful to identify a certain layer of texts supposed to originate from the same letter. For instance, 1:9–17 shows a break with 1:18—3:31, revealing the thematic difference between righteousness and unrighteousness, and then connects with 4:1—5:11 in terms of common theme of righteousness by faith in God. This shows that the texts revealing the issue of righteousness by faith are interrupted by the text treating the theme of unrighteousness.[5] If so, it is likely that 1:9–17 is followed by 4:1—5:11 in a certain layer of Romans. According to Arland D. Jacobson, the composition-critical approach not only shows how the texts fit together but also shows their compositional characteristics.[6] This is an explanation of the essential approach to the study of the compilation of Romans. With regard to the concept of literary unity, Thrall and Hibbard said, "The concept that a literary work shall have in it some organizing principle in relation to which all its parts are related so that, viewed in the light of this principle, the work is an organic whole."[7] In other words, when we connect the parts that show commonality among the separated texts by a redaction-critical approach, each letter could be identified while revealing a literary layer. When the composition-critical approach is applied to Romans, we can achieve the desired result in two respects; one is to see the order that each separate text had in the letter from which it originated, and the other is to see the characteristics of each letter. In this respect, composition criticism must be used to isolate each letter from the current form of Romans.

The redaction-critical and composition-critical approaches will classify four letters that have been compiled into Romans. Then, the next task is to list them in the order according to the order of being written. Another approach is necessary to determine their chronological order;

---

5. Among Paul's letters, a representative case is found in 2 Corinthians. Most critical scholars agree that the content continues from 2:13 to 7:5 with the theme of the meeting with Titus at Troas. This means that 2:14—7:4 has been inserted in between them at the time of compiling 2 Corinthians.

6. Jacobson, *Gospel*, 43.

7. Thrall and Hibbard, *Handbook*, 500. It was quoted by Jacobson, "Q," 372.

for this purpose, I would like to use the "history of ideas." This will make it possible to reconstruct the relationship that Paul had with the Romans and to see how his theological ideas progressively changed and developed in response to their reaction, especially Jewish members represented by Priscilla and Aquila.

The history of ideas is a methodology that studies the development of concepts.[8] This seeks to trace the origins of a specific idea or thought by examining the process by which it was expressed, preserved, and changed throughout history. Above all, it needs to find the unit-idea not only in collective thinking but also in famous thinkers and writers. Accordingly, the history of ideas first focuses on the unit of thought.[9] It begins by distinguishing the characteristics of units of idea and by grouping some of them into new combinations with a view to a particular purpose. The history of ideas then presupposes that each person or generation has mental habits, whether implicit or incompletely explicit, in thinking. This then traces the inherent assumptions that are intellectual habits, having believed that they are so general in some way that they can affect the process by which people react in relation to all topics. Lastly, the history of ideas is to reveal the flow of thoughts and ideas.

When the history of ideas is applied to Romans, it will reveal how Paul developed the thoughts on a specific topic over the course of four letters. For instance, it is to be explained that Paul described the Law in Romans not only in a somewhat positive way but also in an extremely negative way. This appears in the fact that the Law is mentioned in 2:12—3:31 after God's wrath was described first in 1:18—2:11. Paul argued for the uselessness of the Law. This was concluded by a statement that a person is made righteous by faith, not by the works of the Law in 3:28. This means that the Law has a relatively smaller role than faith in God. The inferiority of the Law to faith is again mentioned in 3:31. Paul further stated that the covenant was not based on the Law but only through righteousness by faith in 4:13. The role of the Law was negated with regard to the covenant here. More importantly, it is declared in 4:15 that where there is no Law, there is no transgression. The uselessness of the Law reached its peak here. The above texts refer to the negative role of the

---

8. Lovejoy, *Chain*, 1–23, esp. 19.

9. Having discussed critiques on Lovejoy's theory fifty years after its publication, Daniel Wilson said that while the expression "unit-idea" may be a bit of a misnomer, the methodology itself was very reasonable in linking similar ideas. Wilson, "Lovejoy's," 187–206, esp. 205.

Law. On the other hand, there are also passages that show a slightly reserved stance on the Law. This is the statement that the Law was brought in to increase transgression (5:20), and then it is said that the Law drives people to death due to the sinful lust within them (7:5). At the same time, Paul's view was developed into a positive description of the Law, which states that it is a holy, good, and spiritual being to make people aware of sin (7:7). This position culminates in the statement that Christ came as the end of the Law to bring about righteousness (10:4). In this way, Paul's stance on the Law varies in Romans.

It is then necessary to raise a question whether Paul would have simultaneously shown such diverse positions regarding the Law in a single letter. If he had sent only one letter to the Roman church, he would not have shown such confusion by showing contradictory views on the Law. This shows the possibility that Paul had different positions on the Law depending on the situation while sending letters to the Roman church several times. In this respect, Romans should be approached from a practical rather than a doctrinal perspective.

The history of ideas can explain Paul's different descriptions of the Law. If, as suggested above, four letters from Romans can be isolated by redaction and composition criticisms, the history of ideas will serve to further clarify their chronological order with regard to the process of how Paul developed his thought on the Law. In this respect, the history of ideas will be a useful tool to confirm the fact that Paul sent letters to the Romans on several occasions.

As seen above, a critical approach is essential to reveal the fact that Romans is a composite letter. For this purpose, redaction criticism will first be applied, composition criticism will follow it, and then the history of ideas will be used.[10] If they work properly, they will reveal that Romans is a composite of four letters, show Paul's relationship with the Romans, and identify the changes in his theological thinking. If that happens, the meaning of each text in the current form of Romans will require another level of interpretation. At last, this will allow readers to reconstruct the history between Paul and the Romans as reflected in Romans.

In summary, a critical approach to Romans should be preferred. This is because the traditionally conservative approach blinds readers to the diversity of Romans. The conservative study leads only to the

---

10. I have experienced separating four redactional layers by applying the three critical methods presented above to Q. As a result, the theological characteristics contained in each layer were distinguished. Ra, Q, 21–237.

conclusion that Paul was not an intellectual person who made contradictory statements. A critical approach will reveal the historical fact occurred between Paul and the Romans. This will make readers excavate the theological truth embedded in Romans.

3. DIVISION INTO FOUR LETTERS

Romans is by no means logical in its current form. Although the four short letters were composed according to their own principles, they are not well connected in the current form of Romans. If they can be classified by the critical approaches discussed above, each letter presents its own theme and logic. It is necessary to begin the work of discerning them by approaching critically. This will eliminate the compiler's attempt to turn the four letters into Romans in its current form and reveal the meaning that Paul originally intended to convey to the Romans.

When approaching Romans from a redaction-critical perspective, breaks in the flow are identified in many places. An important clue to confirm this is a sudden change in topic or difference in thoughts. The intelligent Paul would not have written a letter with such varied content in a letter. In any case, it cannot be denied that redaction criticism is a good tool to divide Romans into groups of texts in order to identify four short letters.

First of all, the beginning of letter appears in 1:1–7. There are Paul as the sender, the Romans as the recipient, mission, and greetings. They are essential elements for the beginning of a letter. Paul adopted the titles "apostle" already used in his letters to the Corinthians and the Galatians (1 Cor 1:1; 2 Cor 1:1; Gal 1:1; cf. 1 Thess 2:7) and "servant of Jesus Christ" for the first time in Romans. In addition, it is the first time that Paul stated his status set apart for the gospel of God. This suggests that the gospel is an important topic. The greetings addressed to the Romans clearly informs of the recipient of his letter. However, it cannot be clearly determined from which letter 1:1–7 originated yet. The fact that this text is located at the beginning of Romans does not necessarily guarantee that it is derived from the first letter.

Paul introduced faith in 1:8–17. Faith is something that must be spread, is the foundation of comfort for Paul and the Romans, and is related to the gospel of God. This shows that 1:8–17 can be connected to 1:1–7 by the common theme of "gospel." The connection is further supported by the reference to Rome in 1:7, 15. His intention to visit Rome shows that 1:8-17 was part of the first letter along with 1:1-7. It seems that Paul revealed his intention in advance as he had attempted to visit Rome for the first time to preach the gospel with an expectation of a warm welcome in 1:1-17. This shows that 1:1-17 was the beginning part of the first letter. This is the result obtained by applying redaction criticism and composition criticism.

From a redaction-critical perspective, it can be said that the flow of text is interrupted at 1:18—3:31. This text is structured to focus on the theme of unrighteousness resulting in the wrath of God. Its description resulted from unrighteousness appears in 1:18—2:11, then the theme that people cannot achieve righteousness by keeping the Law is mentioned in 2:12—3:20, and finally the faith of Christ is presented as an alternative to the Law with regard to God's righteousness in 3:21-31. It is insisted that people cannot avoid the wrath of God because they are inherently unrighteous regardless of whether they have the Law or not. Paul rather presented the faith of Jesus Christ as an alternative to the Law with regard to becoming righteous before God. In this respect, a coherent flow of theme is found in 1:18—3:31 that can form a single letter without logical gaps or breaks. As a result, unrighteousness described in 1:18—3:31 is in contrast with righteousness by faith in God mentioned in 1:1-17. It seems that the editor of Romans placed the two texts in sequence to make a contrast between righteousness and unrighteousness.

It is necessary to determine from which letter 1:18—3:31 originate. To be honest, there is still no external clue to decide its origin. However, it is important to observe that Paul challenged the Jewish members of the Roman church with rhetorical questions (2:21-23, 26-27; 3:1-6). This reflects the fact that Paul responded to question or critique of the Romans. If so, this shows that they raised questions about or critiques of the content of earlier letters. Then, it can be said that 1:18—3:31 belonged to at least the second letter. This is supported by the fact that in this text, there is no expectation of welcome, which is characteristic of the first letter. Then, it can be said that 1:18—3:31 has been written later than 1:1-17 originated in the first letter. They were put together in the present order by an editor at the time of compiling Romans.

Righteousness by faith in God is addressed again. This theme reappears in 4:1—5:11, which can be largely divided into two parts. Having introduced Abraham as an example, Paul dealt with the issue of righteousness by faith in God in 4:1-25 and then described how God sent

Jesus Christ to make people righteous in 5:1-11. Abraham was introduced as a type for Jesus Christ in terms of faith in God. If so, the story of Abraham's faith becomes the gospel of God in light of its definition (1:2). This shows the possibility that 1:1-17 and 4:1—5:11 originated from the first letter because they carry the same theme, that is, righteousness by faith in God. If this kind of composition-critical analysis is acceptable, it becomes more clear that 1:18—3:31 is a text interpolated in between 1:1-17 and 4:1—5:11. The three texts listed above clearly reveal the contrast between righteousness and unrighteousness.

It is necessary to apply the history of ideas to 1:1—5:11. This establishes to some extent a chronological order between the two letters embedded in this text. For this, it needs to take a look at what Paul argued for the righteousness by faith, not by works, and the stated the role of the Law bringing about wrath and transgression in the first letter (4:3, 15). Having read it, the Romans, mostly made up of Jews represented by Aquila and Pricilla (cf. 16:3), could not accept it and asked Paul to explain why he had described in that way. In response, Paul had to explain his thought on it and said that righteousness cannot be achieved by the works of Law but by the faith in 1:18—3:31. Then, it can be strengthened that while 1:1-17; 4:1—5:11 belonged to the first letter, 1:18—3:31 originated from the second letter. Since this is the first case of applying the perspective of the history of ideas, it is necessary to leave the above analysis as a provisional conclusion. For a clearer conclusion, more cases are still needed.

From a redaction-critical perspective, another gap appears in connection with sin in 5:12—8:30. Paul focused on the issue of sin in its relationship with the Law. After the contrast between sin begun with Adam and grace given by Jesus Christ was described in 5:12-21, the life freed from sin with Christ Jesus is addressed in 6:1-11. The lesson that a person must live as a servant of righteousness rather than a slave to sin is addressed in 6:12-23. Then, sin through the Law and life through the spirit are contrasted in 7:1-25, and the opposition between the law of the spirit of life in Christ Jesus and the law of sin and death is narrated in 8:1-11. At last, a life led by the spirit rather than the flesh is discussed in 8:12-30. From the fact that sin is dealt with so intensively, the above texts seem to be originated in a coherent letter. From the fact that 5:12—8:30 is different from 1:18—3:31 in terms of issue, it is likely that this was part of a new letter. This shows the relationship between sin and the Law is different from the righteousness and unrighteousness mentioned in

1:1—5:11. In addition, it is noteworthy that no request to welcome Paul appears in 5:12—8:30. Its absence informs that 5:12—8:30 was part of a letter written later than the first one.

It is necessary to discuss the origin of 5:12—8:30. From a perspective of the history of ideas, it can be said that the Law is treated more theologically in 5:12—8:30 than in 1:18—3:31. Having stated that the Law convicts of sin in the second letter (3:20), Paul made a more developed statement by focusing on the relationship between the Law and sin in 5:12—8:30. This reflects the situation that the Romans found it hard to accept Paul's claim written in the second letter. Thus, they raised a question about the relationship between the Law and sin, and Paul had no choice but to answer the question for the clarification. It seems he had no choice but to reply that the Law was holy (7:12). In this way, Paul showed a reserved view of the Law in 5:12—8:30. This analysis leads readers to consider 1:18—3:31 and 5:12—8:30 as belonging to letters written at different times. This is as same as the situation that as Paul related the Law to wrath and transgression in the first letter (4:15), the Romans raised questions rather than accept his instruction, and then Paul had to answer the questions in the second letter. Therefore, 5:12—8:30 seems to have been written later than 1:18—3:31 because with regard to the role of the Law, a more developed concept is found in 5:12—8:30 than in 1:18—3:31. If so, it can be tentatively concluded that while 1:18—3:31 was part of the second letter, 5:12—8:30 originated from the third letter.

The flow of content shows gaps once again in 8:31-39. The redaction-critical approach tells that the main theme of God's love described in this text is different from the relationship between the Law and sin mentioned in 5:12—8:30. In addition, while difficulties caused by external factors such as hardship and persecution are mentioned in 8:31-39, religious conflict caused by internal factors such as sin and unrighteousness by the Law among the Romans is treated in 5:12—8:30. The difference refers to the possibility that 8:31-39 might be originated from a letter other than that 5:12—8:30 belonged to. From a composition-critical perspective, it can be said that the theme of God's love is reminiscent of 5:1-11 in which the same theme appears. In addition, the content flows naturally from 5:1-11 to 8:31-39 in that the death and resurrection of Christ are followed by his role as mediator at the right hand of God after the ascension to heaven. Therefore, this leads reader to the conclusion that 8:31-39 along with 5:1-11 originated from the first letter.

From a perspective of the history of ideas, it is necessary to pay attention to the subject of mediator. Whereas Paul presented the spirit as the one acting the mediatory role in 8:18–30, Christ Jesus was described as a mediator at the right hand of God in 8:31–39. Having used the words "intercede for us" in 8:26, Paul showed a theologically advanced aspect over the use of word "intercede" in 8:34. This shows that Paul changed his thought on the mediator progressively. The difference found in the immediate context also supports that 8:31–39, in which general suffering is described, was written earlier than 8:18–30 where eschatological one is referred to. The differences make it likely that 8:31–39 is a text derived from the first letter written earlier than the third letter to which 8:18–30 belonged.

A new topic is presented in 9:1—12:2. From a redaction-critical perspective, it is identified that the salvation of gentiles is treated anew here. This shows a totally different content from that found in 1:1—8:39. Although Paul spoke of gentiles in his first letter, he acknowledged some degree of Jewish priority in 1:14-16 and 4:12. On the other hand, having mentioned a critique raised against Jews who had the Law in 2:17—3:8, both the circumcised and the uncircumcised were acknowledged to be righteous by faith equally in the second letter (3:28). However, this implies that the priority of Jews began to be shaken. It is worthy to note that Paul used the Adam-typology in 5:12—8:30, presenting Adam as the ancestor of both Jews and gentiles. The door was open to gentiles in the third letter. This means that favorable view toward gentiles has grown as time went by. However, in 9:1—12:2, a new perspective is revealed with regard to the salvation of gentiles due to the stubbornness of Jews. This suggests that 9:1—12:2 was part of a new letter, probably the fourth one.

It is necessary to look at the position of 9:1—12:2 from a perspective of the history of ideas. Having taken a look at the Law, it is not mentioned much here compared to previous letters (9:4, 31; 10:4-5). Nevertheless, it is evident that the concept of the Law has developed, as it is increasingly described from a christological perspective. In the first letter, the Law was mentioned from a negative perspective in general (4:15). Then, Paul emphasized the priority of faith to the Law since he stated that faith establishes the Law in the second letter (3:31). Moreover, in the third letter, it is acknowledged that the Law is holy and that the commandments are good, holy, and righteous (7:12). Finally, here in the fourth letter, Christ is presented as the end of the Law for righteousness for all who believe (10:4). Paul added a christological perspective to the Law positively. Having compared to the views reflected in the three letters written earlier, the view on the Law described here is considered quite positive. This shows that 9:1—12:2, unlike previous texts, was a text belonging to the letter written later than the first three ones. Then, it can be concluded that 9:1—12:2 was derived from the fourth letter.

As seen above, Romans is most likely composed of four letters. Perhaps before the formation of the New Testament in the mid-second century CE, an editor compiled them into the present form of Romans as it now appears. So far, it can be suggested that the editor centered on the texts of the first letter (1:1–17; 4:1—5:11; 8:31–39), inserted those of the second and third letters in between them (1:18—3:31; 5:12—8:30), and finally added that of the fourth letters at the end (9:1—12:2). As a result, Romans reveals breaks in the flow of content in many places, leaving behind editorial evidences. The compilation made it difficult for readers to understand the theological logic embedded in the present form of Romans. This is because leaps and differences in logic are revealed. If so, analysis should now be done on the remaining texts.

Lessons about the life of saints are listed. In the following text of 12:3—15:13, there are also many cases where the flow of content is not fluent. This makes it possible to see the texts belonging to the four different letters, as was the case with the main texts discussed before. If so, the texts listed in 12:3—15:13 should be classified according to topic. Then, we can isolate the letters from which they originated. When this work is completed, the outline of each letter will be revealed. In addition, the theology and context of each letter will also be emerged. If the four letters can be distinguished, the compilation of Romans concluded earlier will be more credible.

First of all, 12:3–13 follows 9:1—12:2. Although they are connected by a linking word "body" (12:1, 4), the redaction-critical approach informs that they have different focuses. While it is used in connection with spiritual worship in 12:1–2, it is related to exercising the gifts given according to the measure of faith in 12:3–13. The expression "according to the measure of faith" is emphasized as it is used twice in 12:3, 6. From a composition-critical perspective, the emphasis on faith in 12:3-13 is to be connected to that mentioned in 1:1–17; 4:1—5:11; 8:31–39. If so, it can be said that 12:3-13 derived from the first letter along with the texts listed above.

Then, it is necessary to look at 12:14—13:7. Here, 12:14-21 and 13:1-7 are connected to each other by two elements: the linking word "wrath" (12:19; 13:4) and the theme of "good and evil" (12:17; 13:3). Then, it can be said that 12:14-21 and 13:1-7 are to be considered consecutive texts. From a redaction-critical perspective, 12:14—13:7 shows a break in flow of content with 12:3-13. While the internal relationship that the Romans had to be united to form one body is dealt with in 12:3-13, the attitude they should have toward external forces is focused in 12:14—13:7. From a composition-critical perspective, the word "wrath" and the theme of "good and evil" used in 12:14—13:7 are found in 1:18—2:11. These two elements make it likely that both texts originated from the same letter. From a perspective of the history of ideas, it can be said that Paul's dealing with the attitude of the Romans toward the external forces was written later than the general instruction on the internal relationship among them supposed to have been given in the first letter. Having received their response to the first letter, Paul seems to have been able to give specific advice about the situation the Romans faced in the following one. In this respect, 12:14—13:7 is believed to have been part of the second letter.

A redaction-critical break appears in 13:8-10. This is enough to form a unit on the theme of love for neighbors fulfilling the Law. It should be then considered an independent text in that it is distinct from 12:14—13:7, which deals with the issue of wrath. From a composition-critical approach, the description of fulfilling the Law in 13:8-10 is in line with what has been written in 8:4 that the requirements of the Law had to be fulfilled. Furthermore, it should be noted that the word "commandment" used in 13:10 is also found in 7:8-12. In this respect, it can be said that 13:8-10 derived from the letter from which 7:8-12 and 8:4 originated. From a perspective of the history of ideas, it can be said that the instruction on the love of one's neighbor for the fulfillment of the Law in 13:8-10 seems to be developed further than that on the love of brothers written in 12:10 supposed to be part of the first letter. In addition, the fulfillment of the Law by loving neighbors is to be considered a more advanced idea than the establishment of the Law by faith in 3:31 supposed to be part of the second letter. If so, 13:8-10, along with 5:12—8:30, is to be considered part of the third letter.

The text of 13:11-14 must be examined carefully because it emphasizes the theme of eschatological salvation. The redaction-critical approach shows a disconnection in the flow of content from 13:8-10, which deals with the issue to fulfill the Law by loving neighbors. From a composition-critical perspective, the imminence of salvation makes readers think of the atmosphere embedded in 9:28 in that God will quickly carry out the work of salvation. Moreover, the reference to "time" may be related to the time when the number of the gentiles will be fulfilled (11:25; 13:11). From a perspective of the history of ideas, 13:11–14, which conveys an eschatological view of ethics, can be seen as written later than 13:8–10 because of a more theologically developed aspect. If this analysis is valid, it is likely that 13:11–14, along with 9:1—12:2, came from the fourth letter.

If my analysis discussed above is acceptable, the editor showed a principle in his or her own way. Having attached the texts of ethical lesson (12:3—13:14) to the main body of four letters (1:1—12:2), the editor arranged them according to the chronological order of being written. A text of the first letter was placed first in 12:3-13, and then a portion of the second letter was attached in 12:14—13:7. Then, the editor placed a text of the third letter in 13:8–10, and it is followed by that of the fourth letter in 13:11–14. So far, we have seen only one case where the texts of ethical teachings were located according to the chronological order of being written.

A similar principle of editing appears in the two cases treated above. This means that the texts of the second to fourth letters were inserted or added to the main text of the first letter. In this respect, the editor appears to have maintained his or her own principle for the compilation of Romans. This is not believed to be an accidental phenomenon. If this principle were to be found in the rest of the text, it would be even more evident and valid. Thus, it is necessary to look at the following texts of Romans.

The theme of faith appears again in 14:1–12. From a redaction-critical perspective, this text shows a break with 13:11–14 in that it does not show anything in common. Since 14:1–12 was independent from 13:11–14, it seems that they originated from different letters each. If so, it is necessary to trace the letter from which 14:1–12 originated. From a composition-critical perspective, it can be said that having based on the theme of faith, 14:1–12 can be connected to 1:1–17; 4:1—5:11; 8:31–39; 12:3–13. Especially the issue of dying and living for the Lord can be linked to the issue of dying for someone (5:6-8; 14:8). Above all, the issue of Christ's death and resurrection is reminiscent of those of the Son of God (1:4; 5:10; 14:9). In this respect, 14:1–12 seems to have formed the first letter along with 1:1–17; 4:1—5:11; 8:31–39; 12:3–13. From a perspective of the history of ideas, the lesson about relationships with others based on faith is to be noted (14:1–12). This belongs to basic and general teachings about religious life, enough for Paul to write about in his first letter. This contains fundamental teachings about living for the Lord Christ. In this respect, the compiler of Romans seems to have linked 14:1–12, originated in the first letter, to 13:11–14 belonged to the fourth letter.

Then, the issue of relationship to brothers is described in 14:13–23. This follows 14:1–12 with the elements of relationship and faith. However, from a redaction-critical perspective, they show differences in various ways. First of all, stronger conflict and critique are reflected in 14:13–23 than one's evaluation on others described in 14:1–12. When Paul used the expression not to criticize one another again in 14:13–23, this presupposes his previous comments on general reference to criticism as written in 14:1–12. This means that 14:13–23 is to be considered to be independent from and written later than 14:1–12. From a composition-critical perspective, the statement that defines "not following faith" as a sin reminds readers of the one that faith establishes the Law and it convicts of sin (3:20, 31; 14:23). Moreover, 14:13–23 is to be connected to 2:7–9 in that the issue of "good and evil" is mentioned in both places. The fact that the issue of eating and drinking is described in relation to the kingdom of God is in line with what was described previously in relation to enemies (12:20; 14:17). Then, it can be said that 14:13–23 was in line with 1:18—3:31 and 12:14—13:7. It is likely that the texts listed above seem to be parts of the second letter. From a perspective of the history of ideas, it is necessary to look at the topic of eating and drinking in order to strengthen the location of the texts listed above. For instance, while the matter of eating is mentioned as a rule that had to be kept among the Romans in general in 14:1–12, the issue of eating and drinking is related to the kingdom of God in 14:13–23. This shows that the latter was written later than the former in that a more theologically developed aspect is found. If this analysis is reasonable, it can be said that 14:13–23 originated from the second letter.

In addition, teachings on reciprocity are described in 15:1–13. It seems that this text follows the preceding one by a connecting word "spirit" (14:17: 15:13). However, from a redaction-critical perspective, this text shows a break in terms of content. A new theme appears that the Romans should be able to embrace the strong and the weak, and the circumcised and the gentiles, following the example of Christ Jesus. They were required to participate in the mission to Jews and gentiles. From a composition-critical perspective, the resemblance of Christ Jesus reminds readers of the theme of unity with Christ (6:3–4). In order to become the people of God, they were to be united with Christ by baptism that means to have died and been buried with him and live in new life through his resurrection. From a perspective of the history of ideas, the teaching in 15:5–7 that the Romans had to become imitators of Christ Jesus is considered more advanced than the description of those who serve him as written in 14:18. In this respect, 15:1–13, along with the text of 6:3–4, was part of the third letter written later than the second one to which 14:18 belonged.

Moreover, it is necessary to pay attention to 15:14–21, where Paul's self-consciousness is clearly revealed. From a redaction-critical perspective, this is completely different from 15:1–13 in that Paul described himself as a servant of Jesus Christ for the gentiles and a priest of the gospel of God. From a composition-critical perspective, this claim is reminiscent of 9:1—12:2, where the salvation of gentiles is emphasized. The expression of offering gentiles as sacrifices reminds readers of Paul's teaching that gentiles should be offered as living and holy sacrifices pleasing to God (12:1–2; 15:16). From a perspective of the history of ideas, the emphasis on preaching the gospel to gentiles is an improved teaching over that found in 15:8–9 where it is said that the Romans should praise God with the Lord's people of nations. In this respect, 15:14–21 may have been part of the fourth letter written later than 15:1–13 derived from the third letter.

The four texts covered above were arranged according to the chronological order. The text of the first letter was supplemented by the texts of the second through fourth letters. Just as in the case of 12:3—13:14 where the texts originated from four letters appear one after another, so also here in 14:1—15:21. This clearly seems to be the intended result. Perhaps the compiler of Romans wanted to keep his or her own editorial principle. So far, the compiler of Romans has shown almost similar editing principles three times. If there were traces of this principle being used again in the rest of the text, this would further reinforce the fact that Romans was compiled.

Finally, Paul wanted to close his letter at 15:22—16:27. However, this is also believed to have been compiled with four letters. There are writings about Paul's purpose for visiting Rome, the deliverer of letter, greetings, and exhortations. They are supposed to have consisted of texts from the four letters. Then, there is no doubt that it is necessary to see whether the editorial principle inferred above is found in the following texts as well.

First, Paul described the purpose of sending the letter to the Roman church in 15:22–29. This focuses on the subject of financial support for the mission to Spain and delivery of collected money to the Jerusalem church. This journey centered on Paul's visit to Rome in order to preach the gospel and give grace. Then, 15:22–29 is believed to belong to the first letter in that the intention to visit Rome was written as it was in 1:13–15. If so, it can be said that 15:22–29, along with 1:13–15, was part of the first letter in which Paul had revealed the plan to visit Rome in advance and asked for a warm welcome.

A similar account of a visit to Jerusalem is given in 15:30–33. Although this text follows 15:22–29 by a connecting word "Jerusalem," the context is quite different. While Paul had not mentioned any feelings about Jerusalem in 15:22–29, he expressed fear of visiting in 15:30–33. From a redaction-critical perspective, it is believed that the two texts originated from letters written at different times. It is likely that as the time came closer to visit Jerusalem, Paul could not help but feel increasingly nervous. It is because he had been subject to checks of the apostles of the Jerusalem church in connection with his mission to gentiles since the theological debate over the gentile table in Antioch (Gal 2:11–14). Moreover, the blessing described in 15:33 also marks the end of a letter. Then, it can be said that 15:30–33 originally belonged to a letter written later than the first one from which 15:22–29 originated in terms of changed attitude toward the Jerusalem church. From a composition-critical perspective, 15:30–33 seems to be consistent with the text that spoke of wrath and unrighteousness against Jews in 1:18—3:31. In this respect, it can be concluded that 15:30–33 was part of the second letter.

In addition, the person delivering the letter to Rome appears in 16:1–2. The deliverer was Sister Phoebe, a member of the Cenchrea church. Paul had to mention her as a deliverer because she had been unknown to the members of the Roman church. If she had been known to them, Paul would have needed her to confirm his letter to them. The introduction of deliverer is considered an element that must appear in the first letter. Paul asked them for welcoming and treating her well. In this respect, it is likely that 16:1–2 was part of the first letter.

Paul wrote a closing message to the members of the Roman church in 16:3–16. The request to greet one another informs that he knew many of them, including Priscilla and Aquila. Having listed the names of all the people he knew, Paul emphasized the relationship that he had kept with them. Although nothing is said about how he came to know them, the description reflects the fact that they interacted with each other. His intimacy with them was presented for the purpose of receiving a warm welcome. In addition, requests for missionary funds may have been expected. If so, this text would have belonged to the first letter.

Then, Paul delivered a harsh warning in 16:17–20. From a redaction-critical perspective, this text is contextually in contrast with 16:3–16 in that a harsh warning does not fit with the closing greetings of the first letter. This perhaps reflects Paul's uneasy relationship with the Romans at the time of writing a later letter. If so, this refers to the situation in which the Romans received a request for missionary support from Paul and expressed their intention to refuse. Then, the appearance of a blessing for greetings shows that this text constitutes the ending part of a letter (16:20). From a composition-critical perspective, this text is reminiscent of parts of the third letter in that it deals with the relationship between life and death and speaks of good and evil (5:17; 7:19). Moreover, the expression that Satan will be crushed under the feet of the Romans reminds readers of oracle given to Eve, the wife of Adam, in her relationship to the serpent in the garden of Eden (16:20; Gen 3:15). In this way, the allusion to Adam and Eve refers to the fact that the Adam-typological approach was used from the beginning to the end of the third letter (5:12–14). In this respect, 16:17–20 is believed to have been part of the third letter.

Paul wrote greetings and blessings in 16:21–24. From a redaction-critical perspective, this text presents a different context from the harsh warning described in 16:17–20. A greeting from Paul with a company of coworkers refers to the end of a letter. The ghostwriter's greeting shows that this is also the last part of the letter (16:22). The blessing for greetings informs readers of the ending of a letter (16:24). From a composition-critical perspective, 16:21–24 can be connected to 16:3–16 on account of greetings. Paul wanted to finish the letter well in order to be welcomed by the Romans. In this respect, 16:21–24 is considered the final part of the first letter.

Then, a text follows that has a problem in its manuscript. It does not appear in some ancient manuscripts (16:25–27). However, if it was part of Paul's authentic letter, it should be determined to which it belonged. It seems to originate in the fourth letter on account of various reasons. First of all, the expression "intended for all nations to believe" reminds readers of the narrative for the mission to gentiles in the fourth letter (16:26). Then, the word "mystery" is used commonly (11:25; 16:26), and the character of God is linked to wisdom (11:33; 16:27). Moreover, the expression "'forever and ever" appears frequently (9:1; 11:36; 16:27). Finally, this text is considered suitable as the ending part of a letter in terms of giving glory to God. The elements discussed above allow this text to be part of the fourth letter.

It is important to observe that a certain principle of editing is found in 15:22—16:27. This means that the texts derived from the first letter formed the main axis and then those from the second and third letters were interpolated in between them, and that from the fourth letter was added to them. The same principle was already used in 1:1—12:2. As revealed above, Paul used the principle twice. This means that Paul intentionally chose this method of compiling. This is believed to be no coincidence.

The principle of compiling Romans was clearly revealed. The editor had a habit of connecting the texts of other letters to those of the first letter; however, it takes two slightly different forms. The first one is that while the texts derived from the first letter formed the main axis, those from the second and third letters were interpolated in between them and the text of the fourth letter was added at the end. This is found in 1:1—12:2 and 15:22—16:27. The second one is that the text of the first letter was supplemented by those of the second through fourth letters in sequence. This was used in 12:3—13:14 and 14:1—15:21. It is then clear that the editor had his or her own principle for the compilation of Romans. This strengthens the argument that Romans is possibly a composite of four letters.

Based on the preceding analysis, it is clear that Romans was developed into its current form through compiling. Romans is believed to be a composite of four letters. From the first to the fourth letters, they may be named Rom(A), Rom(B), Rom(C), and Rom(D). The compiling process of Romans can be diagrammed as follows.

Rom(A)	Rom(B)	Rom(C)	Rom(D)
1:1–17			
	1:18—3:31		
4:1—5:11			
		5:12—8:30	
8:31–39			
			9:1—12:2
12:3–13			
	12:14—13:7		
		13:8–10	

Rom(A)	Rom(B)	Rom(C)	Rom(D)
			13:11–14
14:1–12			
	14:13–23		
		15:1–13	
			15:14–21
15:22–29			
	15:30–33		
16:1–16			
		16:17–20	
16:21–24			
			16:25–27

The above diagram does not explain everything; however, it does show how four short letters have been compiled into the present form of Romans in the New Testament. This shows that having used Rom(A) as the framework, the texts of Rom(B), Rom(C), and Rom(D) were interpolated into it. They are believed to have been written at a relatively later time among the sixteen letters sent by Paul.[11] If so, each letter will reveal its

11. In the five of seven authentic epistles of Paul are found editorial works for compilation. They are composed of at least two or more short letters. It seems that whereas 1 Thessalonians and Philippians are composed of two short letters each, 1 Corinthians and 2 Corinthians consist of three short letters each. In addition, as shown before, Romans can be divided into even four letters. Only Galatians and Philemon are integral letters. When they are arranged according to the chronological order of being written, it will be as follows. Thess(A) (1 Thess 1:1—2:16; 4:1–8; 5:26–27), Cor(A) (1 Cor 1:4–9; 3:16–17; 6:9–20; 10:1–22; 11:2–16; 12:31b—14:1a; 14:20–22, 33b–38; 16:5–6, 10–11, 13–14; 2 Cor 6:14—7:1), Cor(B) (1 Cor 1:10–17; 5:1–5, 9–13; 6:1–8; 7:1–17, 25–40; 8:1–13; 10:23—11:1; 11:17–29, 33–34; 12:1, 4–12, 14–31a; 14:1b–19, 23–33a, 39–40; 15:12–28; 16:1–4, 12, 15–18), Thess(B) (1 Thess 2:17—3:13; 4:9—5:25, 28), Phil(A) (Phil 3:1b—4:3; 4:8–9), Cor(C) (1 Cor 1:1–3; 1:18—3:15; 3:18—4:21; 5:6–8; 7:18–24; 9:1–27; 11:30–32; 12:2–3, 13; 15:1–11, 29–58; 16:7–9, 19–24), Galatians, Cor(D) (2 Cor 1:1—2:13; 7:5—8:24; 13:11–13), Cor(E) (2:14—6:13; 7:2–4; 9:1–15), and Cor(F) (2 Cor 10:1—13:10), Rom(A) (Rom 1:1–17; 4:1—5:11; 8:31–39; 12:3–13; 14:1–12; 15:22–29; 16:1–16, 21–24), Rom(B) (Rom 1:18—3:31; 12:14—13:7; 14:13–23; 15:30–33), Rom(C) (Rom 5:12—8:30; 13:8–10; 15:1–13; 16:17–20), and Rom(D) (Rom 9:1—12:2; 13:11–14; 15:14–21; 16:25–27), Phil(B) (Phil 1:1—3:1a; 4:4–7, 10–23), and Philemon. Ra, *Paul*, 5–6, 31–55. For the contention by critical scholars of the past that 1 Corinthians was composed of three letters, see Hurd, *I Corinthians*, 45. He lists the opinions of scholars how 1 Corinthians was composed of three shorter letters. His study is based on those of scholars such as Johannes Weiss, Alfred Loisy, Paul-Louis Couchoud, Maurice Goguel, Johannes Zwaan, Walter Schmithals, and Erich Dinkler. For more detailed information about my research, see Ra, *Corinthians*, 9–332.

own context and theme contained within it. In addition, as each letter was written, the relationship to its previous letter will be revealed to some extent. As researches on this progress, the changes in Paul's relationship with the Romans will be emerged and the process how he developed the theological thoughts will be revealed.

4. CONTENTS OF EACH LETTER

It is necessary to examine each of the four letters compiled into the current form of Romans separately. When we examine them in the order of being written, the relationship that Paul had with the Romans will be emerged. In addition, the process by which the theology he sought to convey was changed will be identified. If these studies are established exactly, what Paul wanted to convey to the Romans at each stage will be highlighted. To this end, it is also essential to carefully examine the circumstances reflected in each stage of writing. Then, the real history that Paul had with the Roman church will be reconstructed.

If my fragmentary analysis of Romans presented above is acceptable, the contents of the first letter Rom(A) are as follows.

1. Beginning Part (1:1–7)
2. Purpose of Visiting Rome (1:8–15)
3. Righteousness by Faith in God (1:16–17; 4:1–25)
4. Jesus Christ the Love of God (5:1–11; 8:31–39)
5. The Ethics of Saints (12:3–13; 14:1–12)
6. Plan for Itinerary (15:22–29)
7. Recommendation (16:1–2)
8. Greetings (16:3–16)
9. Closing Part (16:21–24)

Rom(A) was written to convey the core of the gospel and to request financial support in return from the Romans. Paul wanted to complete the mission all the way to Spain, which was located at the western end of the Roman Empire. Rom(A) proceeds along two axes: the gospel and financial support for the mission to Spain. Righteousness by faith was presented as the core of the gospel. It is important here that Abraham and Jesus Christ were presented as the examples of faith. Especially, the atoning death and salvific resurrection of Christ were presented as a way to express the highest level of faith. This was defined as the love of God and presented as the life that people of faith should emulate. At the same time,

Paul showed a negative attitude toward the Law, saying that it leads to wrath and transgression. Rom(A) primarily reflects a strong Jewish perspective because the Roman church was dominantly composed of Jews. For the completion of the mission to gentiles, Paul desperately needed the cooperation of the Romans. However, he probably did not know that his critical comments on the Law would become an obstacle to him. And anyway, these contents are appropriate enough to compose the first letter sent ahead of the first visit to Rome.

The process by which Paul wrote Rom(A) is as follows. Having gone to as far as Illyricum the western end of Macedonia for the mission to gentiles (15:19), Paul visited Corinth for the third time as he had announced (1 Cor 16:7; 2 Cor 12:14; 13:1).[12] This is inferred from the fact that Gaius, who was a member of the Corinthian church, was mentioned (16:23; 1 Cor 1:14). Moreover, the archaeological evidence that Erastus was an officer of Corinth in the middle of the first century CE also supports the possibility that there was the place where Paul sent Rom(A). Lastly, the fact that this letter was delivered by Phoebe of Cenchrea, close to Corinth, further strengthens the fact that Rom(A) was written there (16:1). It is certain that it was written before Paul left Corinth for Rome via Jerusalem (15:25–26).[13] In this way, Paul showed the courtesy of giving notice before visiting.

---

12. Paul visited Corinth three times as written in the letters to the Corinthians. The first visit was supposed to be made around 47 CE for spreading the instruction of Jesus Christ and establishing a church there; however, it was not recorded or reflected in any text of his epistles. This visit took place under the leadership of Barnabas, as confirmed by the fact that his name was already known to the Corinthians (1 Cor 9:6; cf. Gal 2:1). During the first visit, Paul probably met Priscilla and Aquila (cf. Acts 18:2). The greetings of Priscilla and Aquila reflects the fact that they had been known to the Corinthians (1 Cor 16:19). For the further discussion on the possibility that Paul visited Corinth during his first missionary trip before the apostolic meeting at the Jerusalem church, see footnote 14 that follows. The second visit was predicted to take place after passing through Macedonia and later confirmed (1 Cor 16:5–6; 2 Cor 13:2). Afterwards, he retreated to Ephesus, revealing that he had been staying with Priscilla and Aquila (1 Cor 16:8, 19). Having made a promise to visit with a purpose there, Paul announced the third visit.

13. It is described in Acts that having left Corinth, Paul went to Jerusalem via Ephesus (Acts 18:18–23). However, Paul did not mention going from Ephesus to Jerusalem in his letters. It is then stated in Acts that Paul came to Ephesus from Jerusalem later (Acts 19:1) and then went to Greece (Achaia) via Macedonia (Acts 19:21–22; 20:1–2). If this description is correct, this would be the third visit to Corinth that Paul mentioned in 2 Corinthians. However, in Acts, it is introduced as his second visit. Anyway, according to Acts, having spent three months in Greece (Achaia), where

Paul sent Rom(A), with an expectation to be welcomed by the Romans. It seems that the Roman church was founded by Priscilla and Aquila who had learned from him while staying in Corinth or Ephesus (16:3; 1 Cor 16:19). It is presumed that the couple met Paul for the first time in Corinth around 47 CE and learned about Jesus from a Jewish perspective as reflected in Q.[14] As time passed, they added some knowledge written in the three letters, Cor(A), Cor(B), and Cor(C), believed to have been compiled into the current form of 1 Corinthians.[15] It seems

---

Corinth is located, Paul arrived at Troas via Macedonia and then headed to Jerusalem by ship (Acts 20:3-6, 13-16). If this description is correct, it means that Paul took relief offerings to Jerusalem as revealed in Romans (15:25-26).

14. Knox argues that Paul already visited Corinth before the apostolic meeting in Jerusalem ("Chapters," 346-47). Later, having been acquainted with his view, Lüdemann argues for Paul's first visit to Corinth around 41 CE before the apostolic meeting (*Paul*, 184, 401, 495, 625 of 3299). To my judgment, it is not realistic that having left Jerusalem in 38 and established churches in various places, Paul arrived in Corinth in 41. Rather, it is likely that Paul was in Corinth around 47 two or three years before returning to Jerusalem for the meeting with apostles supposed to be held in 49. This is because Corinth of Achaia was located in the furthest region while Paul was engaged in the first missionary journey that started and ended in Jerusalem (Gal 1:18-21; 2:1-2). However, according to the author of Acts, Paul visited Corinth after the apostolic meeting and stayed there for eighteen months (Acts 18:11). It is, however, unclear whether this is historically accurate. In my view, Paul's first visit to Corinth occurred before, rather than after, the apostolic meeting. This is supported by the fact that Barnabas was known to the Corinthians (1 Cor 9:6). If he had not visited Corinth with Paul before the apostolic meeting, there would be no reason for his name to be mentioned in 1 Corinthians written after the meeting. Barnabas parted ways with Paul in Antioch after the apostolic meeting (Gal 2:13), so he cannot have visited Corinth afterwards. A similar case appears in the case of the Galatian church. This shows that Paul had already visited Galatia before the apostolic meeting when he informed the Galatians that he had gone up to Jerusalem with Titus a Greek (Gal 2:1-2). In addition, the title "a Greek" shows the possibility that Titus was from Corinth, which is supported by the fact that it appears in 1 Corinthians other than Romans (1 Cor 1:22, 24). On the contrary, in Acts, Paul visited Galatia for the first time after the apostolic meeting (Acts 16:6). It is believed that the author of Acts arranged Paul's journey according to his own intentions. If so, the incident of Paul's eighteen-month stay in Corinth should be regarded as something that happened at the first visit during the first missionary trip before the apostolic meeting.

15. It seems that Cor(A) was written in Thessalonica as a notice for the second visit to the Corinthian church around 52 CE before the trip through Macedonia (1 Cor 16:5-6). Then, Cor(B) is believed to have been written in Athens of Achaia just before the second visit (1 Cor 16:16-18). At last, Cor(C) was written in Ephesus in 53 since he had been forced to retreat there after the challenge by some Corinthians during the second visit and before the upcoming trip to Corinth via Illyricu through Macedonia (1 Cor 1:12; 16:7-8, 19). Cf. Ra, *Paul*, 33-42.

that Priscilla and Aquila had left Ephesus for Rome around 54 CE before Galatians was written at the peak of the challenge against Paul by some gentiles sponsored by the apostles of the Jerusalem church.[16] This means that the couple were not familiar with his teaching that everyone should become righteous by faith in God following the example of Abraham as written in Galatians (Gal 3:6–18). Accordingly, having headed for Rome from Corinth via Jerusalem, Paul would have been full of ambition to spread the gospel which had been developed but not exposed to the Romans gathered together around Priscilla and Aquila. He may have written Rom(A) with an expectation of a welcome from them.

It seems that having read Rom(A), the Romans reacted in their own way to it. If they had decided to welcome Paul, he would have had no reason to write another letter. Paul wrote Rom(B), whose contents would have been as follows.

1. The Wrath of God (1:18—2:11)
2. The Law and Sin (2:12—3:20)
3. The Faith of Jesus Christ (3:21–31)
4. The Ethics of Saints (12:14—13:7; 14:13–23)
5. Closing Part (15:30–33)

Rom(B) progresses along two axes. One is the wrath of God, and the other is the role of the Law. Paul insisted that the wrath will be given in the judgment at the end and that the Law does not bring righteousness of God. Paul emphasized that one can be justified by the faith of Jesus Christ in God, not by keeping the Law. This was done in the direction of strengthening the claim that the Law convicts of sin. Paul seemed to have reflected here many of the words and themes used in Galatians written when the challenge against him reached the peak. Thus, the Romans, mainly composed of Jews, seemed to have become more suspicious of him.

Based on the contents of Rom(B), it can be inferred how the Romans reacted to Paul's instruction, that is, the gospel, written in Rom(A). Having read it, the Romans, mainly composed of Jews led by Priscilla and Aquila, did not show a favor to him because of his teachings that one can become righteous by faith in God and that the Law brings about wrath and transgression. As Jews, they clearly believed that people at the time could be justified by keeping the Law. Accordingly, they were nervous with his teachings and decided to ask Paul to clarify the issue of

---

16. Ra, *Paul*, 39, 48. It is clear that Cephas was sent to the Corinthian church by the apostles of the Jerusalem church (1 Cor 1:12).

righteousness by faith and the role of the Law. Having listened to their questions or critiques, Phoebe returned from Rome back to Corinth or a certain place appointed with Paul and reported whatever she had heard and seen in the Roman church. Then, Paul had to make the case clear in Rom(B), focusing on the issue of the Law. Accordingly, it started with a mention of wrath and continued to mention transgression, with the proposition that the Law makes one realize sin.

Having considered Paul's friendship with Priscilla and Aquila, the Romans' reaction was quite surprising. The couple seemed to be unaware of the situation Paul had been in. Paul had a heated argument about the Law with the Galatians who had challenged him under the sponsorship of the apostles of the Jerusalem church. It was against his gospel from a Jewish perspective. They tried to erase Paul among the gentile churches. Accordingly, Priscilla and Aquila did not seem to know that having stood against their attacks, Paul expressed an extremely negative view of the Law to the Galatians (Gal 3:19). As a result, the Romans seemed to have had a hard time accepting Paul's negative view on the Law and the instruction on righteousness by faith in God.

Paul sent the third letter Rom(C). This reflects the fact that the Jewish members of the Roman church were not satisfied with what Paul had written in Rom(B). Accordingly, the contents of Rom(C) seem to be as follows.

1. Death and Eternal Life (5:12—6:23)
2. The Law and Faith (7:1–25)
3. Christ and the Spirit (8:1–30)
4. The Ethics of Saints (13:8–10; 15:1–13)
5. Closing Part (16:17–20)

In Rom(C), Paul developed the topic of death and eternal life on the basis of the core of the gospel. This was conveyed through various contrasts, all of which were used to reveal the Adam-typological perspective. In addition, it is necessary to see Paul's reserved stance on the Law, which was the only way out; he had no choice but to choose. According to him, sin took advantage of the commandments to fulfill all kinds of greed, and sin is dead without the Law. The Law was also defined as holy and good. Accordingly, Paul retreated from the extremely negative view on the Law. At the same time, he strengthened the claim that gentiles could also become the people of God through Christ. Having written his passion for the gentile nations, Paul maintained the plan to spread the gospel, even to Spain.

Based on the texts of Rom(C), it can be inferred that Paul had to answer the question raised by the Romans. They would not accept Paul's instruction written in Rom(B) that no one is justified by the Law but that it makes people aware of sin. In addition, a question could have been raised about the lesson that Jews can become God's people on the same lines as gentiles. In response to these questions, Paul pointed out that sin is the main cause of taking the commandments, representing the Law, captive and driving people to death. His explanation on the relationship between the Law and sin was enough to make the Romans released. The reserved stance on the Law resulted from his trial to win over the hearts of the Romans for the financial support. However, Paul continued to indicate that gentiles could also become the people of God. This could still cause discomfort to Jewish members. In this way, when this letter is interpreted in relation to previous letters, its role and meaning are clearly revealed.

The Romans, represented by Priscilla and Aquila, had never encountered the teaching that the Law convicts people of sin. Paul also never conveyed this kind of teaching to other gentile churches. If so, this was delivered for the first time in Rom(B), and the Romans could not help but be uncomfortable with him. It seems that Paul realized the seriousness of the situation and faced the reality of having to appease Jewish members. Without solving this problem, not only he could not preach the gospel in Rome, but also he could not expect their financial support for the mission to Spain. Accordingly, Paul seems to have found a solution by turning to a reserved stance on the Law in Rom(C).

The Romans appear to have been consistently unfriendly to Paul. This is reflected in the fact that he had to send the fourth letter Rom(D). Its contents are listed as follows.

1. Paul's Passion for Jews (9:1–5)
2. The Election of God (9:6–29)
3. The Way of Salvation (9:30—10:21)
4. Jews and Gentiles (11:1—12:2)
5. The Ethics of Saints (13:11–14)
6. Closing Part (15:14-21; 16:25–27)

The texts listed above infer that the salvation of gentiles was the main theme in Rom(D). Paul did not deny the salvation of Jews but argued that their stubbornness had opened the way to the salvation of gentiles until their number would be fulfilled. Since Paul was successful to persuade the Romans regarding the Law, he could describe Christ as the end of the

Law in Rom(D). However, he still seemed to have not been able to establish a justification for the extraordinary mission to Spain. This means that they did not accept the request to provide him with financial funds for the mission to gentiles.

It is reflected in Rom(D) that the Romans, mainly composed of Jews, did not agree with Paul's insistence on the mission to gentiles as written in Rom(C). When they read it and questioned its legitimacy, Paul had to present his theological position on this matter in Rom(D). Accordingly, he presented God's grand plan to the Romans who thought not to be responsible for the proclamation of the gospel to gentiles. Thus, Paul insisted that the Jews were so stubborn that God gave gentiles the opportunity for salvation and that this would continue until their numbers would be fulfilled. However, this argument did not seem to have captured the hearts of the Romans.

Priscilla and Aquila knew that Paul was engaged in missionary work in gentile areas. However, unlike Paul, the couple had not received any mission to gentiles ever. It seems that they simply had the information about Jesus from a Jewish perspective that Paul had taught before the challenge from some gentiles sponsored by the apostles of the Jerusalem church. As a result, a new movement was unfolded in Rome by Priscilla and Aquila from a Jewish perspective. However, they did not seem to have gone outside the church and actively engaged in missionary work among Greeks in Rome. It may have been to the extent of accepting Greeks who were interested in the Jewish instruction and joined a new religious movement. Accordingly, it was not at all easy for Paul to convince them of the mission entrusted by God.

Paul appears to have finally arrived in Rome.[17] However, it is not clear whether he had a chance to preach the gospel there and receive financial support from the Romans. Perhaps he failed to get it in that no description related to this appears in the New Testament. Rather, it seems that Paul was imprisoned in Rome. This is reflected in the words "binding" and "guard" and in the statement that he had fellowship with members of Caesar's household (Phil 1:13; 4:22). From the fact that these texts belong to Phil(B), the later letter of the two compiled into Philippians, they reflect that Paul was imprisoned in Rome and was unable

---

17. On the contrary, according to Acts, it is described that Paul was transported from Jerusalem to Rome (Acts chaps 21–28); however, it is not clear whether this was historically true.

to reach Spain. The mission to gentiles that Paul claimed to have been entrusted by God seems to have stopped in Rome.

The relationship between Paul and the Romans appears to be the opposite of that described in Acts. He fell into an increasingly bad relationship with them, and it seems that the mission to gentiles that God had given him had virtually come to an end in Rome. The fact that Paul had to send letters to the Romans four times shows that his relationship with them was more complicated than generally expected. Because of this, it seems that the later editor did not want to make this unfortunate ending known to Christians of his time and later generations. Accordingly, it seems that the editor made it impossible to see the historical context while compiling Romans in order to spread the image of Paul described in Acts.[18] Since this interpretation was made under the assumption that Romans is a composite of four letters, further research on historical facts will need to be conducted.

---

18. Ra, *Paul*, 11–56. It must be acknowledged that the historical life of Paul reconstructed from his seven authentic letters differs greatly from that described in Acts written by the third party.

I

Rom(A)

PAUL SENT THE FIRST letter, Rom(A). This was to reveal his plan to carry out the gospel all the way to Spain. On the way there, Paul wanted to visit the Roman church and give grace by proclaiming the gospel, and then, in return, he expected financial support to carry out the gospel to Spain. Accordingly, he tried to draw the attention of the Romans by introducing the core of the gospel centered on the righteousness by faith in God. Rom(A) proceeds with the theme of faith as its framework.

Although the Roman church was not founded by Paul, he was able to send a letter on the basis of friendship formed in faith. This began when he met Priscilla and Aquila in Corinth and continued until they parted ways in Ephesus (1 Cor 16:8, 19). While staying with him, the couple learned about Jesus Christ from a Jewish perspective and acknowledged the lessons reflected in 1 Corinthians. The couple later moved to Rome and founded a church on the basis of Jewish tradition and the lessons about Jesus Christ learned from Paul. Accordingly, having hoped that the Romans would welcome him warmly, Paul sent a letter Rom(A) prior to the first visit. He had no choice but to write it as carefully as possible in order to complete the mission to Spain with the financial support of the Romans.

The core of the gospel has been recorded in Rom(A) that begins with Abraham and continues with Christ. This was already described in Galatians. However, since it was new to the Romans represented by Priscilla and Aquila, it seems to have been in the midst of some controversy. In particular, a negative view on the Law was enough to provoke critique against Paul by the Romans, especially Jewish members. Because of this, Paul, who had expected a warm welcome, seemed to have instead become an object of avoidance.

The contents of Rom(A) can be divided into nine sections. Having started with the beginning part of letter (1:1–7), Paul introduced the purpose of visiting Rom (1:8–15). He then explained the righteousness of God by faith (1:16–17; 4:1–25) and then described Jesus Christ as the love of God (5:1–11; 8:31–39). These themes constitute the core of the gospel he had wanted to share with the Romans. After explaining the ethics of saints (12:3–13; 14:1–12), he expressed the intention to visit Rome again (15:22–29). Then, Rom(A) included recommendation (16:1–2), greetings (16:3–16), and closing part (16:21–24). Paul sent Rom(A) in the most formal way possible to visit the Roman church.

1. BEGINNING PART (1:1–7)

When Paul sent a letter to the Romans, he adopted a format that had been customarily used at the time. This not only introduces the sender but also mentions the recipient and greetings. They are considered the necessary elements of the beginning part of a letter. Paul tried to show intimacy with Jews, who made up the majority of the Roman church, by describing each element from a Jewish perspective. In this way, he expressed the wish to be welcomed.

Paul introduced himself as a "servant of Christ Jesus" (1:1a). The title "servant of Christ Jesus" was used for the first time in Rom(A). The Corinthians were once advised to become "servants of Christ" (1 Cor 7:21–22), and Paul referred to himself as a "servant of Christ" in Galatians (Gal 1:10). Therefore, the title "servant of Christ Jesus" can be a more developed one from a theological perspective. This is believed to be based on the Jewish background of "servant of YHWH." Having revealed the Jewish perspective, Paul tried to create intimacy with the Romans, supposed to be composed mainly of Jews represented by Priscilla and Aquila. In any case, having mentioned the sender, this text shows the beginning of Rom(A).

Another title, "apostle," follows. Paul had been "called to be an apostle" (1:1a). The title "apostle" was applied to those sent by God in Greek. It was already used in the letters for the Corinthians and the Galatians who had challenged him against the gospel and his apostolate (1 Cor 1:1; 2 Cor 1:1; Gal 1:1). It is interesting that Paul added the expression of "being called." Having presented the Jewish concept of "being called and sent by God," Paul identified himself under the prophetic tradition. The Jewish perspective provided a point of contact between Paul and the Romans because the Roman church was supposed to be mainly composed of Jews.

Paul went on to define himself as a person "selected for the gospel of God" (1:1b). The issue of selection was already written in Galatians that God had set him apart in his mother's womb (Gal 1:15; cf. Jer 1:5). However, in Rom(A), Paul described himself as the one chosen for the gospel of God. Having revealed the self-consciousness, Paul tried to inform that the Romans should accept him as a prophet delegated by God to preach the gospel. This is also a narrative based on Jewish tradition.

The gospel is mentioned here as an important element. Paul presented the gospel to the Corinthians in a summarized form, consisting of the death, burial, resurrection, and appearance of Christ (1 Cor 15:3–5). Priscilla and Aquila would also have known about this. However, Paul linked the gospel of Christ to Abraham in Galatians supposed to have been written after the couple left Ephesus for Rome (Gal 1:7; 3:8). Accordingly, the gospel of God could be mentioned in Rom(A), which was an expression centered on God to create intimacy with the Romans. In this way, Paul implied that the gospel would play an important role in Rom(A).

The definition of the gospel is described in detail. This is what God promised in advance through the prophets in the Scriptures about his Son (1:2). The word "Scriptures" is important here, as it was already used to introduce the gospel to the Corinthians (1 Cor 15:3–4). It would have been known to Priscilla and Aquila while staying with Paul in Ephesus. Afterwards, the gospel was explained to the Galatians as what God told to Abraham, so that the gentiles would be blessed through his Son Jesus Christ (Gal 3:8). In this way, Paul presented as the gospel what was known through Abraham, the ancestor in faith. Accordingly, Paul was able to present the definition of the gospel in a more elaborate form in Rom(A). Accordingly, Paul introduced himself as a preacher of the gospel from a prophetic perspective. There was no letter before Rom(A) that emphasized the gospel like this from the beginning part of a letter.

In order to understand Rom(A) better, it is necessary to decide the category of teachings that Priscilla and Aquila learned from Paul. It is clear that the couple learned something regarding Jesus Christ from the time they first met him in Corinth until they parted ways in Ephesus. To this category at least belongs what Paul taught the Corinthians in letters written not only before the challenge arose against him by those sponsored by Cephas, an apostle of the Jerusalem church, but also after he retreated to Ephesus (1 Cor 1:12; 16:19). The contents are currently recorded in the three letters compiled into 1 Corinthians. However, Galatians seems to have been unknown to Priscilla and Aquila because it is believed to have been written after they had left Ephesus for Rome. This kind of historical situation will be of great help in understanding the contents of Rom(A).

Paul gave a detailed description of the Son of God. This constitutes the contents of the gospel (1:3–4). He is the Lord Jesus Christ, who was born of David's lineage according to the flesh, raised from the dead according to the spirit of holiness, and declared to be the Son of God with power. Above all, the Son of God was mentioned in connection with David for the first time here. This was to give Christ Jesus a messianic character from a Jewish perspective because it has been known that Jews were waiting for a Davidic Messiah. Second, it is stated that the Lord Jesus Christ has been risen from the dead by the spirit of holiness. This is reminiscent of Christ who died but was raised on the third day according to the Scriptures (1 Cor 15:3–4). Accordingly, Paul developed the contents of the gospel further by saying that the spirit of holiness was the driving force for the resurrection of Jesus Christ. The theology of resurrection also reflects the Jewish perspective handed down by the Pharisees. Third, there appears a declaration that Jesus Christ was proclaimed to be the Son of God with power. The interpretation that Christ Jesus was declared the Son of God through resurrection appears for the first time here. The Son of God must be understood in connection with the previously mentioned David in that he was announced as the beloved son of God (Ps 2:7). Paul wrote it from a Jewish perspective in order to create intimacy with the Romans, supposed to be mainly composed of Jews. In any case, this is the core of the gospel that will dominate Rom(A).

The status of Paul was described in relation to the Lord Christ Jesus. This is the claim that through him Paul received grace and an apostolate to make all gentiles obey him by faith (1:5). Paul understood the apostleship given to him as the grace of God. It has been emphasized that he had been called to be a minister for gentiles. This reminds readers of what he said in Galatians that he had received the mission to preach the Son of God to gentiles (Gal 1:16; 2:7–8). Then, Paul was able to say in Rom(A) that he had been given a mission to make the gentiles obedient to the Lord Jesus Christ by faith for his name. Having specified his mission at the beginning of Rom(A), Paul asserted his spiritual authority as a minister sent by God to people in all regions beyond Rome. This was something that could have been mentioned in the first letter.

Here, it is necessary to pay more attention to faith. The issue of faith was already treated in the expression of "Christ's faith" with a reference to the trust of Christ in God (Phil 3:9; Gal 2:16; 3:22). This does not mean people's faith in Christ because Paul did not describe Christ as the object of faith in his letters. Paul put it in parallel with "Abraham's faith" in order to introduce their trust in God's promise in Galatians (Gal 3:6). In a similar manner, Paul conveyed the trust of the Romans in God with the word "faith." In this respect, Paul maintained the issue of faith in God from a Jewish perspective. Having addressed this at the beginning, Paul hinted that it will be continually treated in Rom(A).

Paul spoke about the position of the Romans (1:6). They were defined as those called by God among all the gentiles to belong to Jesus Christ. This does not mean that they were of gentile origin. Rather, the Romans were those who had been called by God while living among gentiles in Rome. In any case, it is important to observe that the expression of "being called and become of Christ Jesus" is reminiscent of what Paul mentioned earlier about himself (1:1). In other words, the Romans, like him, were called by God to become the servants of Christ Jesus. With these expressions, Paul attempted to show a sense of intimacy with them from a Jewish perspective. In this respect, his definition of the Romans is worthy of being included in the first letter, Rom(A).

In addition, the region where the letter was delivered was mentioned (1:7a). This appears in the expression "in Rome." The intended recipients were the members of the Roman church. Paul already mentioned the region where the recipients lived according to the custom in previous letters (1 Cor 1:2; 2 Cor 1:1; Gal 1:2; Phil 1:1; 1 Thess 1:1). It is then clear that Paul sent a letter to the Romans. Rome was the capital of the Roman Empire at the time of writing Rom(A). In this way, Paul clearly identified the recipients at the beginning of the letter. Such a statement is considered worthy of being part of the first letter.

Then, the love of God was applied to the Romans (1:7b). This was a value universally transmitted within Judaism. However, there seems to have been a special reason that Paul defined the Romans as those loved by God. This is to be interpreted against the backdrop of linking the Son of God with David in the previous text (1:3). Just as David was declared to be the beloved son of God (Ps 2:7), so was Christ Jesus as the lineage of David. Paul then applied the same rule to the Romans. They were also the beloved sons of God from a Jewish perspective. Having applied the love of God to them, Paul showed the familiarity with the Romans and expected a warm welcome. This description was also worthy to be included in the first letter.

Moreover, the phrase "calling to be the holy people" was applied to the Romans (1:7c). It is in parallel with "calling to be of Jesus Christ" mentioned earlier (1:6). This derives the meaning that a saint is a person of Jesus Christ. Paul once applied the expression "sanctified in Christ Jesus and called to be saints" to the Corinthians (1 Cor 1:2). Accordingly, Paul was able to mention the master-servant relationship of the Romans with Jesus Christ in Rom(A). It is because he already defined himself as a servant of Christ Jesus at the beginning (1:1). Having mentioned the issue of election, Paul tried to make the Romans focus more on the status as the holy people of God in connection with Jesus Christ. As a result, the statement that God called Paul to be an apostle and the Romans to be saints indicates the equality among them in spite of differences in duties. This was part of Paul's attempt to gain a welcome from the Romans by revealing the affinity with them.

Paul's greetings was quite formal. He prayed for grace and peace to be with the Romans (1:7d). Here a question comes to the fore with regard to the source of grace and peace because it can be interpreted in two ways based on Greek grammar. The first is "being given from God, the Father of ours and Christ Jesus," and the other is "being given from God our Father and the Lord Jesus Christ." The former emphasizes uniqueness of God, while the latter focuses on the equality between God and the Lord Jesus Christ. This was an expression that Paul used as a formula toward various gentile churches (1 Cor 1:3; 2 Cor 1:2; Gal 1:3; Phil 1:2; Phlm 3). To my judgment, the former is preferred to the latter because nowhere in his letters did Paul see God the Father and the Lord Jesus Christ on the equal level. This is supported by the fact that Paul considered gentiles to be "sons of God" just like Jesus Christ to be "the Son of God" (Gal 4:4–6). If my interpretation is correct, it can be said that Paul showed a Jewish perspective while demonstrating a faith centered on God.

In summary, When Paul sent the first letter Rom(A), he presented a point of contact at the beginning to draw the attention of the Romans. This was approaching them from a Jewish perspective. Paul tried to gain favor from Jewish members, the major group of the Roman church. They would have accepted Paul's introduction of himself without difficulty. It is clear that they are elements to be located at the beginning of the first letter.

2. PURPOSE OF VISITING ROME (1:8–15)

Paul expressed the intention to visit Rome, so that he could preach the gospel of God and bear good fruit among the Romans. This shows an attempt to win favor with the Romans. Having informed them of his visit in advance, Paul would have expected a warm welcome from them.

As in the case of other letters except Galatians, Paul described the gratitude to the recipient of his letter. A couple of factors were related to thanksgiving (1:8). First of all, Paul declared that he was thankful to God through Jesus Christ for everything the Romans had done. Gratitude for everything that comes from Jesus Christ is theologically close to an idiomatic expression. This kind of expression was previously applied to the Thessalonians (1 Thess 1:2ff.). Accordingly, having expressed his gratitude to the Romans for everything, Paul tried to get closer to them. Second, Paul was thankful to God on account of the Romans because their faith had been reported all over the world. Paul probably heard of news about the Romans from time to time while being engaged in the mission to gentiles in Macedonia and Achaia. This kind of general reputation reflects the fact that he did not yet have an intimate relationship with the Romans. Gratitude in this general sense was something that Paul could have included in the first letter asking for a warm welcome.

Paul described what he had prayed for the Romans. It is said, "God, whom I serve with my whole heart in preaching the gospel of his Son, is my witness how constantly I remember you" (1:9). Paul presented God as a witness to give strength to his words. This reminds readers of what he told to the Corinthians: that the spirit of God took a role of a deposit guaranteeing what is to come (2 Cor 1:22). Accordingly, having mentioned God as his witness in Rom(A), Paul tried to let the Romans know his earnest attitude towards them. Paul then revealed that he kept praying for the Romans. Having exhorted the Thessalonians to pray without ceasing (1 Thess 5:17), Paul was able to declare in Rom(A) that he had prayed without ceasing for the Romans. This shows that he always had them in mind and that he was trying to win their hearts. This was a way of expressing his expectation that they would welcome him warmly.

Finally, Paul revealed the contents of his prayer for the Romans. It is said, "Now at last by God's will the way may be opened for me to come to you" (1:10). If so, Paul claimed that his visit to Rome would be done according to God's will. Once the "will of God" was told to the Galatians from a soteriological perspective (Gal 1:4). However, in Rom(A), Paul linked God's will to the intention to visit Rome. Furthermore, having mentioned the opening of the way to Rome, he expressed the wish to be welcomed by the Romans. This shows that Paul spoke in strong terms about the visit to Rome. In any case, the description of his intention to visit Rome is an integral part of the first letter sent before the first visit.

An introduction to meeting with the Romans was recorded with a positive sentence. It is said, "I long to see you" (1:11a). Paul showed the earnest desire to see the Romans. This reveals that he had never been to Rome yet. On the one hand, it seems that Paul's desire made the Romans nervous. On the other hand, they would have prepared to welcome him, whom they had heard about from Priscilla and Aquila. It is believed that this type of statement could be recorded in the first letter that mentions the upcoming visit.

Paul summarized what he wanted to do in Rome into three points. First, it was sharing spiritual gifts (1:11b). Paul once introduced spiritual gifts to the Corinthians, listing various categories such as prophecy and tongues (1 Cor 12:4, 8–11). Priscilla and Aquila would have known about this type of spiritual gift. On the other hand, in Rom(A), having mentioned the words "spiritual gifts," Paul did not specify them. In any case, Paul expressed the intention to contribute something spiritual to the Romans. This would have made them wait for him with expectation. Second, Paul stated the reason to go to Rome. It was to strengthen the Romans from a spiritual point of view (1:11c). Having built the Romans up firmly by sharing the spiritual gifts, Paul would have been able to strengthen his spiritual authority. Third, Paul wanted the mutual benefit. It is said that he and the Romans could get mutual comfort by faith (1:12). However, Paul did not clearly explain the consolation that he had sought. The pursuit of mutual benefit reflects the fact that Paul had not yet formed any kind of spiritual relationship with the Romans yet. At any rate, having mentioned the word "faith" three times (1:5, 8, 11), Paul tried to develop Rom(A) based on it. In this way, a description of the purpose of visiting Rome was something that could be included in the first letter.

The passion to visit Rome is revealed. This is found in the statement that Paul did not want the Romans to be unaware of his previous attempts to visit Rome (1:13a). He already gave notice in advance before visiting the Corinthian and Thessalonian churches (1 Cor 16:5–7; 2 Cor 12:14; 13:2; 1 Thess 2:17–18). As such, it is natural to mention the intention to visit Rome before the first visit. In addition, having mentioned that he had tried several times, Paul expressed the strong desire to visit Rome for the first time. Moreover, the double negative expression that he did not want the Romans to be unaware of his attempt reveals his strong will to get their consent or permission. While his excessive enthusiasm for the visit may have made the Romans wait for him, it may also have caused them to be wary of his purpose.

Paul revealed the purpose for visiting Rome. This was to bear fruit among the Romans as well as among other gentiles (1:13b). Having mentioned the mission to gentiles in earlier text (1:5), Paul once pointed out that the Roman church was also located in a gentile area. This point provided him with justification for the need to go to Rome; however, this does not mean that all Romans were of gentile origin. Paul simply wanted to show that he was God's servant for gentiles. Here, "fruit" means that their faith became more mature by the gospel he had wanted to preach. Paul was sure of results that would happen to the Romans, just like in the case of other gentile churches. The reason Paul made this statement was to win over their hearts.

Expressions of regret also appeared. This is detected in the description that the road to Rome had been blocked until the time Rom(A) was written (1:13c). Paul did not specifically explain why the visit to Rome had not been possible. Similar expression was once applied to the case of the Thessalonian church. While Paul had attempted to visit the Thessalonians once or twice, he had been blocked by Satan (1 Thess 2:18). This is probably written against the backdrop of representatives sent by the apostles of the Jerusalem church who instigated them to reject Paul at the time. However, Paul simply stated in Rom(A) that the way was blocked. This means that there was no one who had criticized or challenged Paul at the time of writing Rom(A). So he revealed that whenever he prayed, he had asked God for a path to be opened. In any case, Paul tried to win over the hearts of the Romans.

Paul mentioned the attitude in preaching the gospel. This appears in the expression that he was a debtor to all men, both Greeks and barbarians, wise and foolish (1:14). Paul sublimated the responsibility of preaching the gospel to gentiles into the concept of a debtor. Paul's mention of Greeks and barbarians was a way of distinguishing among gentiles. The Greeks were recognized as wise people, while the barbarians were recognized as foolish people (cf. 1 Cor 1:22–24). Paul did not mention his debt to Jews, probably because he was convinced from the beginning that he was called and elected as an apostle for gentiles (Gal

1:16). Having presented all gentiles as the target of preaching the gospel, Paul emphasized the necessity to visit Rome for the mission to gentiles.

The will to visit Rome was expressed once again. This is revealed when Paul said that he had wanted to preach the gospel as much as possible in Rome (1:15). Having defined the gospel in earlier text (1:2), Paul wanted to spread teachings centered on the prophecies about the Son of God Jesus Christ. This implies that he would deliver new contents to the Romans. They knew only what Priscilla and Aquila had delivered on the basis of lessons learned while staying with Paul in Corinth and Ephesus. Therefore, it is presumed that they did not know about the gospel that Paul had developed after their departure from Ephesus to Rome. If so, it seems that Paul wanted to introduce the message developed anew as being written in Galatians. Otherwise, Paul would not have been able to emphasize the desire to preach the gospel to the Romans.

In summary, Paul expressed a desire to visit Rome. This was for preaching the gospel about something that Jewish members, represented by Priscilla and Aquila, were not familiar with. Paul mentioned the gospel in a way that the Romans would be interested in. However, it is unclear whether the Romans would had been looking forward to new teachings. In any case, Paul's passion to visit Rome could have been included in the first letter, in which Paul asked them for a warm welcome, ahead of the first visit to Rome.

3. RIGHTEOUSNESS BY FAITH IN GOD (1:16–17; 4:1–25)

Paul taught that the gospel leads people to righteousness by faith in God. This is the key lesson he wanted to convey to the Romans. Having based on the case of Abraham, Paul insisted that people can be righteous by faith that leads to salvation. This kind of content was new to the Romans and was enough to attract their attention.

The Gospel and Faith (1:16–17)

Paul introduced the core of the gospel to the Romans. This focuses on the righteousness by faith in God. Having presented the core of the gospel, Paul began to open the main text of the first letter.

Paul was confident in the gospel he would preach to the Romans. This is seen in the declaration that he had not been ashamed of the gospel (1:16a). Paul was proud of preaching the gospel to the Romans. As presented earlier, the gospel was related with Paul's new interpretation of what God had said in advance through the prophets about his Son (1:2). Since Priscilla and Aquila, who represented the Roman church, had not known much about this, Paul wanted to present the gospel that he had realized anew. Accordingly, he said with confidence that he was not ashamed of the gospel. Paul was able to mention his attitude toward the gospel in the first letter, which opened the relationship with the Romans.

It is then necessary to explain the difference between the gospel that Paul claimed and the instruction that Priscilla and Aquila had learned from him about Jesus Christ. To clarify the difference between the two, it is necessary to look at Paul's missionary journey. Having received the revelation about the Son of God, Paul probably received the tradition about Christ in Damascus (Gal 1:16–17; 1 Cor 15:1–5) and learned about Jesus three years later at Jerusalem from Cephas on the basis of Q (Gal 1:18). Accordingly, it seems that Paul had gone to gentile areas and preached teachings about Jesus Christ from a Jewish perspective during the first missionary journey. At that time, Paul met Priscilla and Aquila in Corinth and taught them until they parted ways in Ephesus. Therefore, it seems that the couple was well aware of the contents of 1 Corinthians supposed to be a composite of three short letters written before they left Ephesus for Rome. However, when the challenge of the gentile Galatians against Paul reached the peak under the sponsorship of the apostles of the Jerusalem church in the aftermath of theological debate over the gentile table in Antioch (Gal 2:11–14), he developed his own gospel as a breakthrough and began to preach it. This is well reflected in Galatians in connection with Abraham as an example of those who had kept faith in God. At the same time, Paul fiercely criticized the Jewish teachings that the apostles of the Jerusalem church preached to gentiles about Jesus, defining them as a "different gospel" (Gal 1:6–9). It is believed that Priscilla and Aquila did not know what had happened to the Galatians because they had already left Ephesus for Rome. In other words, the Romans did not know specifically the contents of the gospel that Paul would deliver.

The gospel was defined as the power of God. According to Paul, the gospel is the power of God that brings salvation to all who believe (1:16b). Paul imposed a salvific function upon the gospel. As it was declared to the Corinthians that those who believe in the gospel would be saved, the tradition of Christ was introduced as the contents of the gospel (1 Cor 15:3–5). It seems that Priscilla and Aquila would have learned in Ephesus about the salvific function imposed on the gospel regarding Christ. Accordingly, the Romans would have waited for Paul's visit with a mixture of anticipation about what more they could learn related to the gospel and wariness about new things.

Paul once again mentioned the issue of faith. This appears in the statement that salvation is given to those who believe (1:16c). However, Paul did not specify the object of faith. Given the context, faith can mean accepting the gospel. Paul once told the Corinthians that if they hold fast to the gospel and do not believe in vain, they will be saved (1 Cor 15:1–2). Priscilla and Aquila might have known that Paul wrote these things while staying in Ephesus. Accordingly, having returned to Rome and established a church, the couple delivered the tradition of Christ to the members of the Roman church as the gospel (1 Cor 15:3–5). However, they did not know what Paul later developed further with regard to the contents of the gospel as introduced in Galatians (Gal 3:6–27). Accordingly, the Romans would have been unable to guess about the contents of the gospel that Paul would preach with confidence to them.

Those who would be saved by faith were listed. This is found in the expression of "Jews first and then Greeks" as a pair (1:16d). Paul gave Jews priority over Greeks in terms of the order of salvation. Paul once made a distinction between them because Jews and Greeks had sought for different virtues other than the message of the cross (1 Cor 1:22–24). This would also have been known to Priscilla and Aquila. However, at the time of writing Rom(A), Paul had no choice but to give priority to Jews over Greeks because the former made up the majority of the Roman church. This shows that having sent the first letter to the Romans, Paul could not help but consider those who held leadership in the church. Paul tried to win their favor.

Then, Paul dealt with the issue of righteousness. This is presented in the statement that the righteousness of God is revealed in the gospel (1:17a). Paul insisted that if one believes the gospel, he or she will be righteous in front of God. The issue of righteousness by faith started when Paul wrote a letter to the Philippians. It is said that righteousness is through the faith of Christ—the righteousness that comes from God (Phil 3:9). However, since the issue of righteousness by faith was not told to the Corinthians, Priscilla and Aquila had no opportunity to hear about it while staying with Paul in Corinth or Ephesus. Rather, the righteousness by the faith of Jesus Christ was strongly raised in Galatians believed to have been written after the couple left Ephesus for Rome (Gal 2:16;

cf. 3:5). The Jewish teachings of Jesus that Priscilla and Aquila learned from Paul on the basis of Q did not include anything about the theme of righteousness by faith. If so, they could not help but be surprised when they encountered the statement in Rom(A) that the righteousness of God in the gospel is revealed only by faith. The Romans should have been nervous to the new claim of Paul because they had been accustomed to the instruction on righteousness by keeping the Law. Having emphasized the righteousness by faith in Rom(A), Paul could impress himself on the Romans before the first visit.

A verse from the Bible was quoted. It is said, "The righteous will live by faith" (1:17b; Hab 2:4). Paul quoted it to highlight the issue of righteousness by faith. Since this was an important issue to Paul, it was already quoted in Galatians (Gal 3:6). Then, it seems that Priscilla and Aquila had never heard of this proposition while staying with Paul. If so, they must have been quite nervous when they read the proposition written in Rom(A). The Romans, mainly composed of diaspora Jews, did not give up the religious belief in righteousness by keeping the Law. In addition, they maintained the Jewish instruction on Jesus learned from Paul before the challenge against him had occurred under the sponsorship of the Jerusalem church. Thus, the issue of righteousness by keeping the Law was not a big matter of controversy for the Romans. However, when Paul's instruction that one can be justified by faith was presented to the Romans, it must have come across as challenging contents to them. This shows how to attract their attention with a new topic.

To sum up, Paul wanted to give the Romans a new interpretation of the gospel rather than the Jewish teachings they had previously learned from Priscilla and Aquila about Jesus. This must have been quite shocking to them as it was righteousness through faith in God. This could have been conveyed in the first letter in that Paul made known the core of the gospel he had wanted to convey.

Righteousness by Faith (4:1–8)

Paul attempted a theological approach to the issue of righteousness by faith in God. Abraham was presented as the ancestor from the perspective of faith. Paul seemed to have made this description keeping in mind the fact that the Roman church was mainly composed of Jewish members represented by Priscilla and Aquila.

Abraham was presented as a representative example. It is said in the form of question what Abraham, our father in the flesh, gained (4:1). Paul raised this question with an assumption that he had gained something. This would have been enough to stimulate the curiosity of the Romans. Paul presented Abraham as an example regardless of the fact that the Roman church was composed of Jews and Greeks (1:16). Nevertheless, it cannot be denied that he wanted to elicit sympathy from Jewish members who made up the majority of the Roman church. The fact that Abraham was presented as a representative example shows that Paul approached it from a Jewish perspective. Paul did not teach about Abraham while he was with Priscilla and Aquila, as it is reflected in the fact that Abraham was not mentioned at all in 1 Corinthians. On the contrary, Paul did mention Abraham in Galatians written after the couple had left Ephesus for Rome (Gal 3:6–18). These contents would have been quite shocking to the Galatians, who were mainly gentiles at the time. Accordingly, having received and read Rom(A), the Romans, represented by Priscilla and Aquila, should have felt nervous because they encountered the mention of Abraham as the representative example of faith in God. They may have believed that Abraham was the ancestor of the circumcised according to Jewish tradition. In this way, Paul seemed to have tried to draw the attention of the Romans.

Paul began to address the main point he had wanted to deliver to the Romans. This appears in the form of answer to the question raised earlier (4:2). It has been insisted that Abraham did not obtain righteousness by works. Paul pointed out that if a person is justified by works, he or she may have something to boast about before others but not before God. Priscilla and Aquila had never heard about this kind of teaching while staying with Paul in Corinth or Ephesus. This is supported by the fact that the issue of "by works" does not appear in 1 Corinthians. Paul actually mentioned it in Galatians written after the couple left for Rome (Gal 2:16). Paul's argument for the righteousness by faith in God contradicts the conviction of Jews at the time that they were justified by the work of the Law. Therefore, it seems that the Romans represented by Priscilla and Aquila should have been nervous when this kind of interpretation was known to them. In fact, Paul wrote it for those who defined themselves as descendants of Abraham, so that they might stop trying to become righteous by works. It should be noted that only "by works" is mentioned here, while the connection with the Law was removed. This may be because Paul did not want to offend Jewish members. Paul had no choice but to walk a tightrope of winning their hearts while conveying his views.

A verse was cited from the Bible to support Paul's claim. It is said, "Abraham believed God, and it was credited to him as righteousness" (4:3). Having quoted a verse about of Abraham from Genesis (Gen 15:6), Paul rejected works as the way to obtain righteousness and rather emphasized faith in God. This was also something Priscilla and Aquila had never heard of while staying with Paul in Corinth or Ephesus. Paul mentioned this in Galatians written after the couple returned to Rome (Gal 3:6). Therefore, they should have been quite nervous when the Romans read the faith of Abraham in God to be righteous in Rom(A) because Jews had generally believed that they could be justified by the works of the Law. While Jews had prioritized keeping the Law over faith in God, Paul reversed it. He gave more spiritual authority to the case of Abraham, who had been much before the Law was given. This was a lesson that shook the religious beliefs of the Romans, especially Jewish members represented by Priscilla and Aquila.

Paul cited a worldly principle about work to enhance the value of faith. It is said, "Now when a man works, his wages are not credited to him as a gift; but as an obligation" (4:4). Paul argued that if someone is made righteous by his or her works, this is not given as grace but as remuneration. Of course, there is an assumption that it cannot happen in regard to faith. It seems that Paul wanted to show that the level of faith is different from the principle of the world. As a result, in order to accept the gospel preached by Paul, the Romans, especially Jewish members, had to leave the religious beliefs they had maintained until then. They no longer had to try to be righteous by their works but by faith in God following the example of Abraham. These teachings must have confused them.

Finally, God's grace was described in connection with faith. This is found in the statement that even if one does not work, one who believes in God who justifies the ungodly is considered righteous because of that faith (4:5). Paul emphasized God's authority in justifying even the ungodly. While faith in God is an important element for religious life, God's grace that justifies the ungodly should be more highlighted. Paul described the righteousness of God given as grace on account of faith in Galatians (Gal 2:21; 5:4). Accordingly, when the Romans represented by Priscilla and Aquila read these teachings in Rom(A), they could not help but fall into serious trouble. It is because Paul had delivered new teachings different from the religious beliefs they had maintained until then. However, Paul emphasized that God gives grace to those who do not work and are even ungodly. He taught the Romans to have a new level of faith. While Jewish members felt nervous with Paul's new teachings, gentile members probably expressed considerable interest.

Paul cited a verse from the Bible to support his claim again. Having defined righteousness of God without any works as a blessing (4:6), Paul said that blessed are those whose iniquities are forgiven, whose sins are covered, and whose sins the Lord does not acknowledge (4:7–8; Ps 32:1–2). The quoted sayings focus on the liberation from sin by the grace of God. It was a religiously important element for Jews and had to be done in the temple. Accordingly, Paul presented forgiveness of sin and lawlessness without paying any price as a prerequisite for achieving God's righteousness. At the same time, this was defined as a blessing received without any work. Paul wanted to appeal to Jewish members who lived in Rome far away from Jerusalem where the temple was located. However, they would have found it burdensome to accept his new interpretation due to the Jewish tradition they had maintained until then.

It is important to note that Paul quoted the words of David. This is because of previous description that the Son of God was born according to the flesh into his lineage (1:3). Paul tried to support Abraham's righteousness by faith in God with David's words. By doing so, Paul attempted to add authority to his self-defeating argument based on Abraham, the founder of the Jewish lineage, and David, the founder of the royal family of Judah. Paul had the effect of presenting the Son of God as a royal descendant of David. This reflects the Jewish perspective and is believed to have been written with Jewish members in mind. In this way, Paul revealed that the issue of quoting from the Bible was also a matter of strategy.

In summary, having presented Abraham as a representative example, Paul treated the issues of righteousness by faith in God and forgiveness of sin. It is important that righteousness and forgiveness were given by the grace of God. Having read this kind of instruction for the first time, the Romans, represented by Priscilla and Aquila, have been quite nervous because there was no place for the Law. Having written such important contents in the first letter, Paul would have been able to highlight the gospel he would convey.

Righteousness for All (4:9–12)

Paul insisted that Abraham was justified by faith when he was uncircumcised. This was a theological measure to open the door to gentiles. Paul presented the justification that both Jews and gentiles should accept the gospel he would deliver.

A debate began about the beneficiaries of the blessing. This appears in the statement that both circumcised and uncircumcised people must follow Abraham's case (4:9). Paul set up Abraham, who had been considered righteous by faith in God, as an example. However, this kind of claim could not help but offend the Romans, especially Jewish members represented by Priscilla and Aquila. Having stayed with Paul until leaving Ephesus for Rome, the couple knew that he had made no distinction between the circumcised and the uncircumcised (1 Cor 7:18–19). However, this was a lesson to the Corinthians, who were mainly made up of gentiles. On the other hand, the Roman church was comprised mainly of Jews and recognized the distinction between the circumcised and the uncircumcised. When the Romans, especially Jewish members, encountered Paul's claim as recorded in Rom(A), they would have been quite nervous. On the contrary, gentile members would have welcomed it. In any case, Paul argued that whether circumcised or uncircumcised, they should follow the example of Abraham in order to be righteous by faith, be freed from sin, and resultantly be the people of God. This was the core of the gospel Paul wanted to deliver to the Romans.

Paul applied the case of Abraham to all people. This is found in the description that Abraham was justified by faith in God while being uncircumcised (4:10). Whereas Paul had never made this kind of claim before, he expressed the will to make all the uncircumcised the people of God here. Gentiles were the object of mission beyond the racial distinction between Jews and Greeks. It was a claim that could not help but sound absurd to Jewish members because Paul tried to neutralize the religious boundary in terms of circumcision. On the other hand, gentile members were in a position to welcome his claim with open hands because the difficult process of circumcision was exempted. In this way, Paul presented the theological foundation for the mission to gentiles that he intended to carry out.

A new interpretation on Abraham's circumcision was presented. It is said that while he was uncircumcised, he was declared righteous by faith in God and was circumcised as a sign of it (4:11a). Paul had never made this kind of claim before; however, in Rom(A), a priority was given to righteousness by faith in God over circumcision. It seems that Jewish members would have had no choice but to once again criticize him because his claim did not fit with the Jewish tradition that the circumcised become the people of God. Nevertheless, they were unable to provide a theological basis to reject Paul's logic. On the other hand, this must have sounded like good news to gentile members. Paul laid the foundation to push the mission to gentiles even more forcefully.

Paul attempted to create sameness between Abraham and the people of faith. This is detected in the saying, "So then, he is the father of all who believe but have not been circumcised, in order that righteousness might be credited to them" (4:11b). Paul defined Abraham as the forefather of all mankind with regard to faith from a spiritual perspective beyond the identification of him as the ancestor of Jews from a perspective of the flesh. This claim had never been presented before, and it must have provided a startling clue to Jewish members. On the other hand, gentile members were introduced to something new that was different from the lessons they had learned from Priscilla and Aquila. Paul provided them with a theological basis to devote himself to the mission to gentiles. In this way, Rom(A) progressively deals with the issue of faith more logically as it advances.

Abraham was defined as the forefather of all people once again. This is found in the description that he became the father of all those who followed Abraham's example, not only the circumcised but also the uncircumcised (4:12). Having maintained the element of faith, Paul linked all the people to Abraham, whether circumcised or uncircumcised. It is here focused on how Abraham became the forefather rather than how people be the descendants. As Abraham believed in God before being circumcised and was recognized as righteous, all people who are not circumcised can also walk the same path based on the faith in God. However, Jewish members had to give up their privileges; thus, they would have had no choice but to express their discomfort with this kind of instruction. In this way, the claim that one can be justified by faith in God became the logical framework of Rom(A).

To sum up, Paul presented Abraham as the father of all mankind in terms of faith. Accordingly, those who live by faith were defined as his descendants. This is in accordance with Paul's strategy to include gentiles into the people of God. His argument definitely challenged Jewish members because their privileges became meaningless. Paul presented his argument in earnest from the first letter.

Faith and the Law (4:13–15)

Paul finally addressed the most sensitive issue to the Jewish members of the Roman church. This was the negative view on the Law. This was a barrier that Paul had to overcome in order to make his instruction on faith accepted. In any case, Paul ended up touching the disgust of Jewish members.

Paul attempted an interpretation in regard to the heir of Abraham. According to him, "It was not through law that Abraham and his offspring received the promise that he would be heir of the world, but through righteousness that comes by faith" (4:13). Paul linked the issue of heir to righteousness by faith, not by keeping the Law. This claim was something Priscilla and Aquila had never heard before while staying with him. Rather, in Galatians written after the couple returned to Rome, Paul discussed the issue of inheritance of promise that came down from Abraham through Christ in faith (Gal 3:14–29). Accordingly, when Jewish members read the claim in Rom(A), they should have felt a sense of religious deprivation. This is because the role of the Law was denied in relation to the inheritance of promise. On the other hand, gentile members would have accepted Paul's new instruction because the barrier of circumcision was eliminated in achieving the promise. As a result, tensions between Jewish and gentile members were bound to escalate.

The relationship between the Law and faith was addressed in relation to the issue of heir. This appears in the statement that if those who belong to the Law are heirs, faith is in vain and the promise is broken (4:14). Paul insisted that one had nothing to do with the Law in fulfilling the inheritance of promise of God. This is based on the fact that from a chronological perspective, the Law could not be involved because the promise of an heir in faith was given to Abraham earlier. Paul once addressed this issue in Galatians written after Priscilla and Aquila returned to Rome (Gal 4:1–9). However, later when the couple and Jewish members had read the claim in Rom(A), they could not help but protest against it. This is because it would be denying their privileges to be the heirs of promise given to Abraham. On the contrary, it was good news for the gentile members. Nevertheless, Paul claimed that people could become heirs of God's promise, so that he could accomplish the mission to gentiles entrusted to him.

Paul mentioned the negative role on the Law. This is revealed in the statement that the Law brings about wrath (4:15a). Paul presented the reason that those who belong to the Law cannot become heirs of God's promise. This is because the Law brings about wrath. Wrath was used in the context of eschatological judgment against the Thessalonians (1 Thess 1:10). In any case, having claimed for the first time that the Law brings about wrath in Rom(A), Paul made Jewish members quite nervous. This is because his insistence destroyed the reason for Jews to keep the Law. In fact, Paul should not have made this comment. However, it seems to be inevitable for him to put emphasis on faith in order to open the door to gentiles.

The role of the Law was further presented in a negative point of view. It is said that where there is no Law, there is no transgression (4:15b). Paul made an extreme statement linking the Law to transgression. This claim is based on the description in Galatians that the Law exists to produce transgression (Gal 3:19). Although Paul used a slightly relaxed expression in Rom(A), Jewish members must have become emotionally worse as they encountered it for the first time. This is because his claim completely destroyed the Jewish system of belief. On the other hand, gentile members would have received his teachings positively because they were given the opportunity to be free from the Law. Although Paul made an adventurous claim, he recommended that the Romans make faith, not the Law, the primary religious element.

To sum up, Paul ruled out the role of the Law because the inheritance of the promise of Abraham is also achieved through faith. This is a strategic statement to send the message that gentiles could also become heirs. The Jewish members of the Roman church would have thought absurd. In this respect, Paul boldly presented what he had wanted to covey in the first letter.

Abraham the Father of Faith (4:16-22)

Paul returned to the discussion of how Abraham became the forefather of all people by faith. This was to compare the incident of receiving a son from a closed womb through faith in the promise to make impossible

possible. With this, Paul began to show the core of the gospel he had wanted to preach.

The will for the mission to all people was mentioned in connection with Abraham. This appears in the statement that Abraham is the father of both those who belong to the Law and those who belong to faith, because they will inherit the promise of God in grace (4:16). Paul presented Abraham as the forefather of both Jews and gentiles. Of course, all people would become heirs of God's promise given to Abraham on the basis of faith; however, this claim seems a bit unreasonable. In any case, this claim was something that Priscilla and Aquila had never heard of while staying with Paul in Corinth or Ephesus. Paul once wrote a similar lesson centered on Christ in Galatians (Gal 3:16–18) and then developed it into the present one in Rom(A). The Romans would have reacted differently to Paul's description of Abraham. Jewish members would have thought it unfair to become heirs of the promise along with gentile members. They would not have been willing to give up their privileges of being the heirs of promise. In any case, Paul wanted to embrace gentiles rather than exclude Jews. This plan was born out of the belief that he was entrusted with the mission to gentiles by God.

Paul quoted a verse from the Bible and added his own interpretation. It is written that God made Abraham the father of many nations (4:17a). Paul quoted this verse from Genesis in order to provide a theological basis for the mission to gentiles (Gen 17:5). It was once stated in Galatians that gentiles can also become the descendants of Abraham by the faith of Christ (Gal 3:8). In similar manner, in Rom(A), having gentiles in mind, Paul introduced Abraham as the father of many nations. This elevated Abraham, the ancestor of Jews, to become the ancestor of all people in terms of faith. Paul then described God as the one who gives life to the dead and brings into existence things that do not exist (4:17b). This reveals the fact that God was the one who made the impossible possible. For instance, although Abraham had thought to be infertile due to old age, God gave him a son as promised. In other words, although it seems to be impossible to make gentiles the people of God, God will accomplish it. This teaching violated the Jews' idea of being the chosen people. Although Paul made Jewish believers quite nervous, he wanted to convince gentiles that the door to becoming the people of God was wide open. He borrowed the Jewish perspective to convey the lesson he wanted to convey.

Abraham's character was mentioned in connection with the issue of faith. It is said that since he hoped and believed even though he could not hope, God gave him descendants as promised and made him the father of many nations (4:18). Paul emphasized the fact that God gave Abraham a son in a situation that was considered impossible. This is to inform the Romans that such a miraculous thing could happen in their time as well. In other words, Paul wanted to instill in them the confidence that gentiles beyond Jews could become the people of God. For this work, Paul earnestly hoped that the Romans would participate in the mission to gentiles as well as he himself. It is not clear whether Jewish members who received these lessons were open to the mission to gentiles. Paul once again used the Jewish perspective to present a goal to the Romans that went beyond it.

Paul covered the story of Abraham not giving up faith and achieving results. It is told that even though he was over hundred years old and had no ability to have children, he did not abandon the trust in the promise of God, waited for it to be fulfilled, and finally had a son (4:19–21). Paul presented Abraham as an example of maintaining faith, standing firmly on the promise of God, and enjoying the result. In other words, Abraham took after the character of God mentioned earlier. God, who gives life to the dead, revived the dead fertility of Abraham and Sarah and had them give birth to a son. This is the work of God that "calls things that are not as though they were." Based on this example, Paul taught the Romans that although a person cannot be justified by his or her own effort, God can. At the same time, he insisted that not only Jews but also gentiles should be made into the people of God, even if this task may seem impossible. This was delivered to the Romans to accept the gospel he would preach and to participate in the mission to gentiles.

Paul concluded what he had argued so far. According to him, Abraham was considered to be righteous by God on account of the unshaken faith (4:22). Paul emphasized that Abraham was justified by faith in God. Thus, this verse can be the conclusion to the previous argument about the righteousness given to Abraham. Given that this information was not written in 1 Corinthians, it seems that Priscilla and Aquila did not know about it. On the other hand, in Galatians, Paul wrote that Abraham believed in God and was counted righteous (Gal 3:6); however, not much space was attributed to describe how Abraham had gained the righteousness of God. On the contrary, in Rom(A), Paul devoted a lot of space to this topic and wrote about faith at length. In addition, it was written that Abraham was the forefather of all people in faith and told that they were necessary to have faith. Having concluded in this way, Paul insisted that the Romans should change from the Jewish perspective they held at that time to the gospel he would preach anew. This is the teaching that one can be considered righteous by faith in God, not by the works of the Law. This is precisely what Paul wanted to proclaim, to give spiritual grace to the Romans, and to enable them to stand firm. However, it has not been yet known how much the Jewish members of the Roman church tolerated Paul, who presented an interpretation that ran counter to their own traditions.

To sum up, having used the faith of Abraham as an example, Paul presented that he had a son, the heir according to promise, in the form of resurrection from the dead. This is the core of the gospel that the Romans had to accept, and it ends with the lesson that God wants to make gentiles also his people. Jewish members would have been nervous to this kind of instruction. It was sufficient enough to belong to a letter sent in advance for the visit to Rome in that this part introduced the core of the gospel to be delivered to all.

Transition (4:23–25)

Paul showed a transition from Abraham to the Romans through the Lord Jesus. Accordingly, the principle of righteousness by faith was applied to the Romans on the basis of belief in the death and resurrection of the Lord Jesus. In this way, Paul focused on continuing to describe the core of the gospel.

Now the description of righteousness by faith has begun to be expanded. This is found in the statement that what had been recorded as righteousness to Abraham was not meant for him alone (4:23). Paul opened up the possibility that the principle of faith applied to Abraham could be done to others. Of course, Priscilla and Aquila did not hear this kind of instruction while staying with Paul. He delivered an instruction later in Galatians that those who have faith would be blessed along with Abraham (Gal 3:9). Paul probably hoped that the Romans would agree with what he had written in Rom(A). However, Jewish members might have been displeased to see Paul expanding the scope of Abraham's descendants to gentiles.

Paul mentioned the scope of those who would be considered righteous. This appears in the declaration that those who believe in God, who raised our Lord Jesus from the dead, will be justified (4:24). Paul addressed the works of God raising the Lord Jesus from the dead. Priscilla and Aquila had already learned about the resurrection of Jesus Christ from Paul while staying with him in Corinth or Ephesus (1 Cor 6:14; 15:3–5, 15; cf. 1 Thess 5:10). Paul later mentioned it in Galatians even after the couple returned to Rome (Gal 1:1). Accordingly, they would not have found it unfamiliar while reading Rom(A) later in Rome. However, it is necessary to pay attention to the reason that Paul introduced God as the one who had raised the Lord Jesus from the dead. This theme is closely related to the proclamation of Christ Jesus as the Son of God (1:4). Paul hoped that the Romans would also become sons of God like Christ Jesus. In connection with this, Abraham's faith was emphasized, as it was related to the incident having a son in a closed womb. Accordingly, faith is the driving force that brings results that make the impossible possible. Paul developed this logic with the gentiles in mind becoming the people of God. The Romans would have had no particular reason to reject this kind of instruction.

The Lord Jesus was described more theologically in connection with death and resurrection. It is said that he was delivered over to death because of people's trespass but was raised to make them righteous (4:25). Paul put their trespass and his death in contrast with their righteousness and his resurrection. Priscilla and Aquila might learn about the death of Christ for the sin of people while staying with Paul in Ephesus (1 Cor 15:3–5). However, Paul later wrote in Galatians that Christ voluntarily died on the cross because he loved him (Gal 2:20). The impact his death has on people was not mentioned here. However, in Rom(A), Paul described that the Lord Jesus was forced to die because of the trespass of people but was brought back to life for their righteousness. Here, the atoning death of the Lord Jesus is to be paid attention in that his resurrection leading to righteousness is implied as the status of salvation. Having argued in this way, Paul expanded the contents of the gospel in order to make the Romans not only take responsibility for his death but also receive favor resulted from his resurrection. However, it seems that Jewish members did not have plenty of time to reflect on righteousness by faith.

In summary, Paul applied the principle of righteousness by faith to the Romans. Having linked it to the death and resurrection of the Lord Jesus, he wanted to make them know the core of the gospel. The belief in the power of God raising the dead leads them to righteousness. The Romans had to have faith in God who made the impossible possible. However, not everything went as Paul intended for the Romans.

4. JESUS CHRIST THE LOVE OF GOD (5:1–11; 8:31–39)

Paul described theologically the death and resurrection of Christ, which was the core of the gospel to be believed. This was defined as the love of God and represented by including even gentiles into his people. It seems that Paul excluded the role of the Law while preaching the core of the gospel.

Results of Righteousness by Faith (5:1–4)

Paul described the path that a person who has been justified by faith must take. This is to reach hope from tribulation, just as Christ was raised from the dead. Paul wanted the Romans to live lives that reflected the core of the gospel.

First, the premise that one must be righteous was presented. It is said, "Since we have been justified through faith" (5:1a). Paul put an emphasis on the status of being righteous through faith in God. This serves as a transition in that it concludes what was discussed beforehand and opens what will be discussed later. There is a hint that nothing can be the theological basis for becoming the people of God except righteousness by faith. This is achieved by following the example of Abraham so far. Having continuously emphasized it in Rom(A), Paul tried to impress upon the Romans its importance. They probably ended up in a state of psychological discomfort due to the teachings based on his subjective interpretation.

Paul then described two benefits that the righteous will enjoy in their relationship with God. One is to enjoy peace with God through the Lord Jesus Christ, and the other is to gain access into grace. They are summarized in that the righteous rejoice in the hope of the glory of God (5:1b–2). The words "peace," "grace," and "glory" were already used in the earlier texts (1:7; 4:16, 20). They can be said to be benefits enjoyed by the people of God. The role of the Lord Jesus Christ for this was mentioned as essential. Of course, the Romans would have encountered this kind of lesson for the first time.

Then, a series of situations that faith brings were listed. It is said, "Not only so, but we also rejoice in our sufferings, because we know that suffering produces perseverance; perseverance, character; and character, hope" (5:3–4). Paul described the various factors that people may encounter during their lives in ascending order of tribulation, patience, discipline, and hope. This describes the process one should go through while living as a righteous person through faith. This is written against the theological backdrop of Christ Jesus raised from the dead. If so, it is presented as the path that the people of God should walk. This, of course, means the hope for salvation expressed in righteousness. Accordingly, as a result of these instructions, the Romans should have felt quite burdened by the issue of living that follows the death and resurrection of Jesus Christ.

To sum up, Paul described the benefits enjoyed by those who have been justified by faith in God. This means that in order to enjoy grace, peace, and glory, the Romans had to live a life of patience and discipline along with tribulations. This narrative contains following in the footsteps of Christ Jesus, who rose again from the dead. In other words, this is a life living according to the gospel.

The Death and Resurrection of Christ (5:5–11)

Paul attempted a theological interpretation of the death and resurrection of Christ. This resulted in an atoning death and salvific resurrection. Paul defined it as the love of God and presented it as the core of the gospel.

Paul described what the Romans should hope. It begins with the statement that hope does not put them to shame because the love of God has been poured into their hearts through the holy spirit (5:5). Paul spoke of hope in connection with the love of God poured through the holy spirit. Faith allows those who are justified to have a hope even while experiencing suffering, which ultimately results in God's love. Paul made the Romans expect spiritual phenomena caused by the holy spirit, suggesting that it begins with faith, goes through hope, and then leads to love.

An explanation of God's love immediately followed. This is that Christ died for the ungodly at the right time when they were weak (5:6). Paul described Christ as the one died at the appointed time for the ungodly. Priscilla and Aquila learned from Paul that Christ died for people's sin according to the Scriptures (1 Cor 15:3). After their departure for

Rome, Paul said to the Galatians in the form of personal confession that Christ the Son of God had died on the cross for him because he had loved him (Gal 2:20). However, later in Rom(A), it was mentioned in the form of official statement that Christ had died even for the ungodly. In this way, Paul inherited the atoning death of Christ mentioned to the Corinthians and substituted the love of God for the love of Christ described in Galatians. This was written from a Jewish perspective in order that the Romans, mainly composed of Jews, could understand. However, it seems that they were not prepared to accept this interpretation of Paul, which defined them as the ungodly.

Then, the expression "at just the right time" should also be noted. This presupposes the promised time with a reference to the prophecy of prophet regarding the death of Christ. While the expression of "according to the Scriptures" was once applied to the death of Christ (1 Cor 15:3–4), that of "at just the right time" was used in Rom(A). With this expression, Paul presented the death of Christ as an element of the gospel because it had been prophesied (1:2). This is how Paul presented the justification for the Romans to accept the teachings about Christ, that is, the gospel itself. However, Jewish members would not have been able to agree with Paul presenting the core of the gospel. This is because it was so different from the Jewish tradition they had adopted up to that time.

Paul explained why the death of Christ was the love of God. It begins with the acknowledgment that it is not easy for someone to die for a righteous person and that there are some who are brave enough to die for a good person (5:7). Paul created a parallel between the righteous and the good and a contrast between not finding it easy to die and dying courageously. The righteous and the good were contrasted with the weak and ungodly described in the preceding verse. This conveys the meaning that it is more difficult to die for the weak and ungodly. Paul emphasized that Christ endured the death because God loved them. This kind of instruction would have been even more difficult to be accepted by Jewish members because they had never heard of God's love revealed in this way.

The love of God was identified as the atoning death of Christ. According to Paul, Christ demonstrated the love of God by dying for people when they were sinners (5:8). Paul reiterated the death for the ungodly in the form of Christ's death for sinners. This teaching is reminiscent of Paul's gospel that Christ died for people's sin (1 Cor 15:3; cf. Gal 1:4). However, in Rom(A), Paul described Christ as the one dying for sinners. Paul previously mentioned the blessing of being forgiven from sin without any penalty (4:6–8). Then, Paul presented Christ as the one who died to forgive someone's sin without receiving any compensation. This was the core of the gospel that Paul had wanted to convey. However, although the atoning death of Christ was not unfamiliar to the Romans, it would take time for them to accept the atonement through him.

The blood of Christ is mentioned for the first time. This appears in the statement that people can be justified by the blood of Christ (5:9a). Paul suddenly presented it as the way to be righteous. It should be noted that his death is symbolized by blood rather than the cross here. Unlike Paul's presentation of the cross of Christ as the way of salvation to the Corinthians (1 Cor 1:18–23), the blood of Christ was introduced as the way to be righteous in Rom(A). Having used the expression "blood of Christ" instead of "death of Christ on cross," Paul was careful, so that the Romans might not be misunderstood by the authorities due to the cross, which was a tool for executing traitors against the Roman Empire. Thus, the blood of Christ is another expression of his death on the cross, which is the result of faith in God. This reveals that Paul expanded the theme from Abraham to the blood of Christ in terms of faith.

Paul dealt with the issue of salvation in connection with Christ. It is said that those who are justified by the blood of Christ are saved through him from wrath (5:9b). Paul presented the blood of Christ as the way to righteousness that refers to salvation from wrath, and Christ was introduced as a savior. Moreover, salvation could mean freedom from the Law that brings about wrath (4:15). This description had already been handed down to the Thessalonians without being related to the Law (1 Thess 1:10). Accordingly, Paul developed it in the direction of relating it to the Law in Rom(A). However, it would not have been acceptable for Jewish members to link it to salvation from wrath or freedom from the Law. This is because of the extreme and negative description of the Law. Accordingly, the Romans had no choice but to raise questions to Paul and resist him.

In addition, Paul explained the relationship between God and people. This is revealed in the narrative that when people became enemies with God, God opened the way for reconciliation through the death of the Son (5:10a). Paul spoke of restoring the relationship between people and God. The death of the Son of God played an absolute role in turning enmity into a state of reconciliation. This is because it represents God's love. Paul once told the Corinthians that God was in Christ, reconciling the world to himself through the atoning death of Christ (2 Cor 5:15–19).

This kind of teaching might have been unknown to the Romans because it was written after Priscilla and Aquila had left Ephesus for Rome. At any rate, the role of atonement was imposed upon the death of Christ in Rom(A). It is, however, likely that the Romans would have had a hard time accepting the new instruction centered on the death of Christ.

Paul connected the theme of reconciliation with salvation. This appears in the expression that God, who made reconciliation, allows people to be saved "in the life" of his Son (5:10b). Paul presented salvation in the life of Christ the Son of God as the result of reconciliation with him. Here, his life seems to presuppose resurrection. It is noteworthy that although Priscilla and Aquila had learned about the resurrection of Christ and life in him as told to the Corinthians (1 Cor 15:22), Paul did not describe reconciliation with God from a soteriological perspective yet. On the other hand, in Rom(A), he mentioned the salvation of those who have been reconciled to God in the life of Christ the Son of God. It is important to note that the "life" of Christ was linked to salvation. These teachings were based on Paul's interpretation that no one in the Roman church had ever heard before. It is not clear whether they agreed to this.

Finally, the blessings enjoyed by a person who has been saved were described. This means that people received reconciliation as those who had boasted in God through the Lord Jesus Christ (5:11). In this way, Paul emphasized reconciliation with God in Rom(A). To this end, the role of "our Lord Jesus Christ" is added. This shows a deep connection with the fact that he died for those who were enemies of God but came to life. It is necessary to take a look at the phrase "not only is this so, but also," which was already used in connection with tribulation (5:3). With this, Paul encouraged the Romans to think of the death of Christ in the midst of tribulation and to remain as the people of God.

To sum up, Paul put an emphasis on the salvation provided through the atoning death and resurrection of the Lord Jesus Christ Son of God. This was defined as the love of God that characterizes the core of the gospel. However, Jewish members would have had a hard time accepting Paul's claim because the role of the Law would disappear.

The Love of God (8:31–39)

Paul described the condition of those who have achieved salvation through the death and resurrection of Christ. This means that the

Romans had to stand firm as those who had received the love of God. This is a blessing given to those who lived according to the gospel.

Paul went on to talk about the relationship between God and the Romans. A rhetorical question was used to assert that no one could deny what God had done (8:31a). In other words, no one can dispute the fact that God loved sinners and was reconciled to them through the death and resurrection of the Son Christ Jesus, as written in the preceding text (5:5–11). Christ's death and resurrection were the core of the gospel that leads people to salvation. Paul asked another rhetorical question: if God is for the Romans, who can oppose them? (8:31b). This means that no one is able to oppose them because God is for them. Before the challenge against Paul occurred by some gentiles under the sponsorship of the apostles of the Jerusalem church, he had expressed Jesus' life for others with the phrase "for" (1 Thess 5:10; 1 Cor 11:24). However, in Rom(A), it was applied to the relationship with God. This reveals the narrative from a Jewish perspective that God exists for the Romans. Therefore, they had to trust God and not be shaken.

Then, a third rhetorical question appears. It is told that God would give everything to the Romans because he did not spare the Son (8:32). Paul defined God as the one who gives everything freely. Since he did not spare his own Son, he could give everything else that is less precious than the Son. This very action was expressed as God's love. This teaching was developed based on his confession in Galatians that the Son of God gave himself out of love for Paul (Gal 2:20). Accordingly, in Rom(A), this turned into a teaching to consider it a grace that God gave the Son with everything. Paul taught that the Romans had to believe in God and rely on him. Since God provides all things spiritual and material to his people, the Romans should live in faith in God. This is a lesson quite new to the Romans.

Paul raised a fourth rhetorical question. It is said, "Who can accuse the person whom God has chosen?" (8:33). Paul argued that no one can refuse the one elected by God. Every member of the Roman church was to be a person whom God had called to be righteous. This is an exhortation to live with the belief that they were the people of God. Accordingly, whether Jews or gentiles, the Romans had to live by faith in God. It is because they could be also the elected people whom God loves. No one among the Romans would have disliked this kind of instruction.

A fifth rhetorical question was presented. This is "who is he that condemns?" (8:34a). Paul insisted that no one can condemn those who have been elected by God. This is a stronger word than "accuse," and it was used to give authority to God's election. It is important to observe that Christ Jesus was defined as a mediator at the right hand of God and given the authority to condemn (8:34b). This was a possible narrative because of the premise that he rose from the dead and then was supposed to have ascended to heaven. With this description, Paul heightened the authority of Christ Jesus. This narrative delivered a christological message unknown to Priscilla and Aquila. This was developed based on the fact that the promised descendant Christ was described as a mediator in Galatians, written after the couple left Ephesus for Rome (Gal 3:20). In this way, Paul delivered the lesson that Christ Jesus, the mediator, protects those who have been elected by God to be righteous. Having declared that the Romans would not be condemned, Paul asked them to rely upon Christ interceding for them. In this way, Paul developed the Christ-centered logic more and more. It was, however, difficult for the Romans, especially Jewish members, to accept his instruction based on a huge leap forward.

Paul raised a final rhetorical question. It is said that no one can separate Paul and other Romans from the love of Christ (8:35). Paul emphasized union with Christ. Paul once mentioned Christ's love for him in Galatians (Gal 2:20). Following this, the love of Christ was mentioned for sinners in Rom(A) (5:5–10). Paul confidently declared here that nothing, including tribulation, hardship, persecution, famine, nakedness, danger, and sword, could separate them from the love of Christ. This means that no threat in the world can intimidate the Romans to separate from Christ. Paul, who previously introduced the love of God, emphasized both of them while mentioning the love of Christ. The love of Christ would have been understood as the love of God.

Meanwhile, Paul supported his argument by quoting a verse from the Bible (8:36). It is said that they were killed for the Lord all day long and were regarded as sheep to be slaughtered (Ps 44:22). This is quoted to encourage the Romans to endure the tribulation even to death for Christ. In addition, Paul described situations that not only he, but also the Romans, had or could face. This is in line with the previous statement that suffering leads to hope through discipline (5:3–4). With this kind of image, Paul seemed to have taught the Romans, especially those of Jewish origin, to endure hardships from other Jews because they received the gospel of Christ Jesus.

A song of victory due to God was written. This appears as a declaration that Paul had more than enough victory through God who had loved him and the Romans (8:37). Here, Paul emphasized that God enables people to overcome all trials with the love that made the Son Christ to die for sinners. The issue of overcoming has already been told to the Corinthians in the mention of swallowing up death and giving them victory (1 Cor 15:54) and in the mention of God always giving them victory in Christ (2 Cor 2:14). However, in Rom(A), Paul developed the idea that God gives victory through his love that made the Son Christ die for sinners. With this, Paul encouraged the Romans to embark on the path of righteousness, reconciliation, and salvation given through the death and resurrection of Jesus Christ the Son of God. This is the path given to those who live according to the core of the gospel. Accordingly, having defined the Romans as those loved by God and called saints at the beginning of Rom(A), Paul mentioned the love of God here again in order to create an atmosphere to stand firmly in relationship with God.

Then Paul presented a conclusive saying. It is said that nothing can separate people from the love of God in Christ Jesus our Lord (8:38–39). Neither death nor life, angels nor powers, things present nor future, height nor depth, or any other created thing can break the relationship of love. Paul once told the Corinthians that Christ would destroy heavenly beings, including authorities and powers (1 Cor 15:24). In addition, it was said that Apollos, Cephas, the world, life and death, and the present and future all belong to the Corinthians, but they belong to Christ, and Christ belongs to God (1 Cor 3:22–23). In this way, having described various things, Paul ultimately showed a tendency to emphasize the relationship with God. Along this line, in Rom(A), Paul asserted that even such things cannot separate people from the love of God in Christ Jesus. It is important to emphasize here that God's love is revealed in Christ Jesus. In this way, the love of God and Christ Jesus was expressed as one. The Romans who heard this had to have thought that it was still worthy of paying attention to the teachings Paul preached.

In summary, Paul emphasized the love of God revealed through the death and resurrection of Christ Jesus the Son of God that is the core of the gospel. This is deeply related to God's authority to elect even sinners, so that they could stand firmly in the faith of Christ Jesus. This text is believed to have been part of the first letter on the subject of God's love. However, his new teachings would have been unfamiliar to the Romans, especially those of Jewish origin.

5. THE ETHICS OF SAINTS (12:3-13; 14:1-12)

Faith appears as a common element in the ethical teachings for the Romans. Paul advised the Romans to live by applying the principle of righteousness by faith in God. Paul delivered an eschatological lesson that they will stand before the judgment seat of God according to the level of faith.

Life According to the Measure of Faith (12:3-13)

Paul mentioned living according to the measure of faith. For this, various gifts were mentioned, which were the way for the Romans to live. Paul wrote this part thinking of unity in Christ in terms of faith. This is a lesson that can be generally conveyed in relation to faith.

First of all, the qualification to give advice to the Romans was mentioned. It is said that Paul could speak to the Romans because of the grace given to him (12:3a). The grace given to him is reminiscent of apostleship mentioned earlier (1:5). If this interpretation is acceptable, Paul was qualified to give spiritual advice to the Romans as an apostle. Since grace also meant righteousness in connection with faith (5:2), he was able to mention the faith of the Romans. This clearly provides Paul with the justification to insist that they should accept the lessons he had delivered in the previous texts.

The basic principle was presented for the ethical life. It is not to think more highly than they should but to think wisely "according to the measure of faith" that God has assigned to each person (12:3b). Here, thinking wisely according to the measure of faith is an important element for the ethical life of the Romans. Since Paul as an apostle had already taught about righteousness by faith, he was able to convey to the Romans what they should think and do according to the measure of their faith. The expression "according to the measure of faith" shows that Paul assumed that the degree of faith varies from person to person. In addition, this means that having suggested the principle, Paul told them about their lives according to their faith. Accordingly, the Romans would have had the opportunity to examine the defects of their own faith, rather than the degree of their observance of the Law. In conclusion, this gives readers confidence that this text was part of the first letter to the Romans in that faith was the main focus.

Paul used an analogy to explain his instruction. This is found in the description that just as there are many parts in the human body, there are many parts in Christ (12:4–5). Paul had already explained to the Corinthians that the human body has many parts, but that they have different functions in relation to Christ (1 Cor 12:12, 14, 20). This lesson would have been known to Priscilla and Aquila, who had a close relationship with the Corinthians. In the same context, Paul described in Rom(A) that as one body has many members, the Romans had to form one body in Christ. The phrase "in Christ" was used for the first time here in order to emphasize unity with Christ. Therefore, the Romans would have accepted these teachings without serious opposition. Paul simply presented only principles, which did not seem to mean that any dispute or fight occurred among the Romans. Rather, it seems that he was conveying something that could be applied to all members of churches in general. Paul was unable to write down teachings about specific situations when he wrote the first letter to the Roman church.

The way of forming the body of Christ was discussed. This is described as being accomplished by practicing the gifts received according to the grace given to the Romans (12:6a). The gift was already mentioned frequently to the Corinthians (1 Cor 1:7; 7:7; 12:4, 9, 28, 30–31; 2 Cor 1:11). While staying with Paul, Priscilla and Aquila would have had knowledge of this. Paul then mentioned the gift to be given to the Romans in Rom(A) (1:11), and it was mentioned again here. The gifts given to them by grace should be something that had to be considered wisely according to the measure of faith. Therefore, Paul also presented prophecy as a gift that had to be exercised according to the proportion of faith (12:6b). As prophecy was emphasized as an important gift to the Corinthians (1 Cor 12:10, 28; 14:1), so Paul dealt with it in Rom(A) by linking the expression "measure of faith." However, having compared to what was passed down to the Corinthians, the prophecy was only briefly mentioned in Rom(A). Anyway, this text was a part of Rom(A) that was based on the element of faith. Paul attempted to enrich the religious life of the Romans by presenting them with prophecy as a spiritual gift.

Paul introduced various gifts. These include prophecy, service, teaching, comfort, relief, governance, and mercy (12:7–8). Paul presented several new types of gifts. This is revealed when compared to the previous description. Paul once listed various gifts given by the spirit of God to the Corinthians (1 Cor 12:7–10). They are the word of wisdom, the word of knowledge, speaking in tongues, etc. Having been given as the answer to the question of the Corinthians delivered by Chloe's household (1 Cor 1:11), they were gifts that reflect the special situation of the Corinthian church. It seems that Priscilla and Aquila would have been well aware of them. However, Paul mentioned different gifts in Rom(A), and they were ethical elements that believers should generally practice. In listing them, Paul did not seem to have specifically considered the situation of the Roman church; rather, they seem to have been referring to actions performed in the church in general.

The issue of love was addressed. Paul presented the proposition that there is no lie in love (12:9a). While the love of God was already discussed in the previous texts (1:7; 5:8; 8:39), the love that the Romans should have toward their brothers is addressed here. It seems that Paul addressed them to practice love as general content to be followed. Then, various behaviors are listed as the characteristics of those who practice love in general (12:9b–13). To them belong hating evil and practicing good, and loving one another with brotherly love. Also, respect must come first; then, the Romans had to be diligent and not lazy, live diligently with spirit, and serve the Lord. They must rejoice in hope, endure tribulation, and always persevere in prayer. They should provide food for the believers and serve guests. In this way, Paul introduced how to live with love, having used various expressions. This description also does not seem to have been delivered against the background of the special circumstances of the Roman church. Then, there would have been no reason for the Romans to reject this kind of general teaching. Thus, the text that deals with the issue of love is considered to be in the first letter.

In summary, Paul taught that Romans had to walk according to the measure of their faith. For this purpose, the case of gifts and love was used as an example. Paul wanted the Romans united in Christ without conflict. The issue of faith was something Paul consistently described in the first letter to the Romans.

No Evaluation on Others (14:1–12)

Paul presented the lives of the Romans in light of the death and resurrection of Christ. The element of faith plays a central role here to live for the Lord without evaluation on others. Paul presented general guidelines rather than instructions for specific situation among the Romans.

Paul taught consideration for those who were weak in faith. This appears in the teaching to accept those who are weak in faith but not to criticize their opinions (14:1). Paul mentioned the evaluation on the other party and described it as if there was conflict among the Romans. However, it should be noted that this description had appeared before. Paul once taught the Corinthians about those who are weak in faith (1 Cor 8:11–12). This kind of lesson would also have been known to Priscilla and Aquila, who were closely associated with the Corinthian church. Accordingly, in Rom(A), Paul was able to describe those who are weak in faith. In this manner, Abraham was described as the one who was not weak in faith (4:19), and then Christ was described as the one who died for the atonement of the weak (5:6). This reflects the fact that there were people in the Roman church who had strong faith, as well as those who were weak in faith. However, this seems to have been a teaching that could be applied generally rather than that for a special situation of the Romans at the time of writing Rom(A). Paul delivered this instruction because both the strong and the weak in faith had to constitute the body of Christ (12:5). Jewish members were advised to embrace gentile members who formed a minority in the church.

Critique against those of weak faith was explained in connection with food. This deals with the issue not to make an evaluation on others just because they have different attitudes toward food (14:2–3). Paul mentioned people who had faith strong enough to eat everything and those who ate only vegetables because of weak faith. Then, a warning was made against those with strong faith looking down on those with weak faith. A similar issue was addressed to the Corinthians in relation to meat sacrificed to idols (1 Cor 8:10–11). Priscilla and Aquila should have heard of it from Paul while staying with him in Corinth or Ephesus. However, in Rom(A), this was expanded and applied to people who refused meat itself and those who ate only vegetables in relation to the issue of faith in daily life. At the same time, mutual criticism was prohibited. In addition, having mentioned that God accepted those who were weak in faith, Paul presented the justification that the Romans should also accept them. It is because they were all the people of God. The reason that Paul preached this kind of instruction was to prevent the Romans from being engaged in conflicts due to differences in their degrees of faith. This is how they become one body in Christ.

Paul also applied the issue of criticism to social relationships. This appears in the teaching not to criticize other people's servants (14:4). Whether the servant stands or falls, everything belongs to the master's authority; thus, the Romans should not violate the master's authority. At the same time, Paul taught that they should not criticize each other because their establishment also belongs to the Lord God. This statement is in line with what was taught earlier that no one should make evaluation on those who are weak in faith because God had accepted them. In this way, while making a God-centered statement, Paul taught that the Romans should not criticize whether they were Jews or gentiles. This is because God established all of them. This seems to be a kind of instruction that Paul could give under normal circumstances.

Then, the issue of evaluation on seasons was addressed. This appears in the teaching that some people regard one day as better than another, while others consider all days the same, and each must decide in his or her own heart (14:5). Paul once gave teachings about the feasts to the Galatians (Gal 4:10). This means that there are different standards for interpreting and observing the provisions of the feasts specified in the Law, so no one can criticize others. Priscilla and Aquila would have encountered this lesson for the first time in Rom(A). Since they were Jews, their concept of festivals in Rome could be different from that of gentiles. Accordingly, Paul taught that people should not judge each other based only on their own standards. Having dealt with the issue of seasons, Paul allowed each person to make decisions according to their own standards. This is not believed to be a lesson for special situations that can only occur among the Romans. In this respect, this text could belong to the first letter as a general lesson.

It is most important to think about the Lord. To this end, according to Paul, those who value the day consider it important for the Lord's sake, those who have eaten should eat for the Lord's sake—giving thanks to God—and those who have not eaten do not eat for the Lord's sake but give thanks to God (14:6). In other words, if one considers God the most important, it will be accepted no matter which day he or she considers important, and it can be accepted no matter which day he or she does not consider important. Moreover, whether one eats or not, anything he or she does for God is important. In any case, it is important to live with gratitude to God, and it is not important to judge each other on a relative basis. Having written in this way, Paul allowed both Jewish and gentile members to be free in relation to the holidays. This lesson could have been given generally rather than given by Paul with any special situation of the Romans in mind.

Accordingly, Paul emphasized life toward God. This appears in the declaration that no one lives for himself and no one dies for himself (14:7). Paul attempted this description from a perspective of faith. This is in line with what Paul declared earlier that God showed his love by having the Son die for sinners (5:8). In other words, having followed the example of the Lord Jesus Christ who had sacrificed himself for sinners, the Romans had to live such a life. However, almost everyone lives and dies for themselves. Nevertheless, the reason that Paul preached this lesson was to emphasize faith. This presented the identification of the Romans with Christ.

Life for God is emphasized. This is found in the statement that if people live, they must live for the Lord and that if they die, they must die for the Lord. Whether they live or die, they belong to the Lord (14:8). Paul taught that the Romans should live centered on the Lord, and here the "Lord" seems to refer to Christ. Paul once confessed in Galatians that he lived for Christ, who had loved him and given up the body for him (Gal 2:20). In similar manner, in Rom(A), it is written that whether one lives or dies, he or she lives and dies for the Lord. These teachings would have been unfamiliar to the Romans represented by Priscilla and Aquila. This reflects the fact that Paul approached the Romans from a perspective of the gospel centered on the death and resurrection of Christ.

Paul explained the reason that the Romans had to live for the Lord. It is because Christ died and rose again to become Lord of all people, both the dead and the living (14:9). In previous letters, Paul already proclaimed that God had raised Christ from the dead (cf. 1 Thess 1:10; 1 Cor 15:12; Gal 1:1, etc.). Accordingly, in Rom(A), it is written that God raised the Lord Jesus from the dead (4:24). Afterwards, it was stated that those who have been reconciled to God through the death of the Son would be saved even more through his resurrection (5:10). Along these lines, Paul was able to write that Christ died and rose again, that is, becoming the Lord of the dead and the living. In this way, Paul presented to the Romans a life according to the gospel, based on the death and resurrection of Christ. In this way, Paul defined Jesus Christ as the savior of all people.

Now Paul applied the issue of criticism to relationships with brothers. This is revealed in the statement that one should not criticize one's brother or despise him, for all will stand before the judgment seat of God (14:10). Paul dealt with God's judgment upon all people from an eschatological perspective. With regard to the relationships with brothers, it was once told to the Corinthians that they should not sin against their weak brother because Christ had died for them (1 Cor 8:11–12). Priscilla and Aquila would have been familiar with this teaching of Paul. However, in Rom(A), Paul developed and described this from a more ethical perspective. Since Paul had prohibited the Romans from making an evaluation of those who were weak in faith and criticizing other people's servants in the previous texts (14:1–4), he prohibited critique against brothers here. This can be said to be an extension of what was taught earlier about love for brothers (12:10). In this way, Paul delivered a lesson that can be generally applied in all cases.

A verse was cited from the Bible to support Paul's claims. This is what the Lord said: as he lives, every knee will bow to him and every tongue will confess to God (14:11). This was quoted from Isaiah (Isa 45:23), meaning that the living God will be the judge. Here, God is described as "Lord" to emphasize God's sovereignty. Paul quoted this verse because he wanted to make the Romans think again about their lives while looking at the judgment at the end. They were advised not to criticize others while they lived in this world awaiting the eschatological judgment of God. This was a lesson generally delivered to all people.

Paul also described the situation that will occur in the end times. This means that everyone will give an account of his or her affairs to God (14:12). Paul described what would happen before the judgment seat of God from a Jewish perspective. This means that if anyone criticizes his or her brother, that brother will give an account of him or her to God; thus, one should be careful of criticizing his or her brother or sister. This means that one should not carelessly criticize people on account of their weak faith. In this way, Paul wanted the Romans to understand and help each other in order to build a community of faith as the people of God.

To sum up, Paul encouraged the Romans to live by faith for the Lord. This results in imitating the life of Christ who died but came back to life. Paul did not write it to reflect the specific situation of the Roman church; rather, this was something that could generally be applied to all church members with regard to the issue of faith. In this respect, this was sufficient to be included in the first letter.

6. PLAN FOR ITINERARY (15:22–29)

Paul directly mentioned the intention to visit the Roman church. This is to preach the gospel and then expected in return their financial support for the mission to Spain. Having learned of his intention, the Romans would have been burdened.

Intention to Visit Rome (15:22–24)

Paul made it known that he intended to visit Rome several times. He then revealed the plan to go to Spain via Jerusalem and Rome. In this respect, this text shows that the end of the letter is near.

The intention to visit Rome was clearly expressed. This is found in the saying that he had wanted to go to Rome several times (15:22). Paul revealed the intention to visit and implicitly asked for their consent. This was, of course, a courtesy he should have taken ahead of the first visit. Paul once told the Thessalonians that he had tried to visit them once or twice but that Satan had prevented him from visiting them (1 Thess 2:18). Then, at the beginning of Rom(A), Paul said that he would go to Rome and give spiritual gifts to the Romans to strengthen them (1:13). Then, here he mentioned the fact that he had wanted to visit Rome several times, but it did not happen. His desire to visit Rome and the request to welcome him could rightly have been included in the first letter.

Paul specifically described the reason that he had wanted to visit Rome. This appears in the description that he had been planning to go to Spain for several years because there was no place to work in the areas of Asia Minor, Macedonia, and Achaia where he had worked, but he wanted to visit Rome first (15:23). Paul had a plan to preach the gospel to all regions of the Roman Empire at the time. To this end, the Roman church was able to play an important role in Paul's plan. This was not only a place he wanted to pass through on his way to Spain, an unexplored area, but also an institution that could provide him with financial support. Since the Roman church was not founded by Paul himself, he had to politely inform them of his intention and ask for their permission. If he received permission from the Romans, he would gain spiritual and financial support for the preaching of the gospel to Spain. Even at this time, Paul seemed to have been confident that the Romans would welcome him warmly.

The purpose to visit Rome is clearly stated. Paul wanted to go to Spain and preach the gospel with the financial support of the Romans (15:24). To this end, he first wanted to see them as he passed by. It was once told to the Corinthians that he did not want to see the Corinthians any longer when he passed the area (1 Cor 16:7). The Corinthian church was founded by Paul under the leadership of Barbanas, but they challenged him; thus, he no longer visited Corinth in passing but with a special purpose. Then, in Rom(A), Paul was asked to allow his visit.

However, the Roman church was not a church that Paul himself established, nor was it his final destination; thus, he wanted to stop by on his way through. It is then written what he intended to share with the Romans. Paul tried to make them satisfied by preaching the gospel and then go to Spain with their financial support. This reflects the situation in which Paul was no longer able to do his own work without relying on the financial support of gentile churches. This may have caused the Romans to worry about the economic burden.

In summary, Paul expressed the intention to visit Rome ahead of trip to Spain. In order to gain the consent of the Romans, Paul wrote as politely as possible and mentioned preaching the gospel with an expectation of financial support from them. He was probably confident that they would accept him. Having known his intention, the Romans should have felt a great deal of burden. These contents would naturally have been part of the first letter.

Intention to Visit Jerusalem (15:25–29)

Paul revealed the will to visit Jerusalem before heading for Rome. This is to deliver the money collected by the gentiles. To this end, he presented a theology of service, which could also belong to the first letter.

The intention of Paul to visit Jerusalem was mentioned. This appears in the narrative that he would go to Jerusalem to serve the saints (15:25). There is a reason why Paul mentioned this after expressing the intention to visit Rome. This was to demonstrate his determination to keep the promise with regard to money. Paul tried to keep the promise made at Jerusalem after he had completed the first missionary journey (Gal 2:1–10). Accordingly, it is clear that he went on the second missionary trip and collected donations from gentiles for the poor saints of the Jerusalem church. The first place mentioned was the Galatian church, and then later donations were requested from the Corinthians (1 Cor 16:1). Thus, the collection of money was requested several times to them (2 Cor 8:4; 9:1). The reason Paul made this comment was to make the Romans sure that he would keep the promise regarding money.

Paul mentioned the churches that participated in the collection. They were the people of Macedonia and Achaia (15:26). Paul mentioned the fact that the churches in the Macedonia region participated eagerly (2 Cor 8:1; 9:2), and Stephenas, Fortunatus, and Achaicus participated in the collection, probably in Athens of Achaia (1 Cor 16:17). Of course, many people not mentioned here would have donated money. Paul once mentioned in Galatians that there were many poor members in the Jerusalem church (Gal 2:10). This shows that the economic situation in Jerusalem was not good enough to be independent from an economic perspective. In fact, Paul did not have good relationship with the apostles of the Jerusalem church because they asked the gentiles to challenge him after the theological debate over the gentile table at Antioch. Nevertheless, the reason that Paul announced this plan to the Romans was to give them a hint that they should help him financially in preaching the gospel to Spain.

The attitude for the participation in donations was described. First of all, the Romans must participate with a joyful mind (15:27). No matter how much they donated for religious reasons, it is true that it was difficult to give with a joyful mind. However, Paul emphasized that the church members in Macedonia and Achaia were happy to donate because it was to help the poor members of the Jerusalem church. In addition, Paul told the Romans that since the gentiles were spiritually indebted to the Jerusalem church, they should serve with material called charity. Paul once referred to himself as a debtor to the gentiles (1:14), because for their sake he was called to be a preacher of the Son of God. Here, the concept of debtor is applied to gentiles in their relationship with the Jerusalem church. This is much more advanced than the theology of donations that Paul conveyed to the Corinthians (see 2 Cor 8:14; 9:6). In this way, Paul developed the theological thoughts on collections into a spiritual aspect in Rom(A).

Paul mentioned the plan after delivering the collection. It is said that he would go to Rome and show grace to the church members before going to Spain (15:28). Paul clearly revealed the journey he had planned. It is, however, important here that Paul revealed the intention to use the collection for its original purpose. He implicitly informed the Romans that if he received their support, he would definitely go to Spain to preach. In any case, since he still had a long journey to go from Jerusalem to Rome, he asked them to take sufficient time to think about it. It is believed that his request was burdensome to the Romans, even though Priscilla and Aquila received instruction from him on the Jewish view of Christ Jesus.

Finally, hope was given to the Romans. It was a promise that when he went to Rome, he would take the full blessings of Christ with him (15:29). It was already mentioned in earlier text that he would strengthen the Romans by distributing spiritual gifts (1:11). That gift has been summarized so far in the gospel that Paul would preach to them. The gospel of God can be summarized in that people are justified by faith in God and the path to salvation is opened through the death and resurrection of Christ. Accordingly, Paul gave the Romans an opportunity to recognize the gospel, the spiritual gift, as a blessing and to judge it in advance. This kind of statement was made to prompt them to welcome him in the first letter.

To sum up, Paul declared that he was going to deliver the money that the gentiles had donated for the poor saints of the Jerusalem church. This implicitly reveals a demand that the Roman church, which is mainly made up of Jewish members, had to make donations for missionary work to gentiles at the time. The Romans had to be burdened on account of the request for financial support. This content was worthy of being included in the first letter in that it expressed Paul's intention before visiting the Roman church.

7. RECOMMENDATION (16:1-2)

Paul introduced the person delivering Rom(A). It was customary in his time to recommend a messenger when sending the first letter. Paul sent it by the hand of Phoebe, who was in and out of Rome.

Paul mentioned the person delivering the first letter to the Romans. For this purpose, Phoebe, a female worker of church in Cenchrea, was introduced (16:1). Cenchrea was a coastal city about 5 miles south of Corinth. It is not clear whether Paul established the Cenchrean church or the Corinthians did. However, it is undeniable that there is a close connection between the two churches. That is why Paul was able to send Phoebe to Rome. No further information has been known about her. However, it is clear that she was an active woman, as she was chosen for the delivery of a letter to Rome. Additionally, she may have been a woman who had been to Rome. Based on this, it is likely that Paul sent Rom(A) to the Romans from Corinth.

Paul then asked the Romans to take care of Phoebe. This means welcoming her with the courtesy of saints and helping her in whatever way she needed (16:2). Paul the sender of Rom(A) had no choice but to make this request to the Romans. This was a prelude to what he hoped to be welcomed warmly. Paul already wrote this request for Timothy, who delivered the first letter, Cor(A), to the Corinthians (1 Cor 16:10-11). Accordingly, when Paul sent Rom(A), he asked the Romans to take care of Phoebe. Here the proper etiquette of saints is mentioned but not described in detail. This is believed to refer to the custom that was in use at the time. Also, the request to help with whatever is needed probably means that she should be provided with room and board. Although Phoebe was not a preacher of the gospel, Paul seemed to have requested the Romans to treat her accordingly.

The relationship between Paul and Phoebe was described. She was the protector of Paul and many people. This is reminiscent of a patron-client relationship in the Greco-Roman culture of the time. In other words, it is likely that Phoebe was a woman who supported Paul in preaching the gospel. Having judged from this, it appears that Phoebe was wealthy enough to help many people, including Paul. This means that women's abilities and activities were significant in the gentile churches. It is likely that Phoebe was someone who traveled to Rome to do business. In any case, Paul probably asked Phoebe to find out the situation of the Roman church in detail and return to inform him.

In summary, Paul sent the first letter to the Roman church by the hands of Phoebe. An introduction to her is comparable to the contents of his first letter to the Roman church. Having read these contents, the Romans would have had confidence in his letters.

8. GREETINGS (16:3-16)

Paul sent greetings to the members of the Roman church. This is one of his efforts to be closer to them. It is clear that Paul had information about many people in the Roman church.

First of all, Priscilla and Aquila were mentioned as those to be greeted. They were defined as Paul's coworkers in Christ Jesus (16:3). It is likely that Paul had met them in Corinth and then moved to Ephesus (1 Cor 16:8, 19; cf. Acts 18:1-3, 26). They seemed to have returned to Rome and established a church there before the challenge against Paul reached the peak by the Galatians. Accordingly, they could have occupied a leading position in the Roman church. In this respect, Paul defined them as coworkers, and they were the first candidate to be greeted. However, it is not clear whether the couple accepted everything that Paul wrote in Rom(A). At any rate, Paul began his greetings by mentioning them because he had to win their hearts first.

The narrative of Priscilla and Aquila continued. This is found in the thanksgiving that not only Paul but also all the gentile churches are thankful to them because they gave up their lives for him (16:4). The sacrifice that the couple made for Paul was not specifically described. However, when Paul mentioned their sacrifice, it is reminiscent of the statement that it is not easy for someone to die for a righteous person and that there are some who die for a good person (5:7). This means that the couple was those who followed the life of Jesus Christ. Paul elevated them to this level because he expected the Romans represented by Priscilla and Aquila to help him financially for the desired mission to Spain.

Paul also sent greetings to the church in the house of Priscilla and Aquila (16:5a). This shows that the Roman church was formed in their home at the time. This aspect is also found in Philemon, where the church in the house of Archippus was mentioned (Phlm 2). If so, it seems that the Roman church was not so big at the time of writing Rom(A), because there was a limit to the number of people who could gather in their house. Nevertheless, it was a great achievement to gather that many members in a short period of time. It is not clear how much funding Paul expected from them for the mission to Spain.

Then, Epenetus was mentioned. Having introduced him as a loved one, Paul defined him as the first fruit of Christ in Asia (16:5b). This reflects the fact that he received the gospel from Paul and then met Priscilla and Aquila later in Ephesus. At any way, Epenetus seemed to have moved with them to Rome later. If so, it is likely that he was also a diaspora Jew who had been driven out of Rome by Emperor Claudius and returned there after the edict was lifted. The fact that "the first fruit in Asia" reminds readers of "the first fruit in Achaia" shows that Paul had special affection for those who first received the gospel in each region (1 Cor 16:15). This made him introduce Epenetus immediately after Priscilla and Aquila.

In addition, Paul mentioned Mary. She was introduced as a woman who worked hard for the members of the Roman church (16:6). Having judged from this description, it appears that she did a lot of work voluntarily within the church. Since Mary was an important figure in the Roman church, she was introduced immediately after Priscilla, Aquila, and Epenetus. However, since information about Maria is no longer provided, it is not easy to accurately infer her identity. Moreover, the fact that the name Maria was common at the time does not help much. Nevertheless, the fact that she was mentioned next to Aquila, Priscilla, and Epenetus shows that she might have been the first person in Rome to accept the gospel.

Andronicus and Junias were introduced. Paul defined them as his relatives and fellow prisoners (16:7). Paul's relatives were mentioned here for the first time. Moreover, they were imprisoned with Paul; however, since there is no more information about the imprisonment, it is difficult to accurately restore their whereabouts. Meanwhile, Andronicus and Junia were defined as those outstanding among the apostles and those who had been in Christ before Paul. The apostles here may refer to those other than the twelve (1 Cor 15:5–7). They are believed to have been the people who received the tradition about Christ and later passed it on to Paul (1 Cor 15:3). Accordingly, they could be defined as those who belonged to the precedents in regard to the faith of Christ before Paul. Then, at an unknown time, they seem to have moved to Rome and joined the church founded by Priscilla and Aquila. However, the description of this also does not appear anywhere else, so we cannot know for sure.

Paul introduced Ampliatus whom he loved in the Lord. He was defined as someone who was loved in the Lord by Paul (16:8). Here the expression "in the Lord" was applied to him for the first time in the list of greetings, and it seems to be inextricably linked with "in Christ Jesus" applied to Priscilla and Aquila. Moreover, the expression "whom I love" is used, which is in line with the phrase "my dear friend" applied to Epenetus (16:5). Having written in this way, Paul expressed the extreme interest in Ampliatus. In this respect, he seems to have been a person who had a special relationship with Paul. However, Paul did not provide any more information about him.

In addition, an introduction to the two people appears. Paul mentioned Urbanus and Stachys (16:9). Urbanus was introduced as a coworker of Paul, which was already applied to Priscilla and Aquila in earlier text. However, while the couple were defined in apposition to Paul, Urbanus was introduced in apposition to those who were with him. In this respect, Urbanus is believed to have had a less important position in the Roman church than Priscilla and Aquila. Paul then introduced Stachys as the person whom he loved. The expression "whom I love" was also applied to Epenetus earlier. In this way, Paul introduced Stachys in a personal relationship. However, no further information was provided about Urbanus and Stachys.

Paul mentioned Apelles and Aristobulus. Whereas Apelles was introduced as someone who had been recognized in Christ, Aristobulus was mentioned as someone who had accepted Christ with his family (16:10). The fact that Apelles was introduced as a person recognized in Christ means that he was the one who knew the thoughts of Christ. The expression "in Christ," applied to him, had already been used for Andronicus and Junias (16:7). In addition, Aristobulus is mentioned as someone who went to church with his family. Although Paul did not know the details of their situation, he knew that his family participated in the church together. However, his personal relationship with Apelles and Aristobulus was not mentioned at all.

Some relatives of Paul were mentioned. Among them was Herodion (16:11). Paul mentioned his relative Andronicus and Junias before; however, the relationship among the three is not clear. It appears that some of Paul's relatives had advanced to Rome. In addition, Paul also asked for greetings from those related to Narcissus who were in the Lord. This reflects the situation that there were people in his family who accepted the gospel. Of course, information about Narcissus was no longer provided, so no further explanation can be given. However, Paul must have expected their support by revealing that he knew many people who made up the Roman church.

Paul introduced women who labored in the Lord (16:12). First of all, Tryphena and Tryphosa were mentioned. They remind readers of Mary, who worked hard for the Romans. The difference is that the expression "in the Lord" was applied to Tryphena and Tryphosa. Paul then introduced Persis, who labored a lot in the Lord and whom he loved. It is interesting that she was described as a woman who worked harder than Tryphena and Tryphosa. This is the second case that Paul introduced someone whom he loved after he had applied it to Apliatus. Persis seemed to have been someone who was close to Paul personally.

The personal relationship of Paul was revealed in the case of son and his mother. This is about Rufus and his mother (16:13). Paul described Rufus as a chosen man in the Lord. This is reminiscent of the description that the Romans were chosen as saints (1:7). This refers to the fact that Paul defined Rufus as one of God's people. However, no further information of him appears. In particular, Paul showed closeness to Rufus's mother, to the point where he called her "my mother." There can be no title that expresses intimacy more than this. However, her name has not been recorded; however, she is believed to have been well-known to the Romans. This is unique in the fact that a son and his mother were introduced together.

Paul mentioned several people. Mentioned here are Asyncritus, Phlegon, Hermes, Patrobas, Hermas, and the brethren with them (16:14).

No modifiers were given to them. Although they may not have done great things or been close people, Paul seemed to have had a friendship with them. Although Paul had no choice but to mention them, this made him mention in detail the people who made up the Roman church. Of course, Paul did not write anything about the process of getting to know them; however, it seems that he was listening to news from Rome while working in the Macedonia and Achaia regions.

Finally, several couples were also mentioned. They were Philologus, Julia, Nereus, his sister, and Olympas and all the saints with them (16:15). Perhaps they were those who had been in a marital relationship. However, it seems that Paul not only did not know much about them but also did not know about their achievements. However, they were mentioned because they made up the Roman church. This shows that Paul already had a lot of information about the Romans when he sent the first letter.

Paul asked for greetings. The Romans were asked to greet each other with a holy kiss (16:16). With this, Paul mentioned the way how they greeted at the time. The holy kiss is not a new form of action but one that has been given meaning. At the same time, Paul wrote that all churches of Christ greet the Romans. It seems that it was probably a customary sentence. With this kind of description, he taught that the church must communicate and share fellowship in Christ. This is what it means for the churches to become one in Christ.

To sum up, Paul greeted all the people whose names he had known. They were those who had participated in the Roman church. This was to show off his close relationship with them and to ask subtly to listen to what he had wanted. The more intimacy Paul had expressed with many people, the more the Romans would have felt the burden of having to do his bidding. In this respect, the greeting should be considered part of Paul's first letter to the Romans.

9. CLOSING PART (16:21–24)

Paul closed the letter by sending his greetings. In particular, he also conveyed the greetings of those who were with him. This was also part of Paul's work to strengthen the intimacy with the Romans. This is worthy of appearing at the end of the first letter.

Paul personally delivered greetings to the Romans (16:21). This includes himself, Timothy, Nucius, Jason, and Sosipater. They were those who were with Paul at the time of writing Rom(A). Timothy was already a well-known coworker (1 Cor 16:5), and Jason may have suffered in place of Paul there (cf. Acts 17:5–9). If this is correct, Paul would have accepted him when he preached the gospel in Thessalonica before the apostolic meeting at the Jerusalem church held around 49 CE. Later, when Paul visited Thessalonica again during his second missionary journey, Jason seems to have provided Paul with a place to stay. Afterwards, he seems to have helped Paul by accompanying him to Corinth when Rom(A) was written. However, no information has been known about other people.

Then, Tertius was mentioned. He introduced himself as the one who took dictation of Paul's letters (16:22). It was also revealed to the Corinthians and Galatians that someone wrote down what Paul had said (1 Cor 16:21; Gal 6:11). It seems that Paul had someone write down because he was old, his eyesight was blurred, or he was sick (Gal 4:15). Accordingly, it is revealed that Rom(A) was written down by Tertius. This kind of dictation was common at the time when powerful people had writers or servants take dictation without mentioning their names. However, Paul expressed the respect and gratitude for the writer by listing his name and greetings.

Paul conveyed the greetings of Gaius to the Romans. Gaius was introduced as a person who had cared for Paul and the entire Corinthians (16:23). He was a member of the Corinthian church (1 Cor 1:14; cf. Acts 19:29). Then, it is clear that Paul sent Rom(A) from Corinth. In any case, the fact that Paul mentioned Gaius shows that he had been on Paul's side at the time of writing Rom(A) until the end. Gaius is believed to have accepted Paul's gospel, been baptized by him, and served as his patron (1 Cor 1:14).

Paul then delivered greetings from Erastus and his brother Quartus. Erastus seemed to be identified as a director of public works in Corinth if he is the owner of the name engraved on the inscription found there: "Erastus, commissioner of public works, bore the expense of this pavement." It is then to be believed that he also played an important role in the Corinthian church with financial donation. Having judged from this, it seems that at the time Paul wrote Rom(A), there were people of a certain social status within the Corinthian church. It seems that Paul was able to inform the Romans of his status by listing the names of these people.

The blessing as the final greetings has been written. It is said, "The grace of our Lord Jesus Christ be with all of you ever" (16:24). Paul ended Rom(A) with a blessing, as he did with his other letters. It should be noted that no element of God appears here; rather, only Christ is mentioned in connection with peace. This shows that Paul wanted to emphasize Christ at the time of writing Rom(A). In any case, this can be said to be sufficient as the end of a letter.

In summary, Paul showed utmost courtesy as he concluded the first letter Rom(A). This is revealed in the way he tried to strengthen relationships by sending greetings not only of himself but also of those who had been with him. With this, he waited for a response from the Romans with a hope for a warm welcome.

10. CONCLUSION.

Paul sent the first letter Rom(A) to inform of his upcoming visit to the Roman church. This contained a request to accept and welcome him. At the same time, he revealed the intention to preach the gospel to the Romans and receive financial support from them to go to Spain. For this purpose, he had no choice but to give an outline of the gospel in advance. This shows the situation in which he could no longer do self-funded missionary work. Since Paul did not establish the Roman church and was not economically free, he cautiously expected their support while preaching the gospel of God about the Lord Jesus Christ the Son.

In Rom(A), the narrative centered on God. This is because there were many Jews among the Romans represented by Priscilla and Aquila. However, they did not know much about the challenge of the Galatians against Paul. In any case, in Rom(A), he presented the theology of faith in God based on the case of Abraham that was already developed in Galatians. At the end, it only gave a glimpse of atonement and salvation through the death and resurrection of Jesus Christ. The Romans would have had a hard time to understand the gospel because it was new to them.

Much of the gospel based on what Paul preached to the Galatians after Priscilla and Aquila left Ephesus for Rome was reflected in Rom(A). Righteousness by faith in God was the main element of the gospel. It began with a focus on Abraham's faith and ended with the atoning death and salvific resurrection of Christ Jesus. In addition, although it appeared in weakened terms, a negative view on the Law was also presented. The Romans were not familiar with his teachings and seemed to have been deeply troubled about whether to accept them or not. Accordingly, they seem to have taken a stance of casting doubt about his instructions.

Paul sent Rom(A) from Corinth by the hands of Phoebe. It seems to be in early 56 CE. This is based on the reconstructed life of Paul as follows. Having learned about Christ from the religious precedents probably in Damascus around 35 and about Jesus from Cephas on the basis of Q in Jerusalem around 38 (Gal 1:17–18), Paul traveled through Syria, Cilicia, Galatia, Asia Minor, and Macedonia under the leadership of Barnabas even to Corinth of Achaia (Gal 1:21; 2:1; 1 Cor 9:6). This can be considered the first missionary journey. After attending the apostolic meeting held in Jerusalem around 49 (Gal 2:1–10), Paul had a theological debate with Cephas over the gentile table in Antioch around 50 (Gal 2:11–14). Afterwards, Paul is believed to have traveled the gentile regions from Antioch in Syria to Corinth in Achaia in order to visit the churches and strengthen them spiritually for about four years. Having been challenged by some Corinthians sponsored by Cephas (1 Cor 1:12), Paul retreated to Ephesus (1 Cor 16:19). Having heard about the severe challenge of the Galatians there, he sent Galatians. And then, he traveled through the region of Macedonia to Illyricum (15:19) and then arrived at the Corinthian church. It is believed that it took about two years for him to visit Corinth third times. It was then and there that Paul wrote Rom(A) in early 56.

II

Rom(B)

PAUL SENT ANOTHER LETTER, Rom(B), to the Roman church. It focuses on wrath, transgression, unrighteousness, the Law, and Jesus Christ. There is a reason that Paul dealt with these issues. Having read Rom(A), the Romans, especially Jewish members, did not agree with his negative view that the Law brings about wrath and that where there is no Law there is no transgression (4:15). They told Phoebe, who had delivered Rom(A), and then she apparently reported Paul that he had to clear their doubts and critiques. Accordingly, he had no choice but to respond to them. This is because he desperately needed the financial support of the Romans for the mission, even to Spain.

The answer of Paul to the doubts and critiques of the Romans was written in Rom(B). Accordingly, having maintained the negative position on the Law, Paul had to emphasize its relationship with the wrath of God and the transgression of people. Here, a sense of deja vu is formed in that the strong tone of opposition or criticism Paul had shown toward the Galatians also appeared in Rom(B). Accordingly, he adopted the words, themes, and expressions used in Galatians. In addition, since Paul had already explained the gospel on the basis of Abraham's faith in Rom(A), he went beyond it to appeal to the beginning of the world in Rom(B). As a result, Paul took on a more controversial character in Rom(B) than in Rom(A) with regard to the Jewish tradition.

An essential element to note is that the door has gradually expanded to gentiles. It began by asserting that both Jews and gentiles are on equal footing before God, using the beginning of the world as the theological background. Of course, this is a response to the doubts and critiques raised by the Romans, especially Jewish members, with regard to the righteousness of Abraham by faith as written in Rom(A). However, it seems to be Paul's way of expressing of the mission to gentiles that he had been entrusted by God. Although Paul did not directly express the preference for them, it cannot be denied that this trend has become stronger as Rom(B) advances.

There does not seem to be much of a connection with Priscilla and Aquila in Rom(B). This is revealed in the fact that there is strong critique of Paul against Jews and that the connection with the contents of 1 Corinthians has been greatly reduced. Of course, the Romans represented by the couple would have felt uncomfortable with Paul's new teachings. Accordingly, they may have taken the attitude of not accepting his request and rather asking to check. So Paul had to reduce his dependence on them and further strengthened the Christ-centered gospel to fulfill the mission to gentiles. This shows that in response to the critiques from Jewish members, Paul strengthened the teachings according to his own views in Rom(B).

The contents of Rom(B) can be divided into five sections in terms of topic: the wrath of God (1:18—2:11), the Law and sin (2:12—3:20), the faith of Christ Jesus (3:21–31), the ethics of saints (12:14—13:7; 14:13–23), and closing part (15:30–33). The beginning part seems to have disappeared when Rom(B) was compiled into the present form of Romans. Having described God's wrath and the limitations of the Law in Rom(B), Paul presented Jesus Christ as the way to righteousness in response to their critiques. In this way, Paul revealed more of the gospel based on Jesus Christ.

1. THE WRATH OF GOD (1:18—2:11)

The beginning part of Rom(B), where the sender, the recipient, and greetings were mentioned, seems to have been deleted when it was compiled into the present form of Romans. Accordingly, the reconstructed Rom(B) starts with the main topic right from the first sentence. Paul dealt with the issue of wrath of God that leads to the eschatological judgment upon Jews and gentiles alike. This seems to be the part of Paul's response to the Romans' critique against the negative view on the Law that brings about wrath as written in Rom(A).

The Wrath of God (1:18-23)

Paul taught that the wrath of God was bound to come on account of transgression. This resulted from the violation of the Law, as implied in Rom(A) (4:15). Accordingly, Paul stated that people had no choice but to suffer wrath. Having focused on their unrighteousness, this part shows the reason that people commit transgression. The mention of wrath and unrighteousness is not appropriate in a first letter written with the hope of a warm welcome.

The wrath of God was mentioned at the beginning of Rom(B). This is found in the statement that the wrath of God has been revealed from heaven against the ungodliness and unrighteousness of people who suppressed the truth by their unrighteousness (1:18). If this verse was the first sentence of Rom(B), it shows that Paul started it with a reproaching mode. This shows the possibility that the Romans read Rom(A) and took a stance of denying Paul's teaching especially on the relationship between the Law and wrath (4:15). This is because Jewish members were not familiar with Paul's previous views on the Law. For example, it has been written in Galatians that the Law exists for the sake of transgression (Gal 3:19). Having based on this argument, Paul wrote that the Law brings about wrath and transgression in Rom(A). While Paul carefully revealed his view on the Law with a weakened form in comparison with that written in Galatians, the Romans would have been nervous because Paul presented the negative view on the Law as the source of wrath. Thus, they could not help but ask him for an explanation. No doubt, Phoebe, who had delivered Rom(A) to the Romans, made their doubts and critiques known to Paul. In return, he responded with a saying that the wrath of God would come upon all those who suppress the truth by their unrighteousness. This kind of warning is inappropriate for a first letter expressing expectations of a warm welcome. Rather, it could be included in at least a second letter.

It should be noted that the word "unrighteousness" was used twice here. As shown before, the issue of unrighteousness shows a disconnection from God's righteousness addressed in 1:8-17. It is clear that the compiler of Romans located 1:18-23 at the present place in order to draw a contrast between the righteousness of God and the unrighteousness of people. This allowed the theme of unrighteousness to be emphasized in the final form of Romans. Then, it can be inferred that when the Romans did not accept the way of being righteous by faith in God, as suggested in Rom(A), Paul applied the word "unrighteousness" twice to them and declared God's wrath upon them. This shows an aggressive approach toward them.

The only result of unrighteousness suppressing the truth is the wrath of God from heaven. Here, unrighteousness and truth appear in contrast to each other. Truth is an important topic here. It is to be reminded that there were those who prevented the Galatians from obeying the truth (Gal 5:7). They were the representatives sent by the apostles of the Jerusalem church to the gentile churches established by Paul under the leadership of Barnabas during the first missionary journey. They taught that gentiles could be righteous by observing the Law in addition to following the instruction of Jesus. A similar phenomenon occurred in the Roman church. This was a challenge to Paul by Jewish members who had criticized his teachings. Having heard about the negative influence on faith, Paul seems to have felt that the truth needed to be strengthened. Hereto, he declared that the wrath of God would come upon the unrighteous and ungodly who had prevented people from truth in Rom(B). They could avoid wrath by believing that God raised him from the dead, the core of the gospel (5:8–10). This implies that, unlike the situation when Paul had sent Rom(A), there was a certain level of tension between Paul and the Romans at the time of writing Rom(B).

Then, the reason that the wrath of God had been given was described. This starts with the declaration that God has revealed himself to people in a way that is understandable (1:19). The logic behind this is that people did not recognize God. Having received a revelation about the Son of God (Gal 1:16), Paul was able to write in Rom(B) that ungodliness and unrighteousness made people ignore God; thus, they cannot help but become the target of God's wrath. Then, the truth in contrast with unrighteousness and ungodliness refers to what God revealed and made people know. Having delivered these lessons, Paul wanted the Romans to break away from their entrenched beliefs. Then, the argument is established that they should have accepted what Paul had preached.

In addition, Paul provided the Romans with another reason that they had been subject to the wrath of God. This is found in the statement that God has made his invisible qualities, that is, eternal power and divinity, clearly visible to all things he has made since the creation of the world, so that people cannot make excuses (1:20). With these descriptions, Paul argued that God provides people with a way to know him, but they did not recognize his existence. This teaching did not appear in any of Paul's other letters. God was described as someone who can make the impossible possible in Rom(A) (4:17). Accordingly, in Rom(B), God was presented as the one who makes the invisible visible. Paul argued that people in general can recognize the character of God revealed through all things since the creation of the world. Natural revelation was suggested in order to provide a justification that not only Jews but also gentiles could recognize God. For this, no one can make excuses before God.

An uncomfortable relationship was formed between Paul and the Romans. The Romans seemed to have emphasized observance of the Law, even after reading Paul's account that Abraham was justified by faith in God as written in Rom(A) (4:3). Accordingly, Paul emphasized in Rom(B) that even gentiles can recognize God by presenting the fact that God has been showing his power and divinity through all things since the creation of the world. Paul appealed to the era of creation before Abraham, so that not only Jews but also gentiles could find God and that they had to believe in him. This was Paul's work to inform gentiles that the way to be righteous by faith in God had been opened. While the opening to the gentiles was based on Abraham's righteousness by faith while being uncircumcised in Rom(A) (4:11–12), it was expanded to God's inclusion of them since the creation of the world as written in Rom(B). This narrative conveys the lesson that the opportunity for faith was open to gentiles at the same level as Jews.

Paul explained why people have no choice but to be subject to the wrath of God. This is revealed by using the phrase "even though people know God" and listing four actions they used to perform (1:21). Paul believed that people could recognize God because he had shown the eternal power and divinity through all things. Nevertheless, people do not show proper behavior: first, they do not give glory to God; second, they are not thankful to him; third, their thoughts become vain; and fourth, their foolish hearts are darkened. Paul first mentioned two attitudes that people should have toward God. However, he explained that while people did not show the first two states, they ended up in the last two. They are the reasons that people have been driven into a situation to be subject to the wrath of God. In conclusion, it is due to their mistakes. This is in accordance with the purpose of broadening the perspective of the Romans. It was Paul's strategy to bring faith even to gentiles. He wanted to expand the Romans' faith from a Jewish perspective to a pan-humanistic perspective.

A further reason was given that people could not make excuse with regard to recognizing God. This appears by using the phrase "even though people call themselves wise" and then describing two wrong actions they committed (1:22–23). Paul argued that although the Romans thought they were wise, they were not in reality. It is because they exchanged the glory of the incorruptible God for images in the likeness of corruptible man, birds, beasts, and reptiles. Paul insisted that the revelation through the creation of the world should not turn into idolatry. It is definite that idolatry was prevalent by the Law, even in Rome. This probably attracted Paul's attention when Phoebe reported to him what she had seen in Rome. Paul had seen such cases in Thessalonica, so he praised the Thessalonians for abandoning idols and coming to God (1 Thess 1:9). For the Romans, it was a truly wise life that they walked the same path. This was told because Paul might have aimed at gentiles as the main target.

It must be explained why the issue of idolatry was described at the beginning of Rom(B) in connection with the wrath of God. This reflects that idolatry was quite serious in Rome. Paul would not have addressed idolatry in Rom(B) if it had not been an issue related to the Romans. However, because it had such an impact on them, it could not be ignored. Paul had no choice but to define it as an object of God's wrath. In this way, having addressed a more serious issue, Paul was able to avoid the Romans' critiques against the proposition that the Law brings about wrath. Since it described the religious situation of the Romans, this text is believed to have been written after Paul had heard about it from Phoebe who had delivered Rom(A) and returned from Rome to him.

In summary, from the beginning of Rom(B), Paul declared God's wrath against the Romans. The Romans were even criticized because they could not properly see God's divinity embedded in the creation of the world. A reference to the beginning of the world was used in order to include all mankind, both Jews and gentiles, into the objects of wrath. A detailed description of God's wrath would be out of place in the first letter written with the hope of a warm welcome. This is believed to have originated from at least the second letter in that it could have been written due to interactions with the Romans.

The Lust of Human Beings (1:24–32)

Paul described God's reactions toward human beings. According to him, God allowed people to follow their lusts, which lead them to sin not only in their relationship with God but also in their interactions with other people. Having shifted the responsibility to people, Paul justified that they were bound to receive the wrath of God.

A proposition for God's reaction was presented. Paul claimed that God had given people over to their lusts, so that they might dishonor their own bodies (1:24). Paul would like to say about the wrath that came upon those who worshiped idols even though they recognized the divinity of God in the creature. Here, God's reaction of giving people over to their lusts is paired with the results given to people that their bodies had been dishonored. This was given as a religious principle. It reminds readers of the temptation and fall that occurred in the garden of Eden at the beginning of the world (Gen 3:1–6). Adam and Eve disobeyed God's command and ate the fruit from the tree of knowledge of good and evil, only to discover that they were naked in the end due to their greed to become like God. Having tried to explain the matter of lusts and dishonored body against the backdrop of what was occurred in the garden of Eden, Paul described the religious state of the Romans. This shows that events occurred before the time of Abraham were chosen to provide the theological foundation that both Jews and gentiles had no choice but to commit transgression and subject to the wrath of God.

Paul described in more detail how people defile their bodies by following their lusts. This makes the truth of God turn into a lie and results in worshiping and serving creatures more than the creator (1:25). Paul suggested the two most common transgressions people can commit. The first one is that they turned God's truth into lies, and the second is that they served creature rather than the creator. Without doubt, those who commit such wrong behavior will face the wrath of God. Paul was quite sensitive to idolatry because the Romans were believed to be actually in such danger. This kind of lesson is reminiscent of the event occurred in the garden of Eden in that the defilement of their bodies by lust resulted from the disobedience to the command of God and the acceptance of what the serpent had seduced (Gen 2:17; 3:1–6). Paul believed that all people, not just Romans, could commit this kind of transgression. It seems that he wrote this after hearing about the religious situation of the Romans from Phoebe.

Another way people lived according to their lusts was mentioned in connection with homosexuality. This is found in the expression that God gave them over to shameful desires (1:26a). As an example, homosexuality is a way of life that a man and a woman do not live according to nature in a sexual way but live in opposition (1:26b–27). Paul defined homosexuality as a transgression, ranking it second only to idolatry. Homosexuality is a shameful behavior that exposes one's body to defilement due to sexual greed. It goes against God, who created man and woman as complements to each other from the creation of the world (Gen 1:27; 2:20–24). In the end, since homosexuality is unrighteously suppressing the truth, it will result in the wrath of God as retribution (1:18). This reflects the possibility that some Romans enjoyed homosexuality. Having reacted sensitively to this, Paul had no choice but to criticize them. This lesson would also have made the Romans feel uncomfortable rather than made them to repent.

Paul described in more detail the consequences of God abandoning people to their lusts. This appears in the statement that because people do not want to have God in their hearts, he gives them over to their depraved minds and makes them to do what ought not to be done (1:28a). Paul first described the reason that people did not want to care about God. This reminds readers of the statement that they began to worship idols even though they had known God (1:21–22). Paul pointed out that people had rejected God's revelation and put the blame on themselves. It is later stated that God left them to their own lost will (1:28b). This is reminiscent of two similar statements made in previous texts (1:24, 26). It is a new teaching that God leaves people to their own depraved minds because people do unworthy things. As a result, it was declared that people would do unworthy things. This will mean various kinds of transgression other than idolatry and homosexuality. This reflects the situation that the Romans created a condition for themselves to receive the wrath of God.

The transgression that the Romans should not commit was listed. This is found in a long list of transgression (1:29–31). People are full of all unrighteousness, wickedness, greed and depravity. They are filled with envy, murder, strife, deceit, and malice. To their transgression belong gossips, slanderers, God-haters, and revilers. People are insolent, arrogant, and boastful. They are those who plot evil, disobey their parents, betray their promises, and are foolish, heartless, and ruthless. This kind of long list of transgression occasionally appeared in his letters. For instance, Paul once gave a list of unrighteous people to the Corinthians (1 Cor 6:9–10) and a list of works of the flesh to the Galatians (Gal 5:19–21). However, in Rom(B), Paul listed various transgressions because there were those who did not want to give their heart to God and did what ought not to be done. In any case, it is important to observe that the various transgressions prohibited by the Law were listed in Rom(B). This reflects the situation in which Jewish members committed transgression despite their calls for compliance with the Law. Paul provided these examples to admonish the Jewish members of the Roman church who criticized his views on the Law.

Paul made a conclusion to those who had done unworthy things. They are eligible to be sentenced to death (1:32a). Paul presented death as a result of God's wrath. Of course, not all of the unrighteous deeds listed above are punishable by death; however, for some of them, corporal punishment leading to death is prescribed by the Law. While Paul mentioned voluntary atoning death in Rom(A), the death penalty for transgression was dealt with in Rom(B). This reflects the fact that there were circumstances that caused Paul to change his view on death. He probably felt quite hurt by the critique directed at him.

The more important issue is an act that encourages transgression. This is found in the statement that some people not only do what they do but also sympathize with others who do the same (1:32b). Paul pointed out the contagiousness of evil deeds. In this respect, this ultimately amounts to dishonoring one another, as mentioned earlier (1:24). Whereas forgiveness of sin was presented as a blessing in Rom(A) (4:7–8; 5:8), sin that leads to transgression was dealt with in Rom(B). This reflects the circumstances in which Paul came to view the Romans negatively. It is presumed that it happened because the Romans questioned and criticized the gospel preached by Paul. All of the elements presented above are reminiscent of the events that occurred in the garden of Eden. There death was declared, and Eve made Adam an accomplice by making him eat from the tree of knowledge of good and evil. In this way, having used the first human being once again beyond Abraham as the theological background, Paul tried to convey the lesson that both Jews and gentiles are under the wrath of God.

To sum up, Paul said that because the Romans commit various transgressions contrary to the Law, they were to subject to the wrath of God. It was described against the theological backdrop of events in the garden of Eden. Accordingly, Paul conveyed the fact that beyond Jews, gentiles are also under the wrath of God. Paul responded strongly to the critique of Jewish members against his negative view on the Law. This kind of description is something that Paul could have written in the second letter after Phoebe reported Romans' situation.

The Judgment of God (2:1–11)

Paul turned the attention to God's judgment on the Romans. This was presented as the result from their stubbornness without repentance. At the same time, Paul also suggested equality before God in that both Jews and Greeks are exposed to good and evil. This is also believed to have been written after Paul received a report on the situation with the Romans.

A direct reproach to the Romans was mentioned in terms of no excuse. This is found in the phrase "therefore you are without excuse" (2:1a). Having stated that there was no excuse, Paul treated a special matter. The phrase "to be without excuse" has already been used in connection with recognizing the power and divinity of God (1:20). While the phrase was applied to an unspecified number of people there, it is applied to people in a specific situation here. In this respect, Paul narrowed down the subject he wanted to discuss. Such a expression would have been enough to make the Romans uncomfortable.

Paul expressed the intention to teach a lesson about judging others. This appears in the saying, "You who judge others!" (2:1b). Paul specifically stated a person, who judged others, as an object of admonition. The word "judge" was used in Rom(A) in connection with various types of matter: different levels of approach to food, the authority of master over servants, and the relationship with brethren (14:3–4, 10). However, in Rom(B), Paul addressed the issue of judgment in the context of relationships with other members within the church. Paul pointed out that a certain number of the Romans passed judgment upon others in spite of his instruction of not passing judgment upon others in Rom(A). This reflects the situation in which different groups were formed within the Roman church. This was known to Paul because Phoebe informed him of it. In this respect, the text may be derived from at least the second letter.

The theme of condemnation was presented for the first time in Rom(B). Having used the phrase "to be condemned oneself" in addition to "judging others," Paul revealed the relationship between judgment and condemnation (2:1c). In other words, judgment of others leads to condemnation of oneself. The principle of equal revenge seems to be embedded here, which is reminiscent of equal retaliation described in Leviticus (Lev 24:20). Although it was not described who would condemn the one who passed judgment, there seems to be a person with more authority than the person involved. With this kind of lesson, Paul attempted to prevent the

Romans from getting worse in their relationship with others. This seems to reflect the relationship between the major group of Jewish members and the minor group of gentile members within the Roman church.

Paul made it a problem to judge others and still do the same. This is revealed in the description that one who judges is scolded for doing the same thing (2:1d). Paul pointed out that there were people in the Roman church who practiced differently from what they had taught. They were those who taught not to do something and then did it. Paul once said about a person who not only acts what God prohibited but also supports those who do so (1:32). Everyone must be responsible for approving of those who practice what God has prohibited to do. This reflects the situation that the Romans were committing transgressions while emphasizing the observance of the Law. Paul criticized their hypocritical behavior. It seems to have been written after he had learned about the actual situation of the Roman church.

The issue of God's judgment came to the fore in connection with truth. This is shown in the statement that the judgment of God would be done according to truth to those who judge others (2:2a). The judgment of God here is reminiscent of the judgment seat of God, which appeared in Rom(A) (14:10). However, in Rom(B), Paul mentioned the judgment of God according to the truth. This makes readers retrospect that the word "truth" was used against unrighteousness leading to transgressions (1:18). Since "truth" was twice related to the gospel in Galatians (Gal 2:5, 14), it could be consistent with the gospel in Rom(B). This leads to the conclusion that the judgment of God would vary depending on whether one accepts the gospel or not. Then, the truth of the gospel should be a higher standard than the Law. However, Jewish members, who lived based on the Law, would be hesitant to accept the gospel as truth.

Paul presented those who would be judged by God. It is said that people who do things like this will be judged (2:2b). Here in a close context, a person who does this may refer to one who judges others (2:1). On the other hand, in a distant context, this includes people who not only follow their lusts and do things that God has forbidden by the Law, but also support those who do them as righteous (1:24–32). In any case, both verses point out those who commit transgressions. Paul could not help but announce that all who had committed sin would be judged by God. These descriptions were directed at the Romans, who have claimed to follow the Law but were actually committing transgressions. This kind of instruction might have made them feel uncomfortable.

Then, a comprehensive description about hypocrites appeared. This is found in the saying "So when you, a mere man, pass judgment on them and yet do the same things, do you think you will escape God's judgment?" (2:3). Although Paul did not say it clearly, it seems that he had been deeply concerned about the hypocritical behavior occurring within the Roman church. The reference to people who will judge those who violate the Law and then do the same things is a repetition of the previous verse in which it is said that people who judge others do the same things (2:1). Although the Romans said that they had kept the Law, in reality they kept committing transgressions. Thus, they had been classified as those who would suffer the wrath at the time of God's judgment. This reflects the fact that Paul was well-aware of the situation of the Roman church.

Paul appeared to urge the Romans to repent. For this purpose, two sorts of description come to the fore: one is about God's character, and the other is about people's attitudes toward God (2:4a). Paul emphasized God's kindness, tolerance, and patience while waiting for their repentance of transgression. On the other hand, he pointed out people's ignorance of God's endurance (2:4b). The Romans were encouraged to repent. In Rom(A), Paul emphasized forgiveness of sin as God's blessing and Christ's death for sinners out of God's love (4:7–8; 5:6–8). However, in Rom(B), The Romans were asked for repentance that needed their effort to be forgiven of sin. Paul urged the Romans to repent because they did not understand God's will and were committing transgressions while emphasizing observance of the Law as opposed to the teachings of Rom(A) (1:24–32). This suggests that having learned about the response of the Romans to Rom(A), Paul had an uncomfortable relationship with them. Paul had no choice but to deliver a message of warning to repent.

The coming judgment of God's wrath is spoken of in strong terms. This appears in the statement that people have stored up wrath and will be judged before God because of their stubbornness and unrepentant hearts (2:5a). Paul attributed the reason for being judged to the person being judged. This proposition is in line with the statement presented at the beginning of Rom(B) that God will response to unrighteousness (1:18). This shows that 1:18—2:5 is composed around the theme of wrath. The issue of wrath, however, reflects the situation that he had uncomfortable feelings about the Romans when he wrote Rom(B). The reason that Paul issued this warning to them is not explained.

Paul gave a supplementary explanation about the day of wrath. This is the day when the righteous judgment of God is revealed (2:5b).

Paul emphasized that the wrathful judgment of God would be righteous; then, this entirely reflected the Jewish perspective. Paul referred to the judgment at the end of the world as a righteous event, providing forgiveness for God's wrath. This is different from the case in Galatians. When Paul was challenged by some Galatians sponsored by the apostles of the Jerusalem church, he did not use any eschatological teachings. On the contrary, Paul responded to the Romans' critiques with eschatological teachings in Rom(B), so that Jewish members might be alert. It seems that Paul tried to use these instructions to suppress some Romans who rejected and resisted the gospel as introduced in Rom(A).

A supplementary explanation was provided with regard to the righteous judgment. This appears in the declaration that God will reward each person according to his or her deeds (2:6). For this, Paul quoted a verse from Ps 62:12 or Prov 24:12. This seems to be in conflict with the declaration in Rom(A) that Abraham was not justified by the works (4:2). If so, it is believed that Paul changed his position on the deeds when he quoted this verse in Rom(B). This reflects the fact that Paul strengthened the Jewish eschatological perspective of judgment, conscious of the backlash and critique of Jewish members toward the gospel, especially his negative view on the Law as described in Rom(A). Having accepted the critiques of the Romans, Paul responded them with an eschatological instruction in return.

Paul described the retribution that would be given to people according to their deeds. It is written that eternal life is given to those who endure and do good in order to seek glory and honor and immortality, while wrath and anger are given to those who do not follow the truth and rather seek for unrighteousness (2:7–8). Paul mentioned the eschatological retribution to the Romans in the fact that eternal life was in contrast with wrath and anger. Those who do good and seek for glory, honor, and immortality are in contrast with those who are selfish and do not follow the truth but rather practice unrighteousness. This sort of contrast already appeared in Galatians as a comparison between the works of the flesh and the fruits of the spirit (Gal 5:19–23). It is likely that Paul could have developed it into the present form of contrast in Rom(B). In particular, the reference to those who formed a party seems to refer to a group of people within the Roman church who had criticized and rejected Paul. In any case, the contrast between eternal life and wrath was a good way to sound the alarm to the Romans. The dichotomous description reflects the fact that Paul was aware of the divided groups of people in the Roman church.

Once again a pair of contrast appeared. It describes the retribution given to those who do good or those who do evil (2:9–10). Paul argued that while those who do evil would have tribulation and suffering, those who do good would have glory, honor, and peace. Then, on the one hand, tribulation and suffering are in parallel with wrath and anger; on the other hand, glory, honor, and peace are in parallel with eternal life. Whereas Paul spoke of tribulation from a positive perspective for the production of hope in Rom(A) (5:3–4), he took a negative stance by associating it with each person who practices evil in Rom(B). This shows that as the situation changed, Paul's interpretation of it has been also altered. In any case, the dichotomous description of good and evil shows that Paul approached the issue of eschatological retribution with an allusion to the tree of knowledge of good and evil in the garden of Eden. In Rom(A), Paul advised the Romans to hate evil and belong to good because love is sincere (12:9). At that time, the idea that people could choose between good and evil seemed to have been widely accepted. However, having strengthened the distinction between those who do good and those who do evil in Rom(B), Paul seemed to have solidified the unbridgeable gap between the two. It seems to show that Paul entered into a uncomfortable relationship with the Romans because forces emerged within the Roman church that opposed those who favored Paul.

Paul dealt with the relationship between Jews and Greeks in relation to eschatological retribution due to doing good or evil. This appears in the expression "to the Jews first and then to the Greeks." Paul maintained this principle early in his communication with the Romans. Reference to Jews and Greeks was once mentioned in Rom(A), where it is stated that God's power to bring salvation will be given first to the Jews and then to the Greeks (1:16–17). This implies that Jews were ahead of Greeks in terms of the benefit of salvation. However, in Rom(B), Jews and Greeks are mentioned in relation to the consequences of doing good or evil, conveying the instruction that although there may be an order between them, Jews do not always have a better advantage before God. Even Jews can become targets of wrath and anger in connection with doing evil. This implies their equal status with Greeks from an eschatological perspective. In this respect, Paul began to have a different view on Jewish and gentile members. This subtle difference shows that the situation had changed when Paul wrote Rom(B) in that while Jewish members rejected Paul's gospel, gentile members seemed to have accepted it.

A subtle change is identified in the relationship between Jews and Greeks. This appears in the statement that God is no respecter of persons (2:11). Paul wanted to eliminate human discrimination between Jews and Greeks. The expression "no respect of person" once appeared in connection with the apostles of the Jerusalem church in Galatians (Gal 2:6). Paul used this expression to place himself in an equal relationship with the apostles of the Jerusalem church. In similar manner, it was used in Rom(B) in order to show that God did not show favorability for Jews or repulsion for Greeks. Paul declared that God judges both Jews and Greeks fairly based on their deeds. This means that none of the Romans can escape the judgment of God whether Jews or Greeks. The reason that Paul taught it is to heighten their equality. In this way, he seemed to lean slightly towards the gentile Greeks, who were supposed to show favor to the faith in God without the Law, rather than Jews, who took a negative stance on it.

It is then necessary to define the one who passed judgment on others (2:1–11). This should be applied to the relationship between Jewish and Greek members. In other words, it seems that the Jewish members, who made up the majority of the Roman church, passed judgment upon the minor gentile members; accordingly, the former made the latter hurt in their mind. Accordingly, Paul taught that whether Jews or Greeks, they would be condemned by God according to their deeds. This began to suggest equality between them. This kind of instruction reveals the fact that critiques from Jewish members made him put even more effort into the mission to gentiles that Paul had already begun.

In summary, Paul declared that all people since the creation of the world would be subject to eschatological judgment because they did not serve God properly and committed transgressions even after discovering God's divinity. There is no distinction here between Jews and Greeks. With this, Paul internally showed the intention to achieve the mission to gentiles by leaning more toward the Greek members. This was Paul's response to Jewish members' critique against him. In this respect, it is believed that this text could originate in at least the second letter.

2. THE LAW AND SIN (2:12 — 3:20)

Paul responded to the Romans' criticism of his negative view on the Law. Their hypocrisy was focused on relation to the Law. They did not properly enjoy the privileges received from God and were presented as beings under sin along with gentiles. This is considered a theological strategy of Paul to widen the door to gentiles.

The Role of the Law (2:12–13, 16)

Paul presented a claim that God will judge sins regardless of whether they are related to the Law or not. This plays a role of transition to conclude the previous narrative and open a new discussion on the Law. By doing this, Paul emphasized proclaiming the gospel to both Jews and gentiles on the same level.

Paul ultimately denied the role of the Law. This is revealed in the saying that those who commit sin without the Law will perish without it, and those who commit sin under the Law will be judged by it (2:12). Paul argued that the Law serves only partially for those to whom it applied. This shows a more detailed picture than what was written in Rom(A) that where there is no Law, there is no transgression (4:15). Paul emphasized that in God's judgment, both Jews who had the Law and gentiles who did not have it stand on equal footing. Additionally, it is new that the Law was linked to the verb "to commit sin" here. This shows that the role of the Law was more theologically strengthened than that of transgression simply mentioned in Rom(A). In any case, Paul insisted that everyone would eventually commit sin and be judged, regardless of whether they have the Law or not. This kind of instruction would have made the Romans, especially Jewish members who had been proud of the Law, uncomfortable.

Some room was given to the Law. This is found in the description that before God, not those who hear the Law are righteous, but those who do it are righteous (2:13). Paul took a somewhat positive stance on the issue of keeping the Law; however, a conclusion must be drawn after looking at its context, and previous incidents occurred to Paul. For instance, having been severely challenged by some gentiles sponsored by the apostles of the Jerusalem church, Paul emphasized to the gentile Galatians that righteousness cannot be achieved by the works of the Law (Gal 3:10–13). There, Paul delivered a strong warning to the extent of adding the word "curse" to the works of the Law. In similar manner, Paul stated in Rom(A) that Abraham was not justified by works (4:2). However, having been criticized by the Romans, mainly Jewish members, Paul delivered the message in Rom(B) that each person would be punished according to his or her deeds at the judgment of God (2:13) and then spoke of the matter of keeping the Law than listening to it here. It seems that Paul did not want to express too harshly toward Jewish members. Rather, Paul tried to appease their hearts while acknowledging that there is not a single person in the world who can completely observe the Law.

Then Paul revealed his hidden will. This appears in the description of the day when God judges the secrets of people through Jesus Christ as stated in the gospel (2:16). Paul warned that everything would be revealed at the judgment of God. Whether a person has completely followed the Law will be determined at the judgment of God. This should be understood against the backdrop of previous statement that Christ intercedes for people at the right hand of God, as written in Rom(A) (8:34). With this in mind, Paul seemed to have mentioned in Rom(B) that the judgment of secret things revealed through Jesus Christ as told in "my" gospel. It is necessary to examine the reason that Paul said of his gospel. It is because the intercessory role of Christ Jesus had been added to the tradition of Christ, that is, the core of the gospel handed down to Paul (1 Cor 15:1–5). To be more specific, Paul presented a new element by adding Christ's role as a mediator to the traditional gospel concerning his death, burial, resurrection, and epiphany. At any rate, Paul consistently claimed that, contrary to what the Romans insisted, righteousness cannot be achieved by the works of the Law.

In summary, Paul pointed out the limitations of the Law in God's judgment. At the same time, he showed the connection with Jesus Christ, emphasizing that he will reveal all the secrets of people at the judgment seat. By doing this, Paul ignored the privileges of Jews and granted equality to gentiles. This tendency appears as a phenomenon that was seen in the second letter and was becoming established.

The Law and Jews (2:17–24)

Paul criticized the Jewish members of the Roman church in relation to the Law. They were pointed out as not carrying out the Law even though they insisted on keeping it. This seems to be given as a counterattack to their critique against Paul's negative view on the Law.

Much space was devoted to defining Jews. They relied on the Law, boasted in God, knew the will of God through the teachings of the Law, discerned what was best, led the way for the blind, were a light to those in darkness, and provided knowledge and truth in the Law (2:17–20). In this way, Paul was able to clearly describe the role and status of Jews. It is possible that Paul heard about this kind of information from Phoebe, who had returned from delivering Rom(A). At any rate, the Romans were defined as those who set an example, a teacher of children, and a person who believed in himself. Especially, the expression "teacher of children" used in connection with the Law is reminiscent of the "guide of children" adopted in Galatians (Gal 3:24). Then, in Rom(B), Paul listed the self-consciousness that the Romans, who were mainly Jewish, actually had. It is clear that they kept the Law and put an emphasis on their religious self-esteem as the people of God. Having written this way, Paul harshly criticized Jewish members for living a life dependent on the Law. This reminds readers of Paul's critique against the gentile Galatians, who had challenged him and tried to live according to Jewish teachings.

Then, Paul specifically criticized the hypocritical Jews. This is found in the statement that a Jew who teaches others does not teach himself (2:21a). Having pointed out that Jews did not act what they had taught, Paul heightened the hypocrisy that Jewish members had committed in their religious life. Then, this reminds readers of the critique against those who do what God has forbidden and rather support those having done such things as righteous (1:32; cf. 2:1, 3). In addition, it is also a critique against being filled with pride, as listed above (2:17–20). Paul pointed out that Jewish members, like gentiles, had lived by double standards. Having been judged by this, the Romans were in a state that did not deviate much from this. This kind of critique was not something that could have been included in the first letter, in which Paul requested the Romans to welcome him.

Four examples of behavior were listed in order to criticize the Romans (2:21b–23). First, while they teach people not to steal, they actually steal; second, despite they teach people not to commit adultery, they commit adultery; and third, contrary to their prohibition of adoring idols, they steal temple items. Finally, having boasted about the Law, they dishonored God by breaking it. Paul criticized Jewish members because they had not kept the Law as they should. Paul used three provisions of the Ten Commandments in order to criticize them for not practicing what they had taught. This attributed their failure of becoming righteous people despite having the Law to their hypocrisy. Jewish members were criticized for failing to keep the Law because they could not keep even the most basic commandments.

Paul quoted a verse from the Bible in order to criticize Jewish members for not serving God properly. It is a saying from Isa 52:5, which means that the name of God had been blasphemed among gentiles because of Jews (2:24). With this quotation, Paul pointed out that the Romans, mainly Jewish members, were not living properly in connection with the Law. This is believed to be the first case that Paul devalues the Jews of the Roman church in relation to gentiles. Accordingly, Paul taught them not to claim privileges in front of gentiles. With this, interest in gentiles finally came to the fore. This point would have made Jewish members uncomfortable.

In summary, Paul criticized the hypocrisy of Jews in connection with the Law in general. Jewish church members were criticized for their involvement in several transgressions because they did not keep the law. Therefore, Paul had no choice but to respond to their critique against his negative view on the Law. This is a narrative based on Paul's theological strategy of opening the door to gentiles by criticizing the Jews. It is likely that this part was originated in the second letter in that he criticized them rather than asking for a warm welcome.

The Law and Circumcision (2:25–29)

Accusations against Jews continued in connection with circumcision. It was Paul's theological strategy to break down the barrier between circumcision and uncircumcision. As a result, he wanted to open the door to gentiles.

Accordingly, Paul argued for the importance of carrying out the Law. This appears in the statement that if the Romans follow the Law, circumcision is beneficial but that if they break the Law, their circumcision becomes invalid (2:25). Paul reflected the claims of Jewish members about keeping the Law and practicing circumcision. The relationship between the Law and circumcision has already been treated in Galatians, where it was said that those who receive circumcision are obligated to keep the Law (Gal 5:3). However, Paul seemed to have had in mind the premise that no one can perfectly obey it. Accordingly, in Rom(B), he argued that circumcision becomes useless in the sense that no one can keep the Law completely. This shows that the Romans tried to keep the Law by even mentioning the practice of circumcision in response to Paul's negative view on the Law as written in Rom(A). In response, having describe more clearly the relationship between circumcision and the Law, Paul expressed a negative opinion about the validity of circumcision because no one can keep the Law completely.

Paul went one step further with an insistence that uncircumcision could replace circumcision. This appears in the argument that if an uncircumcised person keeps the Law, uncircumcision should be considered the same as circumcision (2:26). Paul argued that an uncircumcised person could overcome the barrier of circumcision stipulated in the Law. It is then necessary to look at Paul's previous perspective on circumcision and uncircumcision. For example, while he placed little emphasis on the difference between circumcision and uncircumcision to the Corinthians (1 Cor 7:17–19), he did emphasize the distinction between the two to the Galatians (Gal 2:7–8). Paul did not make much of a distinction between circumcision and uncircumcision in Rom(A); however, it seems that more weight was placed on uncircumcision. On the other hand, he acknowledged the distinction between the two in Rom(B), written after being criticized by the Romans, probably Jewish members. Then, Paul presented a new view that the uncircumcised could obey the Law and become like the circumcised people. This appears to have been a preliminary measure to break down the wall between Jews and gentiles.

Now value was given to the uncircumcised. This is found in the statement that if an uncircumcised person completely keeps the Law, he or she can condemn those who break the Law in spite of having the "written code" and "circumcision" (2:27). Paul argued that circumcision or uncircumcision itself was not important; rather, whether the Law was kept or not was more important. It is important to note here that the uncircumcised person may condemn the circumcised person. Paul hinted at the possibility that gentiles could be in a better position than Jews from a religious point of view. This means that status may be reversed between Jews and gentiles regardless of being circumcised or not. In this way, Paul emphasized internal and spiritual aspects rather than external and lineage conditions. Having criticized Jews, this played a role of opening the door to gentiles. Hereby, his argument was presented to raise awareness among Jewish members and to justify his mission to gentiles.

Paul pointed out that Jews should give up their privileges. This is detected in the expression that no one who is an outward Jew is a Jew and that outwardly physical circumcision is not circumcision (2:28). Paul wanted to describe what the people of God should have been. Before making this description, it is necessary to look at the previous steps. Paul once taught the Corinthians that those who were called to be circumcised should not be uncircumcised and that those who were called to be uncircumcised should not be circumcised (1 Cor 7:18). This conveys the lesson to become a servant of Christ while maintaining one's original state. However, in Rom(B), Paul presented a direction that denied Jewish circumcision itself. This conveys the instruction that just their Jewish origin and religious circumcision do not guarantee their status as the people of God. Paul seemed to criticize those who had claimed privileges due to their Jewish status within the Roman church. This claim completely reverses the order that Paul presented as "Jews first and then Greeks" in Rom(A) (1:16). After this phrase was used to indicate equality between Jews and Greeks in Rom(B) (2:9–10), Paul presented to the Romans the view that there was a possibility of a reversal between Jews and gentiles here for the first time. This shows Paul revealing the stance on the preference of gentiles to Jews.

Then, a new definition of God's people was presented. It is written that an inward Jew is a Jew and a person with a circumcised heart (2:29a). Paul strengthened the message he wanted to convey by writing in contrast to what was described previously. It was once argued in Galatians that in Christ Jesus neither circumcision nor uncircumcision has any effect but only faith that works through love (Gal 5:6). Paul emphasized to the gentile Galatians that there was no difference between circumcision and uncircumcision in Christ. However, in Rom(B), Paul defined God's people by creating a parallel between inner Jewishness and circumcision of the heart. The instruction that circumcision must be done in the heart appears in the Bible (Deut 10:16; 30:6), and Paul applied it to the Romans. This opened the way for gentiles to become the people of God without being Jewish. As a result, Paul shifted the focus from Jews to gentiles. This shows that having read Rom(A), the Romans argued that gentiles should also become the people of God by obedience to the Law and practicing circumcision. In response, Paul suggested circumcision of the heart from a spiritual perspective in Rom(B). In this way, Paul criticized Jewish members and opened the way for gentiles to become God's people without circumcision.

Paul put an emphasis on the "spirit" (2:29b). This appears in the declaration that circumcision of the heart is in the "spirit" and not in the "written code." While Paul used the word "spirit" a couple of times in Rom(A) (1:4; 5:5), it was in contrast with "written code" in Rom(B). The contrast between "spirit" and "written code" was already addressed to the Corinthians, where it was used in connection with the office of Paul (2 Cor 3:6). However, in Rom(B), Paul used it in relation to the issue of becoming the people of God by practicing circumcision. In this way, Paul adopted the expression of "written code" in order to reveal an inherently negative stance toward the Law. Accordingly, he expressed his withdrawn position on the Law by applying the method he had used to the Corinthians to the Romans again.

The origin of praise was dealt with. This is found in the description that it comes from God, not from people (2:29c). Paul once again showed a God-centered narrative. To be more specific, praise for those who have circumcised in their hearts by the "spirit" comes not from man but from God. Here, praise refers to God's acknowledgment of people, and it belongs entirely to God's unique authority. Accordingly, Paul taught that the distinction between Jews and gentiles in the Roman church was invalid. Before God, Jews were not better simply because they had the Law, and gentiles were not disadvantaged simply because they did not have it. Paul argued that it is entirely within God's authority for anyone to become the people of God. This claim must have made Jewish members uncomfortable.

To sum up, Paul had to provide his own response to the advocation of Jewish members regarding the observance of the Law and the practice of circumcision. Instead of denying them, Paul developed the logic that one should properly understand the inner meaning and act accordingly. His answer would have made Jewish members quite uncomfortable because he told them to let go of their privileges. It is important to note that this opened the door to gentiles. This content would have been included in at least the second letter, given that it was written with knowledge of the situation of the Roman church.

Critique Against Jews (3:1–8)

Paul now began to criticize Jews in earnest. This focuses on their actions contrary to the principles of faith. In this way, Paul attempted preliminary work to open the door to gentiles.

Critique against Jews began with two rhetorical questions. Paul set up a parallel between the advantage of Jews and the benefits of circumcision (3:1). This is a supplementary explanation after Paul had said that if Jews do not keep the Law, they are not different from gentiles. This shows that having read the circumcision of Abraham described in Rom(A) (4:9–12), Jewish members argued for their advantage with circumcision. Having received questions about the relationship between Jews and circumcision, Paul answered in Rom(B) that the circumcised Jews had their own advantages. However, a rhetorical question was used to imply that this was not properly observed.

In addition, beneficial aspects of being Jewish were listed. Among them is that Jews were entrusted with the words of God (3:2). Here, Paul adopted the phrase "words of God," which seems to mean the Bible. This implies that although Jews could have been in a better position than gentiles in relation to God, they failed. Instead, Paul opened the door to gentiles by adopting the "words of God" rather than the "Law." Paul tried to teach that gentiles could also treat the Bible without restrictions as the words of God rather than the Law that Jews adhere to. Ultimately, there is an implication here that even gentiles can become God's people.

Paul then emphasized the faithfulness of God. This is found in the statement that even if a person does not believe the words of God, their unbelief cannot nullify his faithfulness (3:3). Paul would like to say that there were some among Jews who did not believe in the words of God. Having described that this does not invalidate God's faithfulness, Paul hinted at the possibility of God's words leaving Jews and accepted by gentiles. This created the meaning that a way was laid for gentiles to become the people of God. Perhaps Paul suggested here that the words of God preached by him should be received not only by Jewish members but also by gentile members.

The truth of God was declared. This is described in the claim that God is true even though people may be false (3:4). Paul made a contrast between truthfulness of God and falsity of people. On the other hand, a parallel between God's faithfulness and his truth appeared. To support this, a verse was cited from Isa 51:4, which states that God may be proved right when he speaks and that he prevails when he judges. This is an accusation that Jewish members did not accept the gospel as the words of God that Paul had claimed to be. Having put the lies of Jews in contrast with the truth of God, Paul seemed to have created the logic that the words of God had no choice but to go to gentiles because of Jews' mistakes.

Paul once again made a contrast between God and human beings. This appears in the statement that people's unrighteousness reveals God's righteousness and that God brings wrath on them (3:5). Paul justified the wrath of righteous God on the unrighteous. Unrighteousness and wrath are addressed at the beginning of Rom(B) (1:18–23). Paul argued that even if a person reveals God's righteousness in an unrighteous way, that person must receive his wrath. This means that there were people among Jewish members who committed unrighteousness. Having pointed out these facts, Paul established a justification for turning the attention to gentiles. Paul made this claim because Jews lived an unrighteous life.

The righteous aspect of God was described in connection with judgment. This is found in the statement that if God is unrighteous, he can never judge the world (3:6). Paul emphasized that God can judge the world because he is righteous. While the righteousness of God by faith was emphasized in Rom(A) (1:17; 4:3), the righteous aspect of God that judges people is heightened in Rom(B). This reflects the fact that, unlike when Paul sent Rom(A), he became aware of the situation of the Romans, especially those of Jewish origin, at the time of writing Rom(B). They were in a situation where they felt judged by God for deviating from their religious concepts and leading an unrighteous life. Accordingly, Paul told them that in order to avoid the wrath of God, they should listen to the words of God. Accordingly, Jewish members may have begun to have aversion to Paul's description of God's judgment as being possible for them.

Paul then introduced words that were talked about among the Romans. This means that if God's truth is enriched and brought glory to him through lies, there is no need to be judged like a sinner. However, Paul presented here the argument that this should not be the case. An example of this was described earlier, which argued that God's righteousness can be revealed through man's unrighteousness (3:5). If so, it turns out that some members of the Roman church were leading a religious life from an unethical perspective, contrary to the contents that appeared in the greetings described in Rom(A) (16:3–16). The reason Paul states this kind of phenomenon is believed to provide a justification to shift attention from Jews to gentiles.

One more rhetorical question was added. It is said, "Why not say, 'Let us do evil that good may result?'" (3:8a). Paul quoted what some members of the Roman church had said and once again conveyed the meaning that they should not speak in that way. The idea of doing evil to achieve good is absurd. This is in line with Paul's logic that God's righteousness should not be revealed through the unrighteousness of people. The contrast between good and evil has already been dealt with in Rom(A) (12:9), and then the lesson has been delivered that they cannot coexist in Rom(B) (2:9–10). With this question, Paul hinted at the fact that there were some Romans who ignored the process in favor of religious results. This reflects the situation that although Jews had the Law, they did not properly keep it. Accordingly, Paul provided a justification to once again turn his attention to gentiles.

Paul mentioned the slander he and his coworkers faced. This is the fact that some members of the Roman church slandered him and his coworkers by accusing them of saying the words quoted above (3:8b). This is an argument that Paul had no reason to be slandered because he never said such a way. This shows that some Romans criticized Paul after reading Rom(A). Having responded their backbiting, Paul strongly denied it and insisted that anyone who said such a thing would be condemned. The word "condemnation" was already used in the earlier text of Rom(B) (2:1, 27). When Paul used it again here, he scolded the Romans at a fairly severe level. Paul made Jewish members ashamed.

To sum up, Paul continued his critique against Jews. This pointed out that Jews were going down the wrong path. Paul wrote this in response to critique of Jewish members about the core of the gospel described in Rom(A). Of course, they were not happy with his answer. In this respect, this part is believed to be derived from at least the second letter.

The Law and Sin (3:9–20)

Paul shifted the focus from Jews to all people in connection with the matter of sin. This is revealed in the proposition that all mankind is under sin. Paul kept taking a negative stance on the Law, saying that it only makes people realize their sin. His intention was to create a theoretical foundation that would guide people on a path to freedom from sin.

A rhetorical question was given to suggest the proposition. It is said, "What shall we conclude then? Are we any better?" (3:9a). Paul raised this question, so that the answer would be "we are not better." To this belong both Jews and Greeks, and they were all declared to be under sin (3:9b). Only here did Paul begin to describe Jews and Greeks on the same level, ever since equal opportunity had been implied in the statements that there was no distinction between Jews and Greeks in doing good or evil (2:9–10) and that one had to be a Jew inwardly rather than outwardly (2:26, 28–29). Then, this verse constitutes a watershed in Paul's description of the relationship between Jews and gentiles in terms of equality because while it had been described implicitly in the previous texts, it began to be mentioned explicitly here. In this way, Paul established a justification for the mission to gentiles.

A subtle change is found in regard to the issue of sin. Paul changed the focus on sin when he sent letters to the Roman church. For instance, forgiveness of sin and Christ's death for sinners were the main topics in Rom(A) (4:7-8; 5:8). They are descriptions of the benefit given to sinners by God. On the other hand, since the issue of sin was mentioned in connection with the Law in Rom(B) (2:12), it is then declared that all people are under sin here. In this way, when Paul sent letters to the Roman church, he changed the direction from describing the blessing to be forgiven their sin to describing their spiritual situation. This shows that Paul was disappointed with Jewish members. This claim would have made Jewish members uncomfortable.

Paul started quoting passages from the Bible to support the claim that all are under sin. First of all, he cited the words from Psalms: "There is no one righteous, not even one; there is no one who understands, no one who seeks God. All have turned away, they have together become worthless; there is no one who does good, not even one" (3:10b-12; Ps 14:1-3). Having made parallelisms among the righteous, those who understand, those who seek God, and those who do good, Paul presented the justification that all people, whether Jews or Greeks, should become these kinds of people. In Rom(A), Paul stated that Christ died for sinners (5:8). Accordingly, in Rom(B), he insisted that all people had been under sin and defined them as sinners. Having pointed out that in reality there is no one righteous, Paul wrote that all people have become biased and have become useless together. The reason that Paul quoted these verses is to emphasize the fact that even though the words of God were given to the Jews, they did not keep them. This kind of instruction would have made Jewish members uncomfortable; on the other hand, this would have been a lesson that gave hope to the gentile members.

To support the claim raised above, Paul quoted several passages from the Bible. To them belong the words "their throat are open graves" and "their tongues practice deceit" (3:13a; Ps 5:9). Paul wanted to say that the energy of death comes from everyone's hearts and that they ultimately suffer such things themselves due to their deception. In any case, it means that people have no choice but to die due to their own mistakes. In addition, Paul cited a verse that says, "The poison of vipers is on their lips" (3:13b; Ps 140:3). This probably means that everyone is being driven to death through words that are like poison. Having mentioned the poison of vipers on their lips, Paul dealt with the cursing and bitterness that filled the mouth. Among other things, Paul quoted passages about the wickedness of people (3:14; Ps 10:7). This means that people's mouths are full of cursing and bitterness. In this way, people were portrayed as those who do things that kill others mentally and spiritually. Additionally, it is said, "Their feet are swift to shed blood; ruin and misery mark their ways, and the way of peace they do not know" (3:15–17; Isa 59:7–8). This means the state of not being able to enjoy any reward in life. Finally, Paul noted that people do not fear God before their eyes (3:18; Ps 36:1). It was cited to prove that people were under sin. It seems, however, that these citations were not enough. In any case, Paul assumed that people needed to be free from sin and tried to lead them to salvation with the gospel he had preached.

Here, Paul's position on the quoted verses should be examined. Although most of them were quoted from Psalms written by David, no mention of him was made at all. Of course, David could not have been mentioned because there was a quoted verse from Isaiah. However, even though Paul could only quote from Psalms known to be David's writings without quoting a single verse from Isaiah, he did not. When Paul quoted verses from Psalms in Rom(A), he used the expression "David says" (4:6–8). However, in Rom(B), it seems that Paul intentionally avoided any clue to David. This seems to result from the intention to reduce the allusion to David from a Jewish perspective. In this way, Paul tried to have reduced the intensity of alluding to David that Jewish members would prefer.

A negative stance toward the Law continued. It begins with an introductory statement that "Now we know that . . ." (3:19a). With this kind of expression, Paul wanted the Romans to agree with what he had presented. This is that whatever the Law says, it speaks to those who are under it. The expression "those under the Law" was already applied to the gentile Galatians in connection with the expiation brought by the Son of God (Gal 4:4–5). There is reflected a homogeneous relationship between the Son of God and those under the Law. On the other hand, in Rom(B), the expression "those under the Law" was only used to indicate the limitations of the Law and the final judgment of God. This reflects the situation that Jewish members had not properly kept the Law. In this way, Paul maintained the negative view of the Law in Rom(B).

Paul also presented the results that the Law brings. This is that every mouth may be silenced and the whole world may be brought under the judgment of God (3:19b). Paul insisted that those who had kept the Law were ultimately doomed to be judged or condemned without a word before God. It has been suggested that God's judgment would fall upon those who committed sin without properly understanding the divinity revealed through creation (2:2). Then, Paul hinted here that the Law was not that special compared to that. This statement appears to be more severe than his previous declaration in Rom(A) that the Law brings about wrath and that without the Law there is no transgression (4:15). With this, Paul maintained the negative stance on the Law so far in Rom(B). Without a doubt, Jewish members had a hard time facing Paul's views on the Law as they read this.

A negative conclusion about the Law was presented. This means that nobody can be righteous before God by the works of the Law and that it only makes one aware of sin (3:20). Paul linked the role of the Law to sin for the first time here. Then, it can be said that Paul declared in that way here in response to the critiques of Jewish members against what Paul had argued in regard to the Law in Rom(A) (4:15). Then, when the Romans asked for a more detailed explanation, Paul mentioned the judgment with the works of the Law (2:12) and then presented its negative role in relation to sin in Rom(B) (3:20). Accordingly, it is necessary to look at the process by which Paul's perspective on sin changed. Whereas Paul had quoted several verses from the Bible to refer to the blessings that sin is covered and not recognized in Rom(A) (4:7–8), he declared that all people are under sin and the Law makes one realize sin here (3:9, 20). The preceding description shows that Paul developed a more negative view on the Law in Rom(B). His negative argument on the Law would have made Jewish members uncomfortable.

In summary, having presented the proposition that all people are under sin, he emphasized that Jews and gentiles are on equal footing with regard to sin. At the same time, he presented the proposition that one cannot be liberated from sin by the works of the Law and that it only makes people realize sin. This was a preliminary statement for a new breakthrough. In any case, Jewish members who heard these claims would have been uncomfortable, while gentile members would have felt relieved. In this way, Paul increasingly opened the doors to gentiles and established the legitimacy for the mission to gentiles. This text is believed to have originated from the second letter in that its intensive description of the relationship between the Law and sin is more advanced than that between the Law and transgression asserted in Rom(A).

3. THE FAITH OF JESUS CHRIST (3:21-31)

Paul touched on the main point that is the righteousness by faith of Jesus Christ in God rather than the works of Law. This was also a criticism of the Jewish faith and an attempt to widen the door to gentiles. Paul further revealed the core of the gospel centered on the death and resurrection of Christ Jesus.

Christ Jesus and Grace (3:21-26)

Paul dealt with the grace that leads to the righteousness of God through Christ Jesus. This is the redemption given through Christ Jesus, which is the core of the gospel. Just as the case of challenge by the gentile members of the Corinthian and Galatian churches, Paul responded to the critique of the Jewish members of the Roman church with lessons centered on Christ. This presented a way for gentiles to be included as the people of God.

The righteousness of God was offered as an alternative to the Law. This is found in the statement that apart from the Law, the righteousness of God has been revealed to which the Law and the Prophets testified (3:21). Paul opened up about a new way to be considered righteous before God evidenced by the Law and the Prophets. This brings two factors into consideration. First, Paul further separated the righteousness of God from the Law. Second, it was evidenced by the Law and the Prophets, that is, the Bible at the time of the first century CE. While Paul introduced the prophecies of prophets about the Son to define the gospel in Rom(A) (1:2), he linked the Law and the Prophets, that is, the entire Bible, to define it in Rom(B). In this way, Paul gave authority to the righteousness of God. Whereas Paul previously mentioned that the words of God were given to Jews, he added authority by associating the Law and the Prophets with righteousness here. This shows his trial to persuade the Romans to accept the way to the righteousness by the faith in God, that is, the core of the gospel. Paul's claim would have been enough to attract the attention of Roman believers.

Then Paul specifically presented the way of obtaining the righteousness of God. It is defined as being extended to all who believe in God through the "faith of Jesus Christ" (3:22). Paul presented the faith of Jesus Christ in relation to the righteousness of God. In Rom(A), the faith of Abraham in God was emphasized as being earlier and better than the Law (4:3). Then, it was stated that one would be credited to righteousness by faith in God, who raised Jesus our Lord from the dead (4:24). This emphasized personal faith in God. On the other hand, in Rom(B), Paul put an emphasis on the "faith of Jesus Christ" without any reference to the Law. This shows an important transformation in regard to the example of faith in God. This shows that after Paul had received doubts and critiques from the Romans, mainly Jewish members, about the role of the Law as written in Rom(A), he presented the faith of Jesus Christ in God as an alternative for the righteousness of God in Rom(B). In Rom(A), Paul expressed that people are justified through the blood of Christ (5:9). Having expressed the death of Christ in different way, the blood signifies the faith of Christ in God. Then, in Rom(B), Paul argued that righteousness by the faith of Jesus Christ extends to all believers. As a result, the importance of faith in God was maintained as the way of accessing to the righteousness of God. Having changed the model of faith from Abraham to Jesus Christ, Paul showed a deliberate move to escape from focusing on Jews. This also shows Paul expanding opportunities for gentiles to reach the righteousness of God.

Paul explained the relationship between sin and the glory of God. This is found in the saying that all have sinned and fallen short of the glory of God (3:23). Paul first declared that people had committed sin. The issue of sin was important for Jews. Accordingly, in Rom(A), Paul said that Christ Jesus proved the love of God by giving himself for sinners (5:8). Subsequently, he insisted in Rom(B) that all people, whether Jews or Greeks, have committed sins (3:9) and then declared that through the Law they can be conscious of sin (3:20). Accordingly, it was possible for Paul to declare that all people have committed sin here. In addition, it was claimed that people fall short of the glory of God because of their sin. With regard to the glory of God, he declared in Rom(A) that by faith in God one can enter into grace and hope for the glory of God (5:2). However, in Rom(B), sin was considered to be the fundamental reason that prevents people from reaching the glory of God. Then, it can be said that the relationship between sin and the glory of God reflects Paul's shift from an optimistic position toward the Romans in Rom(A) to a neutral or pessimistic one in Rom(B). Paul reacted this way because he had received severe critiques or challenges from them after sending Rom(A).

The theme of redemption was addressed. It is said that people have been righteous by the grace of God through the redemption in Christ Jesus (3:24). Paul introduced the redemption in Christ Jesus as the path to the righteousness of God. This was presented as the grace of God because it is the way to be free from sin. If so, the redemption in Christ Jesus appears to be related to the faith and righteousness of Christ mentioned earlier. The word "redemption" was once used to the Corinthians in the statement that Jesus came from God and became the redemption for the people (1 Cor 1:30). Jewish members would have learned about this from Priscilla and Aquila who had heard about it while staying with Paul in Corinth or Ephesus. Just as the assertion of redemption was informed in a letter written after Paul was challenged by the Corinthians, the same phenomenon was observed in the case of Rom(B) written in response to the doubts and critiques of the Romans, especially Jewish members represented by Priscilla and Aquila. This is, of course, a concept presented against the backdrop of the atoning death of Christ Jesus for sinners and return to life as described in Rom(A) (5:8–10). Accordingly, Paul added the concept of redemption to Christ in addition to the meaning of atonement in Rom(B). Having put forward more Christ Jesus for salvation for the first time in Rom(B), Paul delivered a lesson that completely abolished the role of the Law. The Romans should have felt more uncomfortable about Paul's negative view on the Law and then had no choice but to cast doubts on him.

Paul then described Jesus as a sacrifice of atonement. This is described in the statement that God established Jesus as a "sacrifice of atonement in his blood" (3:25a). Paul used the expression "his blood" in connection with the "sacrifice of atonement." Once in Rom(A), Paul wrote that people could be justified by the blood of Christ and were reconciled to God through his death (5:9–10). Here in Rom(B), having connected the blood of Christ to the "sacrifice of atonement," Paul understood the death of Christ in light of atoning sacrifice from a priestly perspective. This seems to have been a strategic approach of Paul to make the Romans understand the atoning death of Jesus Christ. In addition, the blood of Christ was mentioned instead of cross or crucifixion in order to prevent the Romans from being misunderstood by the authorities of the Roman Empire. In other words, if Paul had mentioned the cross of Christ, the authorities could have misunderstood the Romans as a group of people following the crucified traitor. In any case, Paul took into account the political situation of the Romans and revealed the core of the gospel he wanted to convey one by one. This is how Paul might impart to them some spiritual gift to make them strong (1:11). There is, however, no mention of the resurrection, which seems to reflect Paul's diminished expectations for the Romans. It is doubtful whether the Romans would have accepted this teaching of Paul.

The purpose that God established the "sacrifice of atonement in the blood of Christ" was described. This appears in the statement that God left the sin committed beforehand unpunished in his forbearance to demonstrate his righteousness (3:25b). Paul emphasized the righteousness of God because it symbolized the state of being saved by God. For this purpose, the reason was given that refers to God's long-suffering and overlooking the sin of people. Once in Rom(A), having quoted the words of David (4:7–8; Ps 32:1–2), Paul put an emphasis on the forgiveness of sin. Although how to be forgiven was not stated there, it could only be acknowledged from the context that faith in God was the way of being free from sin. Accordingly, in Rom(B), Paul stated that people's sin can be overlooked because God has been patient for a long time. This made the Romans think of Christ Jesus as the "redemption" mentioned earlier (3:24) and of God's reference to his patience and kindness in leading people to repentance (2:4). Paul taught that people must repent and enter a state of liberation from sin through the blood of Christ. This is a more theologically developed statement than Paul's previous presentation of God's righteousness shown in the story of Abraham's faith as written in Rom(A). In this way, Paul wanted to make the Romans come closer to Christ Jesus.

At the same time, Paul described the results related to righteousness. This is found in the statement that God demonstrates his righteousness and makes those who live by faith of Jesus also justified (3:26). Paul taught that God's righteous character had been transferred to people who lived by the faith of Jesus. As a result, God as well as people share righteousness as a common element. Having written this way, Paul showed that the faith of Jesus that connects God and the Romans has to be conveyed clearly when writing Rom(B). In this way, the faith of Jesus Christ, the core of the gospel, was presented once again. While Paul emphasized that people should believe in God following the faith of Abraham in Rom(A), he reiterates the importance of faith with an emphasis on imitating Christ Jesus in Rom(B). This shows that while Rom(A) was written with Jewish members who had been the major group of the Roman church in mind, Paul approached it from a broader perspective when writing Rom(B). In this way, as time passed, Paul little by little expanded the path for gentiles to become the people of God by following the faith of Jesus Christ. It is, however, to be reminded that this instruction would not have been easily accepted by the Jewish members of the Roman church.

In summary, Paul presented the core message of the gospel. This means that they were redeemed from their sin through the faith of Jesus Christ. Having emphasized the faith of Christ Jesus, Paul widened the path to righteousness for gentiles. This theologically in-depth description of Paul was presented to overwhelm the Jewish viewpoint of the Romans. However, it is not easy to guarantee whether they would have accepted his new instruction. This text is most likely derived from the second letter in that it deals with Jesus Christ beyond Abraham's faith dealt with in Rom(A).

The Law and Faith (3:27–31)

Having concluded that faith establishes the Law, Paul put it beyond the works of the Law for the righteousness of God. Paul did not give up his emphasis on faith and maintained the core of the gospel. This also follows a theological strategy to bring about the result of opening the door to gentiles.

The emphasis on faith reappeared in connection with the Law. This is seen in the declaration that there is nothing to boast about in the Law or works, but only the Law of faith (3:27). Paul presented the Law of faith, not the Law or works, as the reason to be proud of. Although Paul had once pointed out that Jews boasted about the Law (2:23), he completely denied it here. Rather, he linked faith and the Law by presenting the "Law of faith" as an alternative. In other words, the Law should be viewed from a perspective of faith. This statement reminds readers of Paul's question to the Galatians whether they received the spirit by the works of the Law or by hearing with faith (Gal 3:2, 5). However, Paul linked these elements to obtaining the righteousness of God in Rom(B) and presented the importance of faith to Jewish members. This once again shows how Paul responded when he had been challenged or criticized by them. In this respect, this text shows a similar case with that reflected in Galatians. It is, however, doubtful whether this claim was accepted by the Jewish members of the Roman church.

Paul presented his own conclusion with regard to the Law and faith. This is found in the acknowledgment that a person is justified not by the works of the Law but by faith (3:28). The theme of being justified by faith rather than by the works of the Law came to Rom(B) through Galatians and Rom(A). However, it is necessary to take a look at here is the subject of faith. Paul presented the faith of Christ in Galatians (Gal 2:16) and the faith of Abraham in Rom(A) (4:3). Then, in Rom(B), the faith of Christ was presented again (3:22), and finally the faith of people was presented (3:28). This scheme conveys the instruction that people can be justified by faith in God, just as Abraham and Christ believed in God. With this, Paul taught the Romans to properly believe in God according to the way Christ Jesus lived. This is the core of the gospel Paul wanted to convey to the Romans.

The relationship of God with people was presented. This appears in the statement that God is the god of not only Jews but also gentiles (3:29). Having raised two rhetorical questions, Paul declared that God is truly the god of all mankind. Ultimately, this was Paul's strategic statement to embrace all the members of the Roman church supposed to consist of both Jews and gentile Greeks. In addition, this was a way to justify the mission to Spain that Paul had focused on up to that time. Paul urged the Romans to go beyond the distinction between Jews who had the Law and gentiles who did not. In this way, Paul went beyond the schema of "Jews first and then Greeks" mentioned in Rom(A) (1:16). Having reused the expression of "Jews first and then Greeks" to imply the equality between the two groups of people (2:9–10) and stated the equal condition of them under sin (3:9) in Rom(B), Paul at last clarified the equal status of them in their relationship with God here (3:29). In this way, a narrative began to appear that increasingly opened the door to gentiles. This claim would certainly have been seen as unreasonable by Jewish members.

Paul dealt with the role of God in regard to the righteousness of Jews and gentiles. This is found in the description that circumcised Jews as well as uncircumcised gentiles are justified by faith and that the only one who does this is God (3:30). Paul not only showed that he had maintained the perspective on the one God but also presented a new argument that everyone, whether Jewish or gentile, should live a life of faith with Jesus Christ. The parallel between circumcision and uncircumcision was mentioned here with a certain intention. Paul once emphasized uncircumcision more than circumcision in connection with Abraham becoming the forefather of faith in Rom(A) (4:9–12). There, circumcision and uncircumcision do not appear as opposites. However, in Rom(B) that circumcision and uncircumcision are the matter of opposition according to the stance whether one keeps the Law or not (2:25–26). And finally,

Paul argued for the equality between the circumcised and the uncircumcised here in the main section of Rom(B). This is a continuation of mentioning the equality between Jews and Greeks described in the previous text. With these descriptions, Paul conveyed the lesson that the Romans, whether Jews or Greeks, should live by faith according to the life of Jesus Christ. This interpretation shows that Paul tried to lead the Romans to pay more attention to gentiles.

Finally, the relationship between the Law and faith was reestablished. This appears in the declaration that the Law is not nullified by faith but rather upheld (3:31). Paul presented the logic that the Law cannot be completed without faith. Once in Rom(A), Paul described the relationship between the Law and faith as opposites in relation to the Abrahamic covenant and showed a negative perspective linking the Law to wrath and transgression (4:13–15). Later, in Rom(B), Paul argued that the Law makes one realize sin and then concluded that faith establishes the Law (3:20, 31). Still, faith was shown to have priority over the Law. The reason that Paul wrote in this way is to convey the gospel without offending the Romans, especially Jewish members, as much as possible. Nevertheless, it cannot be denied that Jewish members were stimulated by new interpretations of relationship between the Law and faith.

To sum up, Paul tried to establish the relationship between faith and the Law. At the same time, he argued that faith following the life of Jesus Christ completes the Law. In spite of a significant challenge of the Romans, especially Jewish members, Paul emphasized that even gentiles have entered the path to be righteous by faith. This kind of controversial teaching should be considered to have been written in response to their critique against Paul's negative view on the Law as written in Rom(A). This informs that this part originated in the second letter.

4. THE ETHICS OF SAINTS (12:14—13:7; 14:13-23)

Paul also dealt with the ethics that the Romans should observe in Rom(B). This is closely related to the wrath of God against unrighteousness that was mentioned at its beginning. In particular, it reflects the fact that the relationship between the Romans and outsiders has become difficult. This is something that Paul was able to deal with after learning about the specific situation of the Romans.

Good and Evil (12:14–21)

Paul dealt with the ethics that the Romans should maintain between good and evil. This is an application of the lesson about the wrath of God against unrighteousness. In this respect, it can be said that Paul wrote this instruction after facing the critique against his view on the Law and wrath as written in Rom(A).

The issue of persecution was dealt with first of all. This appears in the saying to bless and not curse those who persecuted the Romans (12:14). Paul mentioned the persecution that actually occurred in the Roman church. However, it is not clearly stated whether it occurred due to external or internal factors. Although the issue of persecution was mentioned once in general terms in Rom(A) (8:35), there is no clue to clarify it in Rom(B). First, if the persecution occurred due to internal factors, it may have been perpetrated by Jewish members composed of majority against gentile members composed of minority. However, this kind of interpretation is not supported because Paul addressed this topic to all Romans without distinction between them. Second, if persecution occurred due to external factors, it would be related to the Law and circumcision, which were different cultures to accept at the time. Presumably, Paul may have visited the Jerusalem church as revealed in Rom(A) and then announced that he wanted to spread the gospel via Rome to Spain (15:25, 28). Then, the apostles of the Jerusalem church may have sent representatives to the Roman church, just as they had sent Cephas to the Corinthian church and unknown people to the Galatian, Philippian, and Thessalonian churches (1 Cor 1:12; Gal 4:25; 1 Thess 3:5; Phil 3:2). They may have arrived in Rome before Paul sent Rom(B) and emphasized the observance of the Law and circumcision. When Paul learned of this, he may have defined the Romans as being persecuted, just as he had warned the Galatians (Gal 4:29; 5:11). However, this interpretation has problems because Rom(B) is believed to have been written while Paul was heading to Jerusalem (15:31). Although the relationship between Paul and the Romans was reconstructed as best as possible from a historical point of view, the chronological inconsistency makes it difficult to identify the persecutors as the representatives of the Jerusalem church. Third, it is possible that the Romans suffered persecution from people or institutions around the church in Rome. There is no evidence for this yet, but the possibility should not be overlooked. However, the Romans would have been well-aware of the persecutors mentioned by Paul.

It is necessary to pay attention to the contrast between curse and blessing. The word "curse" was already used in a verse quoted from the Bible for the description of evil sinners in Rom(B) (3:14). However, here Paul proposed to declare a blessing instead of a curse on the persecutors. This could be presented as a representative example of living according to the faith of Christ Jesus who died for sinners (3:26; 5:8–10). Otherwise, Paul would not have been able to convey such extreme teachings to the Romans. Anyway, in Rom(A), Paul gave an instruction to hate evil and belong to good (12:9). On the other hand, having suggested a positive attitude toward those who persecute was presented in Rom(B), Paul went much further to require ethical precepts, such as to bless rather than curse.

Then, Paul taught about emotional attunement. This appears in the teaching to rejoice with those who rejoice and weep with those who weep (12:15). Although Paul put an emphasis on the issue of emotional attunement, little has been known about the situations in which one should rejoice or cry. If it is related to the persecution described above, this may have a connection with the image of blessing instead of cursing. On the contrary, this lesson could be related to something that can generally happen in daily life. If so, this would be a general lesson. In any case, Paul wanted the Romans to be united with each other in responding to pressure from insiders or outsiders, whether in situations of joy or sorrow.

The issue of controlling one's mind was discussed. This is found in the instruction that the Romans should be of same mind as one another, not be high-minded but low-minded, and not be pretend to be wiser than others (12:16). Paul wanted them to control their own minds. This reminds readers of what Paul taught in Rom(A); according to him, each person should not think more highly than he or she should think, but should think wisely according to the measure of his or her faith (12:3). While Paul focused on the fact that a person had to accurately know his or her location in Rom(A), he paid attention to the comparison with others in Rom(B). Besides this, Paul seemed to have developed this into a more diverse direction in Rom(B). First, it is important to observe the prerequisite of being of same mind. This is in line with the suggestion of emotional attunement as mentioned in the preceding text. Second, Paul taught the Romans to set their hearts low, not high. At any rate, it is an instruction that only then will the Romans be able to share their hearts with each other. Third, Paul taught them not to pretend to be wiser than others. This is the conclusion to the instruction about being like-minded or being humble. With this saying, the Romans were taught that it was important to properly know their position. From the perspective of mirror-reading, it can be inferred that the Romans had a high mind and pretended to be wise, and did not accept the gospel he preached. This is believed to be a lesson written in response to what Paul received from Phoebe about the reality of the Romans.

Paul delivered an instruction on the issue of good and evil. This is well reflected in a chiastic structure that can be listed as follows: A. the relationship between good and evil (12:17); B. reconciliation with others (12:18); B'. God's retaliation against enemies (12:19–20); and A'. the relationship between good and evil (12:21). In this structure, elements that intersect with each other are discovered. Paul taught about whether the Romans should treat outsiders as good or evil. Having mentioned the phrase "wrath of God," he revealed that this text belonged to Rom(B) along with other texts about unrighteousness and wrath (1:18—2:11). Additionally, the fact that the theme of good and evil appears in both texts supports the possibility that they originated in the same letter, possibly the second.

Paul treated the issue of doing good. This appears in the teaching to repay no one evil for evil and to seek to do good in the sight of all (12:17). Here the combination of good and evil is the main topic to be considered. Although Paul also dealt with the issue of good and evil in Rom(A) (12:9), he used different Greek words there. While there the relationship between good and evil was delivered from a passive point of view as something to be avoided, here it was conveyed from a positive perspective as something to be overcome. In this respect, it reflects the specific situation of the Roman church. In any case, the theme of good and evil is in line with what was taught earlier that the Romans should bless those who persecute them (12:14). With these teachings, Paul presented the Romans with a level of life that they had never thought of before. It was probably passed down against the backdrop of Jesus Christ, who had given up his body for sinners that was the core of the gospel as written in Rom(A) (5:8; cf. 1 Cor 15:3; Gal 1:4; 2:20). This shows the process by which Paul developed theological themes related to good and evil over time.

The topic of peace was mentioned. This is seen in the form of command to live at peace with everyone if possible (12:18). Paul presented this kind of instruction as an example of life that pursues goodness. The word "peace" is already used in Rom(A) in the teaching that having been justified by faith, the Romans should have enjoyed it with God through the Lord Jesus Christ (5:1). Accordingly, Paul taught them to make peace with all people if possible in Rom(B). This focuses on the relationship the Romans should have with all people, including those who had persecuted them. To be more specific, this includes blessing those who persecuted the Romans, emotional sympathy with them, and an attitude of not being more arrogant than others. Paul was able to convey the instruction on peace in Rom(B) because he was well aware of what was happening among the Romans.

Paul taught about the issue of enemies. This appears in the teachings that define the Romans as "my beloved ones" and say about not taking revenge on people but leaving it to the wrath of God (12:19a). Paul presented a way to put the teachings presented above into practice. This was presented as a way to enjoy peace with all people in order to promote goodness. First, Paul adopted the expression "my beloved" for the first time toward the Romans. This shows that he wanted to have a good relationship with them. Second, the teaching not to take revenge reminds readers of what Paul taught in Rom(A); according to him, God saved his enemies, who were defined as sinners, from wrath by having his own Son die for them (5:10). And then in Rom(B), it was said that the Romans should avoid enmity. In this way, Paul changed his focus on the relationship with God to that with people. As people received salvation from God, they were not to treat others as enemies. Third, it is necessary to take a look at the issue of wrath. After Paul mentioned in Rom(A) that the Law brings about wrath (4:15), he described wrath and judgment in more detail in Rom(B) (1:18—2:11; 12:19a). In conclusion, having emphasized that the final judgment lies with God, Paul encouraged the Romans to leave it to the wrath of God rather than take revenge for themselves. In this respect, this text can be considered to be a conclusion in relation to wrath discussed in Rom(B). This reflects the fact that the Romans were experiencing conflict with those who had persecuted them.

Paul quoted two verses from the Bible to support his teachings. This appears in the saying that vengeance belongs to God and God will repay (12:19b–20; Deut 32:25). Paul showed the Romans a way to achieve peace with all people by not taking revenge for themselves. In addition, another verse is cited: If your enemy is hungry, feed him, if he is thirsty, give him a drink, and heap coals of fire on his head (Prov 25:21–22). This verse is connected to the previous one with a linking word "enemy." Having cited two verses, Paul asked the Romans for a positive act of giving food and water to their enemies beyond a passive act of not avenging them. With these quotations, Paul reflected the situation that the Romans maintained an enemy-like relationship with those who had persecuted them. Perhaps with these quotations, Paul revealed the intention not to criticize Jewish members who had criticized the gospel. Rather, it may be an expression of waiting for God's wrath. This is considered a text written after learning about their situation in that it deals with relationships with people outside the church.

Finally, a conclusion to the previous discussion was presented. This is found in the saying not to be overcome by evil but to overcome evil with good (12:21). Whereas Paul taught people to hate evil and belong to good in Rom(A) (12:9), the issue of good and evil was dealt with to overcome evil with good. The difference between the two is also found in the use of different Greek words in Rom(B) (2:7-10; 3:8; 12:17). Accordingly, Paul was able to mention the conflict between good and evil here, which shows that he more actively advocated the issue of overcoming evil with good. This can be said to be another expression of the teaching not to curse but to bless those who persecute the Romans (12:15). In this respect, Paul showed a consistent view of external forces.

It is necessary to pay attention to the description of good and evil. It is because they were mentioned against the backdrop of the garden of Eden. The conflict between good and evil refers to the way that God originally created humans and had them live there (Gen 3:1-6). As for this, at the beginning of Rom(B), Paul wrote that from the creation of the world, the invisible things of God, namely, his eternal power and divine nature, have been clearly seen and known in all things (1:19-20). He then mentioned good and evil several times. It was no coincidence that Paul addressed the issue of primordial creation and the theme of good and evil together in Rom(B). Therefore, the issue of overcoming evil with good is related with returning to the life before the fall in the garden of Eden. Paul taught the Romans to restore the original state that Adam and Eve had been in. In this respect, it is revealed that Paul's theology on good and evil has gradually developed as time passed.

To sum up, Paul reflected the specific situation the Romans were in and advised them with ethical lessons. It focuses on responding to those who persecute them. The lesson that they had to bless rather than curse and overcome evil with good contains the message that people must restore the original state of human beings living in the garden of Eden. The fact that Paul focused the ethical lessons on the specific situation of the Romans rather than on general matters suggests that this text likely originated from at least the second letter.

Obedience to Authority (13:1–7)

Paul dealt with the matter of social institutions. The issue of obedience to authority and the relationship with external organizations came to the fore. In particular, this text follows the previous one with a common theme of wrath, judgment, and a contrast between good and evil. Perhaps the teaching to bless instead of curse one's persecutors may have been associated with the institution.

The issue of worldly authority was dealt with. This appears in the teaching that each person must be subject to the governing authorities (13:1a). They seem to refer to powerful institutions of the Roman Empire. Paul never mentioned worldly power in any of his previous letters. If so, this reflects the situation that the Romans had been in a conflict over whether or not to obey worldly powers. If Paul had not known about this situation, there was no reason to address this topic. It is thought that Paul probably heard about this problem from Phoebe, who returned from delivering Rom(A) and wrote appropriate instructions in the second letter.

Then, Paul continued describing the issue of worldly authority. This appears in the saying that all authority comes from God and is ordained by God (13:1b). Paul once told the Corinthians that all things exist because of God (1 Cor 8:6). However, having stated that all authority comes from God and that God has established all authorities in Rom(B), Paul put the governing authorities under the divine authority. In this way, Paul added weight to the power of the world. The reason that the subject of obedience to ruling authorities was addressed is not specifically stated. However, given that the theme of authority is described in connection with God, this shows that there were elements causing conflict with the authorities among the Romans.

The issue of submission to the worldly authority was emphasized once again. This is found in the statement that whoever resists authority rebels against the commands of God, and those who resist will bring judgment upon themselves (13:2). Paul presented God as the source of authority and stated that the resistance against it is that against God. Paul once told the Corinthians that Christ would destroy the authority (1 Cor 15:24); however, this is known to refer to angelic beings. However, in

Rom(B), Paul argued that the worldly authority has been given by the commands of God. It seems that the Romans were experiencing conflict in their relationship to worldly powers. Paul's favorable description of the power of the Roman Empire appears to be consistent with the instruction to bless, not curse, those who persecute. This was a way to protect the Romans from the worldly authority of the Roman Empire.

Paul then described the role of ruler. This starts with the premise that those who rule should not be fearful of good deeds but of evil deeds (13:3a). Paul assumed that God's authority was given to "those who rule" and that they were to be feared against evil deeds. The contrast between good and evil works is mentioned several times in Rom(B) (2:7–10; 3:7; 12:21). In this respect, this text must be connected to the previous texts in terms of theme of good and evil. In other words, this is a lesson that those who receive authority from God and rule must do good deeds and overcome evil deeds so that people can obey them. Second, Paul taught that the Romans had to do good deeds in order not to be afraid of authority (13:3b). Although the standard for good is not clearly stated here, it seems to be a matter that should be judged based on the Bible, as in the previous case (12:19–20). Third, the result of doing good deeds was also treated. The Romans will receive praise from those who rule (13:3c). Paul already mentioned the word "praise" once in Rom(B), where praise from God is described (2:29). On the other hand, praise from people seems to be mentioned here because it is a teaching about the ethics of the Romans. In this way, Paul seemed to have taken a positive stance toward worldly powers when he wrote Rom(B).

The role of the ruler was described in more detail. The rulers are defined as the servants of God to do the Romans good (13:4a). With this saying, Paul once supported the statement he made earlier that God established the ruling authority. Anyway, it is important to observe that the phrase "minister of God" was applied to the secular ruler. This shows that he took a positive stance toward worldly powers. However, as was described here for the first time the relationship between worldly powers and the Romans, Paul has not yet fully developed these issues theologically. It is possible that he tried to avoid conflict with the authorities of the Roman Empire as much as he could, keeping in mind that he would have to go to Spain for the mission to preach the gospel. Therefore, the positive stance toward the ruler was probably a conclusion based on his realistic judgment.

Paul also left open the possibility that the Romans would commit evil. This appears in the teaching to fear those who rule when the Romans do evil (13:4b). Paul previously taught that if one does not want to be afraid of the ruler, he or she should do good; on the contrary, here he conveyed this instruction in reverse. The contrast between good and evil was thus constantly used. It is believed that Paul mentioned the contrast between them against the backdrop of the tree of knowledge of good and evil in the garden of Eden. Although this has already been covered in earlier text (12:14-21), it is an interpretation that can be strengthened in that Paul used it once again. Paul may be presenting the justification that not only Jews but also gentiles among the Romans should accept the instruction that he had delivered.

The reasons to fear those who rule were stated. This is found in the statement they have been given the role of being God's agents who use the sword to punish evildoers and retaliate according to his wrath (13:4b). Paul realistically described what those who rule do as agents of God. It is necessary to take a look at the word "sword" as a weapon of wrath held by those who rule. The "sword" could be reminiscent of the flaming sword that surrounded the garden of Eden from a typological perspective (Gen 3:25). This is especially true in that it is used in the context of the judgment according to the wrath of God. Paul seemed to have developed a theological description of worldly power from a typological perspective on the garden of Eden. This also seems to convey the message that there is no distinction between Jews and Greeks, conveying that all of humanity is under God's judgment.

Paul provided the Romans with the reason to submit to those who rule as agents of God. This appears in the saying that obedience cannot be avoided, not because of wrath but because one must follow one's conscience (13:5). Paul presented the reason from the positive perspective of conscience rather than the negative perspective of fear of wrath. Conscience was once presented to the Corinthians as a standard for judgment (2 Cor 1:12). Then, when Paul wrote Rom(B), conscience was considered the standard given by God to everyone to judge situations. Paul emphasized conscience instead of the Law because he had in mind the gentile members of the Roman church, too. In this way, it seems that while writing Rom(B), Paul wanted to convey teachings that could be applied to more people beyond Jewish members.

Specifically, obedience to those who govern was described in relation to the issue of taxation. This appears in the teachings that the

Romans had to pay taxes according to their conscience (13:6a). This reflects the fact that they were in a situation of conflict over the taxes paid to the Roman Empire. Pressure to pay taxes may have been understood as persecution. In response to this, Paul emphasized that they had to pay the taxes they owed. The reason for paying taxes was to enable God's agents to work (13:6b). The idea behind this is that the Roman Empire was also established by God. Accordingly, Paul may have taught the Romans to bless rather than curse. It seems that Paul did not want to create antipathy while preaching the gospel within the Roman Empire. The instruction on paying taxes may be related to the request for financial support for the mission to Spain, as recorded in Rom(A) (15:24). It seems that Paul did not really want to reserve worldly taxes for God's work.

Paul presented the conclusion related to authority. This is found in the statement that it is to be given to everyone (13:7). There are four types of things to give, including both material and immaterial things. Paying taxes to those to whom taxes are owed and customs duties to those to whom customs duties are owed are related to material things. Then, it is immaterial to fear those who should be feared and respect those who should be respected. With these descriptions, Paul asked the Romans to give both their hearts and substance. Paul taught this because they received both material and grace from God. It is then necessary to consider the reason that Paul taught the Romans to obey those in authority and pay taxes and tariffs. This shows that the Romans talked about taxes and tariffs. They probably said that when Paul asked for missionary grants, they could not afford to support him because they had to pay taxes and customs duties. Accordingly, it seems that Paul taught them to pay taxes and customs duties and to provide monetary fund to support the mission to Spain. In any case, Paul tried to fulfill the mission of spreading the gospel even to Spain under the protection of the Roman Empire at the time of writing Rom(B).

To sum up, Paul did not want to clash with the Roman Empire regarding taxes. While teaching people to obey those in power, he also wanted to do missionary work all the way to Spain under the protection of the Roman Empire. Accordingly, he wanted the Romans to support him with financial funds that could be perceived as a tax paid to God. This text is considered to belong to at least the second letter rather than the first, because it was possible only after knowing in detail the situation the Roman church was in.

Prohibition of Criticizing Others (14:13–23)

Paul taught the Romans not to criticize one another. This is particularly related to the issue of eating and drinking with regard to their religious standards. Paul hinted at the situation that there was some kind of conflict within the church.

Paul addressed the issue of critique again. This appears in the statement that people should not criticize one another (14:13a). Paul continued dealing with the issue of critique in Rom(B) by using a different Greek word than that used in Rom(A) (14:1–4). It is important to observe that the Romans criticized each other. It is, however, different from the teaching in Rom(A) not to criticize one-sidedly. This shows that there has been a shift from one-sidedness to mutuality in regard to criticism. This shows that the critique of one another among the Romans occurred within the church after Paul had given advice not to make an evaluation on the opinions of those who were weak in faith in Rom(A) (14:1). This lesson is also considered to be a response to what was reported to Paul by Phoebe. Therefore, in the first part of Rom(B), he mentioned the condemnation that will come to those who judge others (2:1). In this way, contrary to the teaching that the Romans should form one body (12:5), in reality they seem to have been divided among themselves.

More specific advice was given regarding relationships with others. This means that the Romans must be careful not to place stumbling blocks or obstacles in front of others (14:13b). While Paul taught about what should be observed between those who were strong and those who were weak in faith in Rom(A) (14:1–12), the instruction prohibiting interference with brothers in the same position was given in Rom(B). Although there is no explanation about stumbling block and obstacle, it is likely to refer to those who did not fit with each other among the Romans or who could cause harm to the other person in their religious life. Having described in this way, Paul reflected the fact that there was a problem of conflict among the Romans. It is sure that having heard specifically about the mutual critique, Paul wrote this text.

Paul introduced what he had been sure of in the Lord Jesus. This is related with the saying that nothing is profane in itself, but it is profane to the person who considers it profane (14:14). Paul mentioned the importance of each person having his or her own religious standards. Accordingly, it was announced that the same object can be perceived and judged differently. Paul mentioned here, "I am confident in the Lord

Jesus," which is stronger than the expression "I speak to every one of you through the grace given to me" as written in Rom(A) (12:3). This reflects the situation that the relationship had deteriorated to the point where Paul had to speak more strongly to persuade Jewish members who had criticized what was profane. What is expressed as profane in confidence is probably related to something that he mentioned the distinction among food and seasons described in Rom(A) (14:2–3, 5–6). It was told that to some extent, a certain members of church ate different foods and differentiated the importance of each season according to their level of faith. As a result, a distinction inevitably arises between what is considered profane and what is considered sacred. When this phenomenon occurred among the members who received Rom(A), Paul had no choice but to preach warnings against it in Rom(B). It is once again likely that Paul received feedback on the lessons from Phoebe, who had previously delivered Rom(A) and returned to him.

The attitude towards food was dealt with in relation to brothers. This appears as a teaching that if one makes one's brother sad because of food, he or she is not doing it out of love (14:15a). Paul gave an admonition to treat brothers with love rather than criticizing them. The reason Paul mentioned the issue of food is related to what he had taught in Rom(A). He suggested that those who were strong in faith ate all food, while those who were weak ate only vegetables (14:2). Accordingly, having read this, some of the Romans criticized others religiously in relation to food. They, especially Jewish members, probably insisted that dietary regulations had to be observed according to the Law. When Paul heard of this news, he could not help but mention it. To this, Paul added the admonition not to destroy the brother for whom Christ died because of food (14:15b). Having already given this kind of exhortation to the Corinthians (1 Cor 8:1–13; 10:23—11:1), Paul could easily mentioned it again in Rom(B). In other words, it is a lesson not to destroy one's brothers spiritually by considering some foods sacred and other foods profane. Paul pointed out that the Jewish members of the Roman church interfered with the gentile members based on the Law by telling them not to eat certain foods because they were unclean. This kind of interference is equivalent to stumbling block or obstacles mentioned earlier. If it hurts someone's heart, it is not done out of love; rather, it is an act that causes destruction. To this end, Paul taught to put an end to the debate about food and asked the Romans to go beyond the issue of the Law.

Paul presented the role of Christ for brothers. This is found in an admonition not to destroy the brother for whom Christ died (14:15b). Paul considered each and every Roman member to be important in connection with Christ. The expressions of "the brother for whom Christ died" had already been told to the Corinthians (1 Cor 8:11). Paul then emphasized in Rom(A) that Christ Jesus revealed God's love by dying for sinners (5:8–10) and asked the Romans to love their brothers (12:10). However, it seems that these teachings were not implemented properly. Accordingly, Paul had no choice but to address the issue of not loving brothers here in Rom(B) (14:15). Thus, building up brothers for whom Christ died was presented as a way of maintaining the love of God to them. However, Paul's use of the word "destroy" reflects a situation in which a struggle or conflict occurred among the Romans. This shows the possibility that Paul's teachings may have led to differences of opinion among them.

An exhortation appeared regarding relationships among the Romans. It is said, "Do not allow what you consider good to be spoken of as evil" (14:16). Paul hoped that the Romans' good intentions regarding eating would not be misunderstood. This was one of the ways to edify brothers. Paul once preached to the Corinthians that they should not criticize a person who ate food sacrificed to idols with gratitude and without any hesitation (1 Cor 10:30). This acknowledges that the person should act according to his or her conscience of faith. And in Rom(A), it was said not to evaluate food according to the measure of faith (14:3). Accordingly, in Rom(B), Paul stated that attitudes towards food with good intentions should not be slandered. In other words, when it comes to eating food, one should not judge other's action on the basis of the rules that appear on the surface; rather, it is better to judge him or her on the basis of his or her intention. These teachings emphasize a more personal standard than the measure of faith presented in Rom(A). In this respect, the more Paul communicated with the Romans, the more specific his teachings became.

Paul explained why actions done with good intentions should not be slandered. This appears in the statement that the kingdom of God is not a matter of eating and drinking, rather of righteousness, peace, and joy in the holy spirit (14:17). Paul presented an instruction that the kingdom of God goes beyond the matter of eating and drinking. This made the Romans look beyond the issue of eating and drinking based on the Law and look at the kingdom of God from a spiritual perspective. In this way, Paul viewed it as more important for the Romans to enjoy righteousness, peace, and joy in the holy spirit. This means being receptive to what people say with good intentions. This is how they do not criticize one another, how they do not put any stumbling block or obstacles in other's way, and how they love one another in Christ Jesus. This was suggested by Paul in the direction of solving problems arising among the Romans. Accordingly, Paul viewed the kingdom of God from a fairly realistic perspective.

The direction of life that the Romans should pursue was presented. This is found in the expression that those who serve Christ in this way not only please God but also receive praise from others (14:18). Here, the phrase "in this way" probably means living a life of righteousness, peace, and joy in the holy spirit. Having focused on those who serve Christ in this way, Paul presented the core of what he had wanted to reveal. This is a life living like Christ. Paul defined himself as a servant of Christ in Rom(A) (1:1) and then emphasized that the Romans should serve Christ, that is, to be his servants here in Rom(B). Being the servant of Christ is basic to please God, but an additional requirement is to be praised by others. This is related to the previous teaching that the Romans had to be at peace with all people (12:18). While writing Rom(B), Paul wanted the Romans to avoid internal as well as external conflict with others. This reflects the fact that Paul heard from Phoebe more about the specific situation the Romans were facing and had to come up with a solution for it.

Paul mentioned what those who serve Christ had to do. This appears in the statement that they should strive to make people peace and build each other up (14:19). Paul taught the Romans to improve the relationships with others. Peace is an element mentioned in the description of relationships with others and the kingdom of God in Rom(B) (12:18; 14:17). On the other hand, the issue of edifying others was first used for the Thessalonians (1 Thess 5:11) and then frequently for the Corinthians (1 Cor 8:1; 10:23; 14:3–5, 12, 17, 26; 2 Cor 12:19). Accordingly, Paul mentioned the theme of edification toward one another in Rom(B). Paul emphasized peace and edification of others because the Romans created conflict by criticizing each other, especially in relation to the most instinctive elements such as food.

The issue of food was addressed again. It is said that God's work should not be destroyed because of food (14:20a). Paul seemed to be referring to the work of edifying one another by a life of righteousness, peace, and joy enjoyed in the holy spirit of God. Accordingly, although the Romans had different opinions about food due to the Law, they had to refrain from fighting, judging, and slandering each other. This is because living according to the will of God is more important than food itself. The reason that the Romans should not destroy the work of God with regard to food is because all things are clean, but the person who eats with stumbling mind is evil (14:20b). Therefore, if one eats the clean food with reservations, it can be evil for him or her. In this way, Paul taught the Romans not to be judged by the Law when eating food, but to judge according to the conscience given to human beings by God. In addition, having mentioned evil here, Paul continued dealing with the contrast with good in this passage (14:16). As mentioned earlier, this appears to be a typological approach in that the contrast between good and evil may have been written against the backdrop of the tree of knowledge of good and evil. Their contrast is an important element that constitutes the theme of Rom(B) (2:9–10; 3:8; 12:17–21; 13:3–4). In this way, Paul seemed to have developed his own consistent logic.

Paul described the theme of beautiful behavior. This is suggested in the form of negative imperative with regard to eating meat, drinking wine, and causing trouble among brothers (14:21). Paul tried to show that when one decides whether to eat meat or not, or to drink wine or not, it is necessary to do so in a way that does not offend his or her brothers. Paul seems to have concentrated the previously mentioned work of God on causing no offense to his brothers. It was once said to the Corinthians that if food caused his brother to stumble, he would never eat meat (1 Cor 8:13). In Rom(A), criticism between those who eat and those who do not is simply prohibited (14:3). Accordingly, in Rom(B), the matter of causing offense among brothers was added and applied to the Romans. In other words, one must think about peace with others and make decisions in the direction of edifying them. This reflects the situation that at the time of writing Rom(B), there were incidents that the issue of food resulted in the destruction of brothers. This reflects the fact that the Romans did not take well the teachings presented by Paul in Rom(A).

Each one's faith was emphasized with regard to the relationship with brothers. This is found in the instruction that the Romans had to keep their faith before God (14:22a). Paul encouraged those who maintained the faith that he advocated. In Rom(A), Paul tried to win their hearts by mentioning that their faith had been spread throughout the world (1:8). In Rom(B), faith was emphasized, shaking the hearts of especially Jewish members so far as to say that faith establishes the Law (3:31). Accordingly, the Romans were advised to maintain their faith in their lives. Paul changed the focus from faith known to the world in Rom(A) to faith before God in Rom(B). With these teachings, Paul tried to help the Romans get closer to the essence of faith.

Paul felt the need to encourage the Romans in relation to their faith. It is said that blessed is the one who does not condemn himself or herself, just as each one claims to be right (14:22b). Paul did not deny that each person should do what they think is right according to their level of faith. In Rom(A), Paul defined forgiveness of sin by God as a blessing (4:6–8). On the other hand, in Rom(B), it is defined as a blessing that each person acts according to his or her own standard and is not condemned. This shows that the standard for enjoying blessing has changed from God's exclusive grace in Rom(A) to each person's religious belief in Rom(B). The lesson is that there is no need to blame oneself for not being able to live the way others live. Paul taught that those who related their faith to the Law should live as they did, and vice versa. Faith was defined as living according to personal standards with God rather than objective standards according to the Law. In this way, while keeping the position of the Jewish members in check, Paul encouraged the gentile members to practice their religious life more independently.

A conclusion has been drawn with regard to the relationship between faith and food. This appears in the teaching that anyone who doubts and eats must be condemned (14:23a). Paul said that anyone who doubted their faith was singled out for condemnation. In Rom(A), Paul taught that those who were strong in faith should not make an evaluation on those who were weak (14:1–3); on the other hand, in Rom(B), he strongly taught them not to criticize one another (14:14). As a result, it can be concluded that the level of faith can be determined by focusing on individual actions here. With this, Paul once again emphasized the level of each individual's faith rather than the objective standard of the Law. Ultimately, this would have been a way to gain more consent from gentile members than Jewish members.

Paul once again emphasized the importance of faith. This is found in the description that they should follow faith (14:23b). Faith means living according to the standards given by God in one's own way. A person who maintains faith in relation to the Law must live with his or her own stance on food and vice versa. Anyway, it was important for them to live in an attitude of helping each other. This is a lesson for each person to live according to his or her own faith and to live confidently in relation to food. With this, Paul strengthened the instruction that both Jews and gentiles in the Roman church should live according to their level of faith.

Finally, Paul concluded the relationship between faith and sin. This appears in the declaration that "everything that does not come from faith is sin" (14:23c). Paul emphasized the standards given to each person in their relationship with God. Accordingly, if possible, they tried to eliminate any room for the Law to stand. Paul once said that through the Law one becomes conscious of sin (3:20) and then concluded that faith establishes the Law (3:31). Therefore, here Paul was able to define not acting according to faith as committing sin. In other words, anyone who pursues the will of God but does not act according to his or her own conscience commits sin. In this respect, Paul made not only Jews but also gentiles think more freely about the faith he had preached. When Jewish members criticized Paul for violating the Law by saying that the faith was against the Law, he attempted to end the debate by defining not acting according to faith as committing sin.

In summary, Paul taught the Romans not to criticize one another according to their own standards. This means that they should not slander each other based on differences that may arise as they each have different opinions regarding the Law. Accordingly, while describing the issue of food, Paul introduced a way for each person to do God's work. This is to do it according to each one's faith. In this way, Paul presented more specific teachings on the issue of criticism of food in Rom(B) than those recorded in Rom(A).

5. CLOSING PART (15:30-33)

Paul closed Rom(B) with exhortation and blessing. He asked the Romans to pray for him to succeed in what he had wanted to do in future. With this, Paul once again revealed the desire to visit the Roman church.

An exhortation was given in connection with prayer. This is found in the description that he asked the Romans to pray for him through the Lord Jesus Christ and the love of the spirit (15:30). First of all, Paul laid the foundation for the admonition by presenting the unbalanced parallelism between "our Lord Jesus Christ" and "the love of the spirit." This resulted in the emphasis on Jesus Christ and the introduction of the love of the spirit for the first time. In Rom(A), Paul mentioned God's love three times: once in connection with the holy spirit (5:6) and twice without its connection with a reference that God gave the Son for sinners (5:8; 8:39). On the other hand, in Rom(B), the love of the spirit was presented here, showing the fact that the subject is transformed from God to spirit. This is probably because the love of the spirit was a virtue that the Romans should practice among brothers. In this way, Paul wanted to emphasize their efforts to love others.

Then, Paul encouraged the Romans to join forces with him in prayer. In fact, he did not ask the gentiles to pray for him as much as expected. He once asked for prayer after hearing that the Thessalonians were shaken by those sponsored by the Jerusalem church but stood in the gospel (1 Thess 5:25). On the other hand, the difference here is that Paul asked Jewish members to pray, even though he had been criticized by them. This implies that the mission he had to carry out in the future was by no means an easy one. The cooperation of the Romans was essential. Accordingly, it seems that Paul asked them to pray in order to strengthen the relationship.

Paul suggested what should be included in prayer. They are listed in three categories. First, Paul asked for the deliverance from the disobedient people in Judea (15:31a). Although the intention to visit Jerusalem has already appeared in Rom(A) (15:25), Paul expressed in Rom(B) his concern about those who had opposed him since the apostolic meeting and the theological debate over the gentile table at Antioch (Gal 2:1–14). To say in more detail, having a conflict with Cephas over the gentile table at Antioch, Paul broke up with Barnabas and turned his back on Cephas, one of the twelve apostles of the Jerusalem church. Afterwards, they sent representatives to the gentile churches established by Paul under the leadership of Barbanas and asked them to follow the Jewish instruction and refuse what Paul had taught. Thus, Paul faced severe challenges from the Corinthians and Galatians under the sponsorship of the apostles of the Jerusalem church (cf. 1 Cor 1:12; 2 Cor 11:13–15, 22–23; Gal 2:11–14; 4:17, etc.). On the other hand, the Philippian and Thessalonian churches sided with Paul. Because of this, Paul criticized the apostles using various expressions (1 Thess 3:5; Phil 3:2–3; 2 Cor 11:13). Paul knew that it was actually dangerous to bring the donations collected by gentiles to the Jerusalem church. Accordingly, they are defined as disobedient people in Judea in Rom(B).

Second, Paul asked the Romans to pray so that the service to Jerusalem would be acceptable (15:31b). This was the delivery of donations collected by gentiles for the poor saints of the Jerusalem church (15:26; Gal 2:10; 1 Cor 16:1–4; 2 Cor 8:2–4; 9:1). However, as Paul himself was concerned earlier, he did not have a good relationship with the apostles of the Jerusalem church at the time of writing Rom(B). Nevertheless, he wanted to bring the donations he had collected from the gentiles, as he had promised to the apostles. Although he could have been attacked by extreme Jews in the Jerusalem church, Paul wanted to keep the promise. Accordingly, he asked the Romans to pray for the matter to be resolved well. This shows the competitive structure that existed among the leaders leading the churches at the time.

Third, Paul asked the Romans to pray so that he could go to Rome with joy and rest with them according to the will of God (15:32). The expression "with joy" here conveys Paul's hope that the work in Jerusalem would be completed well. Paul considered it God's will to advance to Rome and hoped to be able to rest with the members of the Roman church. It is surprising that Paul expected to rest with the Romans, even though he criticized them. That is how much Paul was concerned about their financial support. It is unknown whether the visit to Jerusalem actually took place. From the description that Paul later imprisoned in the palace guard (Phil 1:13; cf. Phlm 1), it can be known that he arrived in Rome after the visit to Jerusalem. Anyway, in Rom(A), Paul expressed the wish to preach the gospel to the Romans and expected financial support for the mission to Spain in return (15:22–24). However, such content was not mentioned at all in Rom(B). This implies that his relationship with them was getting worse as time went by.

Rom(B) ends with a blessing. This appears as Paul declared that the God of peace would be with the Romans (15:33). Whenever Paul closed a letter, he typically included a blessing. In any case, peace has already been declared to come from God at the beginning of Rom(A) and described as enjoying peace with God through Jesus Christ (1:7; 5:1). Then, in Rom(B), it is described as a relationship that one must have with all people and then even as one of the characteristics of the kingdom of God (2:10; 12:18; 14:17). Therefore, it is natural to close Rom(B) by mentioning peace as a blessing at its ending. Having compared to the blessing written in Rom(A) (16:24), the ending of Rom(B) is appropriate.

In summary, even though Paul was criticized by Jewish members of the Roman church, he asked them to pray for him. This shows that he still expected their support. It is believed that such contents can only be included in a second letter reflecting the actual situation, following the first one written in expectation of a warm welcome.

6. CONCLUSION

In Rom(B), Paul answered the questions and critiques raised by the Romans after reading Rom(A). These were about the claim that the Law brings about wrath and that where there is no Law there is no transgression. In addition, questions seem to have been asked regarding the time when Abraham was circumcised. Accordingly, Paul explained that wrath would come to those who do not recognize God's power and divinity and who live according to their lusts in Rom(B). In addition, having listed various transgressions, he explained that the Law plays a role in making people realize their sin. This interpretation reflects the situation in which Paul did not yet have a close relationship with the Romans, especially Jewish members, at the time of writing Rom(B).

The contents of Rom(B) are well organized in their own way. Having described the wrath of God, Paul dealt with the issue of the Law and the role of Jesus Christ. He then presented the ethics of saints related to the situation that they had faced. A new teaching was delivered in the middle of Rom(B) that Jesus Christ was presented as a new way to obtain the righteousness of God. However, it is observed that Paul entered into an even more difficult relationship with the Romans, especially Jewish members, as he once again made negative statements about the Law.

It seems that Paul was quite disappointed with the Romans, especially Jewish members. He hoped to receive funding for missionary work to gentiles while conveying the core of the gospel to them; however, all that he received in return was suspicion and critique. Accordingly, since Paul harshly criticized Jews in Rom(B), it seems that the relationship with them was getting worse. This tendency was enough to provoke a backlash from the Jewish members of the Roman church.

Rom(B) has elements reminiscent of many features in Galatians. This is acknowledged in that many of the situations and solutions reflected in Galatians also appear in Rom(B). When Paul was challenged by some gentiles of the Galatian church sponsored by the apostles of the Jerusalem church, he refuted their claims based on the gospel. When this phenomenon also led to critique from the Jewish members of the Roman church, Paul refuted their claims. Accordingly, the core of the gospel, which consists of the death and resurrection of Christ, was not mentioned in depth. This shows that Paul used similar strategies when he was challenged and criticized.

Paul revealed the equality between Jews and gentiles in Rom(B). This began with the fact that a theological approach to the beginning of the world was presented. This is confirmed by the fact that as Rom(B) progresses, typological approach to the tree of knowledge of good and evil in the garden of Eden increasingly developed with the contrast between good and evil. Paul might have taken this stance while dealing with the Jewish members of the Roman church who criticized and opposed him. However, it was also ultimately due to the mission to gentiles, which he had believed to be entrusted by God. In this respect, it can be said that Paul revealed his true intentions in Rom(B).

The place or time for the writing of Rom(B) has been never mentioned. However, having considered his concerns about visiting Jerusalem to deliver the collected donations, it is believed to have been written after he had left Corinth for Jerusalem. It is not clear whether he went on foot or by ship, so it is impossible to say exactly where he wrote Rom(B) and sent it to the Romans. Nevertheless, Rom(B) was probably written at least a few months after Rom(A) had been supposed to be sent in early 56 CE. If so, it is likely that it was written in mid-56.

III

Rom(C)

PAUL SENT THE THIRD letter, Rom(C). It seems that it was written in response to the question and critique raised by the Romans, especially Jewish members, with regard to the relationship between sin and the Law after reading Rom(B). It is apparent that references to sin and the Law appear frequently in Rom(C). However, Paul took a reserved stance on the Law by stepping back from the negative stance. This was made to enhance the relationship between Paul and the Romans getting deteriorated as time went by. This reflects the fact that the Romans were unwilling to move in the direction Paul had suggested.

Dichotomous description is dominant in Rom(C). It was used to clarify the core of the gospel. Accordingly, having started with the contrast between death and eternal life, then it continued between the Law and faith, and the flesh and the spirit in pairs. The combination was formed in order to make all mankind enjoy the eternal life that is an expression of salvation. For this, a typological approach to Adam in the garden of Eden was adopted from the very beginning of Rom(C). Having tried to simplify the argument with dichotomous description, Paul did his best to lead the Romans to accept the gospel.

In Rom(C), Paul wrote in a direction of equal status between Jews and gentiles as developed in Rom(B). However, it cannot be denied that a slight preference to the latter was implied with the emphasis on the mission to gentiles. This is most clearly seen in the biblical quotations at the end of Rom(C). This is believed to be something that could offend Jewish members because this showed a tendency to alienate them. In any case, Paul wanted to guide both Jews and gentiles to become the people of God.

The contents of Rom(C) can be broadly divided into five sections. Having dealt with the relationship between death and eternal life (5:12—6:23), Paul discussed the issue between the Law and faith (7:1–25) and then described the role of Christ and the spirit (8:1–30). It is followed by the ethics of saints (13:8–10; 15:1–13). Finally, Rom(C) ended with closing part (16:17–20). This structure shows that the core of the gospel was the most dominant issue. Paul then tried to deal with it by relating the Law to Jesus Christ. This style of development has already appeared in Rom(A) and Rom(B).

1. DEATH AND ETERNAL LIFE (5:12—6:23)

It seems that the beginning part of Rom(C), which includes the sender, the recipient, and greetings, was deleted when it was compiled into the present form of Romans. The main body of Rom(C) starts with the description of death and eternal life followed by the debate over the relationship between sin and the Law. Here, the main text delivers the lesson that life has been given through one person, Jesus Christ. Paul advanced various narratives based on the core of the gospel.

Sin and Grace (5:12—6:2)

The main body of Rom(C) seems to have begun with the issue of death and eternal life. Having focused on the word "one person," Paul compared Adam and Christ. Their role presents sin and death in contrast to grace and life. The Adam typological description adopted here was more developed than the allusion to the beginning of the world and the tree of knowledge of good and evil reflected in Rom(B).

Paul mentioned the process by which sin and death came into the world. This appears in the statement that sin entered the world through one person and death through sin (5:12a). Paul treated the issue of sin and death together for the first time. Once the blessing of being forgiven from sin was mentioned in Rom(A) (4:7–8); here, sin was described as standing in a passive position as something that must be forgiven. On the contrary, in Rom(B), it was claimed that everyone is under sin and the Law makes people aware of sin (3:9, 20). At that time, the prevalence of sin is revealed in inseparable relationship with people. However, in Rom(C), it is said that sin entered the world through one person and that sin has led people to death. Paul portrayed sin as quite active and aggressive. This shows the circumstances in which the Romans read Rom(B) and raised a question with regard to the connection between the Law and sin. And then, Paul explained the nature of sin in more detail in Rom(C). The concept of sin embedded in Rom(C) is to some extent more advanced than those described in Rom(A) and Rom(B). The above descriptions show that the more letters Paul sent to the Roman church, the more he developed the theological interpretation of sin.

The Adam-typological description was adopted to explain the relationship between sin and death. This is found in the statement that sin and death came into the world because of "one person." Paul used the word "one person" for a typological explanation. It was once said to the Corinthians that death came into existence through "one person" (1 Cor 15:21). Without doubt, that person refers to Adam. However, in Rom(C), sin was added to the issue of death. Accordingly, Paul mentioned "one person," sin, and death in order to make the Romans think of Adam, who had been pronounced to death on account of committing sin in the garden of Eden by breaking the command of God (Gen 3:1–19). In addition, Paul was able to use the Adam-typology at the beginning of Rom(C) because he already used a typological approaches to the beginning of the world (1:20) and to the tree of knowledge of good and evil in Rom(B) (2:9–10). This shows how Paul developed a typological interpretation in the later letter based on the previous one.

Paul then expanded the case of "one person" to all people. This is revealed in the statement that death spreads to all people because all have sinned (5:12b). Paul generalized the special case of "one person" by saying that people face death because of sin. This generalization was also described in the case of Abraham in Rom(A) (4:23–25). Anyway, Paul took a more negative view here than in the previous claim that all people have sinned and therefore fall short of the glory of God as written in Rom(B) (3:9, 23). Paul approached the relationship between Adam and all people from a typological perspective so as to establish him as the ancestor of all people. In Rom(A), Paul once established Abraham as the ancestor and presented him as an example with regard to righteousness by faith in God (4:1, 12). On the other hand, in Rom(C), Paul established Adam as a type of all people for making Jews and gentiles the people of God. As a result, a theoretical basis for putting all mankind, Jews and gentiles alike, under the category of being the people of God was founded.

The relationship between sin and the Law was presented. This appears in the statement that sin had been in the world before the Law was given and that when there was no Law, sin was not considered sin (5:13). Paul addressed the priority of sin to the Law from a chronological perspective. This is seen as a supplementary explanation to what Paul said, "Where there is no Law, there is no transgression" in Rom(A) (4:15) and "Through the Law people become conscious of sin" in Rom(B) (3:20). However, in Rom(C), Paul said that although there had been sin before the Law came into existence, people did not recognize it as sin. Rather, only after the coming of the Law, they came to know transgression as sin. In this respect, the claim in Rom(B) that the Law convicts of sin is made more concrete in Rom(C). It is, however, important to observe that the function of the Law was not the focus but the existence of sin. In other words, Paul pointed out the fact that sin had been already in the world before the Law was given. Since this kind of logic was new to the Romans, it is not clear whether they would have accepted it.

Paul then described the relationship between sin and death. It is said that from Adam to Moses, death reigned even over those who did not commit sin before the coming of the Law (5:14a). Paul presented the universality of sin by the statement that death "reigned as king." In other words, this is an insistence that everyone dies because of sin regardless of the Law. Paul tried to focus more on the relationship between sin and death while viewing the role of the Law in a limited way. The underlying premise is that since not only Jewish members but also gentile members were targeted, they had to find a way to escape from sin and death. Having gone beyond the teaching that people realize sin through the Law as written in Rom(B), Paul argued in Rom(C) that sin existed even before the coming of the Law. In this way, Paul lessened the role of the Law in the relationship with sin and death.

Subsequently, a typological relationship was declared between Adam and the "one to come." This appears in the statement that Adam is a type of the "one to come" (5:14b). Paul used the word "type" for the first time here and established a Adam-typological relationship with a contrast between Adam and the "one to come." Paul once hinted at the Adam-typology to the Corinthians with the expression of death and resurrection due to "one person" (1 Cor 15:22). And then it is said that just as Adam the first man had become a living soul, the last Adam became a life-giving spirit (1 Cor

15:45). This shows how Paul presented the typological relationship between Adam and Christ. Accordingly, while Jesus died as a descendant of Adam, Christ became a being who rose to new life through resurrection. It is believed that the Romans learned this kind of typological interpretation to some extent from Priscilla and Aquila, who had been associated with the Corinthian church. Paul developed it into the Adam-typology between Adam and the "one to come" with the word "type" in Rom(C). In any case, it was suggested that both Jews and gentiles would achieve the same result through Adam or the "one to come." This means that while all mankind had no choice but to follow Adam and die physically but that a solution could be found in the "one to come."

Paul presented the role of the "one to come." This is mentioned in the saying that his function is not the same as Adam's trespass that brought about the death of people, but the gift from God and Jesus Christ overflowed to many people (5:15). The "one to come" who took Adam as the prototype was identified as Christ. Then, Paul mentioned the consequences that Adam and Christ brought to people. This appears as a contrast between death and gift overflowing to many people. Accordingly, Paul put the death of all people due to Adam's sin in contrast with the gift given by the grace of Jesus Christ. It is justified that all people who are descendants of Adam should accept the fate given to them as the gift by the grace of Jesus Christ, whether Jews or gentiles. Paul attempted to break down the barrier between Jews and gentiles through a contrast between Adam and Christ. With this dichotomous description, Paul made a theological effort to expand the recipients of gifts through grace from Jews to gentiles. It was a bit uncomfortable for Jewish members to be treated equally with gentile members

Then, the result that Adam and Jesus Christ have given was described. This is found in the contrast between the judgment of condemnation due to one sinful man and the gift leading to the righteousness of God from sin (5:16). Paul put the judgment of condemnation resulted from Adam's sin in contrast with the gift of righteousness through Jesus Christ. It is necessary to look at the process by which Paul's description of how a person becomes justified changed. In Rom(A), Abraham's faith in God and the blood of Christ were presented as the way that leads to righteousness (4:1, 12: 5:9). Then, Paul argued in Rom(B) that the Romans were to be justified freely by God's grace through the redemption in Christ Jesus (3:22–24). This is expressed as a gift that leads to righteousness from many trespasses in Rom(C). Having used the Adam-typology,

Paul attempted to present the "one to come" as a worker of God who will lead both Jews and gentiles to righteousness that refers to the saved status. As shown above, the role of Jesus Christ in making people righteous grew bigger and bigger as time went by. It seems that the Romans, especially Jewish members, would not have accepted the typological interpretation of Paul without the role of the Law.

Paul once again explained the results brought about by Adam and Christ Jesus. This appears in the statement that just as death reigned over the descendants on account of Adam's transgression, those who have received the gift of grace and righteousness in abundance will reign in life through Jesus Christ (5:17). Having used pairs of contrasts and comparisons, Paul presented the way to life. It was once written to the Corinthians that while death had come through "one person," Adam, life came through "one person," Christ (1 Cor 15:21–22). In addition, it is necessary to observe that Paul applied the expression "reign" to both death and life in Rom(C). This word was already used for the Corinthians in the statement that Christ would reign until he had put all his enemies under his feet (1 Cor 15:25). If so, then the Romans should have learned it from Priscilla and Aquila, who were familiar with the instruction that Paul had given to the Corinthians. Then, the Romans were able to understand easily what Paul developed into an Adam-typological narration in Rom(C) when it was described that those who have received the gift of grace and righteousness through Jesus Christ will reign as kings. Paul argued in this way, so that not only Jewish members but also gentile members could become the people of God. It seems to have been written in order to establish a strategic base for the mission to gentiles with the financial support of the Romans.

Another contrast was presented between Adam and Jesus Christ. It is said that just as one trespass led to condemnation for many, so one righteous act led to righteousness and life for many (5:18). Paul pointed out the contrast between the trespass and the righteous deeds on the one hand, and the condemnation caused by Adam and righteousness resulted from Jesus Christ on the other hand. The antithetical relationship is highlighted between the condemnation due to Adam's trespass and the righteousness due to Jesus Christ's righteous deeds. Jesus Christ's righteous deeds refer to his death for sinners, as already mentioned in Rom(A) (5:8). Having mentioned the contrast on the basis of Adam-typological point of view, Paul continued to present dichotomous explanations to simplify what he had intended to deliver. This is in accordance with Paul's strategy to bring life to gentile members, including Jewish members, by focusing more on Jesus Christ without any reference to the Law. It seems that the Romans did not necessarily reject Paul's intention.

The contrast between sinners and righteous people was developed around the theme of obedience. This appears in the statement that just as through one person's disobedience many became sinners, through one person's obedience many became righteous (5:19). Paul once again drew a typological contrast between Adam's disobedience and Christ's obedience. The word "one person" is used here, signifying a continuation of the previous contrast between Adam and Christ. With this, Paul preached the lesson that the Romans had to turn from death due to Adam's disobedience to righteousness and life through Christ's obedience. This kind of Adam-typological contrast can be said to be a characteristic of Rom(C) in order to simplify the thesis to be discussed. This conveyed the lesson that all Romans, regardless of whether they were Jewish or gentile, should be led to a spiritual life through Christ. With this, Paul increasingly revealed the interest in the gentiles beyond the Jews.

Paul drew a conclusion about the relationship between the Law, sin, and grace. It is said that the Law was brought in to increase trespass, but where sin increases, grace abounds all the more (5:20). Paul suddenly mentions the Law here. This shows that the previous description was a process of preparing for an explanation of the Law. Once in Galatians, Paul said that the Law was given to increase transgression (Gal 3:19). Then, it was stated in Rom(A) that where there is no Law, there is no transgression (4:15). And Paul argued in Rom(B) that the Law convicts of sin (3:20). Accordingly, in Rom(C), Paul was able to say that the Law seeks to increase trespass in spite of the fact that Jewish members had cast doubt on his negative view on it. Paul did not change his basic position on the Law but simply used the word "trespass" instead of "sin" in order to show a somewhat reserved stance of retreat. However, since he thought that his argument would result in serious consequences, Paul presented an alternative, that is, where sin increases, grace abounds even more. Here sin and grace are contrasted with the emphasis on the life of righteousness. Paul urged the Romans to embrace the grace of God and Jesus Christ rather than the Law. This reflects the fact that the Romans, especially Jewish members, consistently showed obedience to the Law rather than following the Christ-centered gospel in spite of Paul's admonition in Rom(A) and Rom(B).

A contrast appeared once again, centered on the word "reign." This is seen in the statement that just as sin reigned in death, grace also reigns through righteousness, leading to eternal life through our Lord Jesus Christ (5:21). Here, Paul put sin and death in contrast with grace and righteousness, emphasizing eternal life through Jesus Christ. This explains the process by which people are liberated by grace from death due to sin and reach righteousness, that is, eternal life. Ultimately, Paul presented eternal life as a gift given to those who achieve righteousness. This is reminiscent of the tree of life in the garden of Eden that God have kept to give to people one day (Gen 3:22–25). This also shows that Paul reached the conclusion from an Adam-typological perspective. Paul provided the answer to the Romans' critique against his claim that the Law convicts of sin as written in Rom(B) (3:20). Instead of mentioning the Law, Paul tried to deal with life and grace rather than sin and death. This was to give Romans a choice. As a result, his argument is believed to have had more impact on them.

Paul presented the direction in which the Romans should live. This is revealed, as it begins with a rhetorical question about what they should say and ends with another question about whether they should not continue to commit sin so that grace may abound (6:1). Paul showed that he sought the consent of the Romans with the first rhetorical question. He then expressed the view whether one should continue to commit sin in order to increase grace. Here, sin and grace are once again in contrast, which suggests the necessity of living according to grace rather than committing sin. Paul increasingly focused on the issue of sin while also emphasizing grace as an alternative. Since it was previously stated that where sin increases, grace abounds even more (5:20), the rhetorical question could be asked here whether the Romans would continue to commit sin in order to increase grace. In this way, sin and grace were presented as an antagonistic relationship that cannot coexist. When the Romans had raised a critique against the message that the Law convicts of sin as written in Rom(B) (3:20), Paul tried to make them understand with this description in Rom(C). Accordingly, he wanted to lead them to the grace of God and Christ Jesus, that is, life. There was no reason for these lessons to be rejected either.

The answer to Paul's own question was provided. It is said, "By no means! We died to sin; how can we live in it any longer?" (6:2). Paul insisted that the Romans should not live in sin in order to gain more grace. Because God-believers have died to sin, they can no longer live in it. Paul once said in Galatians that if one tries to be justified in Christ and is revealed to be a sinner, he or she can never do that because he or she is making Christ a person who causes sin (Gal 2:17). And then it was said that because of the Law, one died to it in order to live to God (Gal 2:19). Accordingly, in Rom(C), Paul made a contrast in that one cannot live in sin in order to gain grace. In this way, as time passed, Paul developed the theological thoughts in the direction of being free from sin. Both Jewish and gentile members of the Roman church would have had no choice but to accept Paul's instruction.

To sum up, Paul created a contrast between Adam and Jesus Christ from a typological perspective. It was emphasized that whether Jewish or gentile members, they were doomed to death due to Adam's sin but must come to life through the grace and righteousness of Christ Jesus. Having presented Adam as the ancestor of mankind from an Adam-typological perspective, Paul suggested that both Jews and gentiles were on the same path to righteousness. Paul rarely mentioned the Law, the standard of Jewish life, in order to show favor to gentiles.

Union with Christ (6:3–11)

Paul presented baptism as a way of union with Christ to be liberated from sin and become righteous. This symbolizes the process of dying, being buried, and then being resurrected with him. Baptism was ultimately presented as a way to bring people to eternal life. By doing this, Paul presented baptism as a way for the Romans to live according to the gospel.

Paul presented union with Christ Jesus as a way to enjoy grace. This is to participate in his death by being baptized into Christ Jesus (6:3). Paul imposed the meaning of union with Christ upon baptism. This kind of interpretation was already made in Galatians (Gal 3:27). However, the difference is found in that the death of Christ was linked to baptism in Rom(C). It is then necessary to take a look at Paul's description of Christ's death. Paul once wrote that Christ died for sinners in Rom(A) (5:8); and then, in Rom(C), baptism is presented as a way of dying with him. While the focus was on the death of Christ in Rom(A), the emphasis was on the death with him in Rom(C). Baptism was presented as an act in which sinners had to die in union with Christ Jesus who died for them. In this respect, sharing in Christ's death was defined as dying to sin (see 6:2). Thus, Paul described baptism as a sign of forgiveness of sin. This shows that Paul's interpretation of baptism was given in response to the critique of the Romans against his previous declaration that the Law convicts of sin as written in Rom(B) (3:20). To be more specific, according to Paul, sins are not forgiven by keeping the Law but rather by dying together with Jesus Christ. Paul made a new claim that the Romans should receive forgiveness of sin through baptism.

Another meaning was added to baptism. It is said that people were buried with Christ Jesus through baptism into his death (6:4a). Paul connected baptism with the burial of Christ Jesus. This was completely new to the Romans represented by Priscilla and Aquila. Paul once received the tradition of the gospel that having died, Christ had been buried (1 Cor 15:1–5). However, baptism is not connected to the burial of Christ in Galatians (Gal 3:27). On the other hand, the instruction that people should be buried with Christ Jesus appears for the first time in Rom(C). The focus was shifted from the burial of Christ to the direction that people had to be buried with him. This is a theological description of living along the path taken by Jesus Christ. In this way, in Rom(C), the religious actions that the Romans should perform were emphasized. It is, however, unclear whether Paul's insistence would have been persuasive to Jewish members.

Paul continued the description of baptism in connection with the resurrection. This appears in the statement that, just as Christ was raised from the dead by the glory of God the Father, people should also walk in new life (6:4b). Paul taught that just as Christ died, was buried, and then raised, the Romans had to walk the same path and gain new life through baptism. New life means eternal life gained in Christ through grace (5:21). While Paul taught that salvation would be achieved through the resurrection of Christ the Son of God in Rom(A) (5:10), it was presented as a way for those who have been baptized to gain new life in Rom(C). Then, salvation refers to the new life of believers given as the result of union with Jesus Christ through baptism. In this way, the resurrection of Christ described in Rom(A) was theologically developed into the meaning of walking in new life in Rom(C).

The union with Christ Jesus was described in connection with his death and resurrection. This appears in the statement that if a person has been united in a death like his death, he or she will also be united in a resurrection like his resurrection (6:5). Paul emphasized that the Romans should be united with him through death and resurrection. It should be noted that only the death and resurrection of Christ are mentioned here.

They were presented in Rom(A) as the elements that constitute the core of the gospel and that lead people to salvation (1:2–4; 5:6–10). Paul presented baptism as a symbol of living a life according to the gospel. Accordingly, it was announced that new life would be gained. In addition, Paul had in mind a theological message with the death and resurrection of Christ. This was the way for them to become the sons of God, just as Christ Jesus was declared the Son of God through resurrection by the spirit of holiness (1:4). However, it would not have been easy for the Romans to accept baptism as a ritual for life because they were fixed on the tradition that life would be gained through the Law.

Paul attributed the meaning of atonement to the death of Jesus. This appears in the statement that one's old self was crucified with Jesus, so that the body of sin would die and he or she would no longer be enslaved to sin (6:6). Although Paul did not specify with whom the Romans should crucify their "old self," it could refer to Jesus from the context. It shows Paul's great care to ensure that they should not be suspected by the Roman Empire by omitting the name "Jesus." Anyway, Paul described the complete liberation from sin through one's crucifixion. It was once explained to the Galatians that since Paul was crucified with Christ, he no longer lives for himself, rather for Christ, who gave up his body for him (Gal 2:20). However, it is said in Rom(C) that the Romans, including Paul himself, were advised to crucify their "old self." It was described against the backdrop of crucifixion of Jesus. Having mentioned the blood of Christ in Rom(A) and Rom(B), Paul presented it as the path to righteousness (3:25; 5:9). However, in Rom(C), the voluntary crucifixion of the Romans was mentioned as a way to atonement. This means salvation in which one becomes free from sin by dying of the body of sin and no longer being a slave to sin. This is the result of union with Christ through baptism. However, Paul's teaching that one's "old self" must die with Christ would have been a difficult requirement for both Jewish and gentile members.

Righteousness is mentioned as a result of atonement. This is revealed in the statement that the person who died was freed from sin and was justified (6:7). Paul presented crucifying "old self" as the method by which people become free from sin and be righteous. Here, it is necessary to look at the process by which the relationship between righteousness and sin changes. In Rom(A), Paul wrote that God justified people by having his Son die for sinners (5:8–9). Then, in Rom(B), it was stated that God revealed his righteousness by overlooking people's sins in his patience

(3:25). However, in Rom(C), the Romans were requested to crucify their "old self" to be free from sin and become righteous. This means that they die as descendants of Adam and gain new life as people of Christ. It was the way for atonement and salvation. In this way, in Rom(C), the Romans were required of doing something religious and spiritual for their redemption and salvation. This is to be considered Paul's response to the claims of Jewish members who continually sought to be righteous by the works of the Law. It is, however, unclear whether Paul's teachings were persuasive enough to them.

Paul once again mentioned union with Christ in connection with death and resurrection. It is believed that if a person dies with Christ, he or she will live with him (6:8). Paul dealt with the issue of dying and living with Christ. It was already said that if one has been united with Christ in the same way as he died, he or she will also be united with him in resurrection (6:5). The death and resurrection of Christ was mentioned in indirect connection with atonement in Rom(A) (5:10). Later in Rom(C), this was developed into the saying that those who die with Jesus will be resurrected with him and will enjoy new life. In other words, the death and resurrection of Jesus Christ the Son of God were described as having the same effect on those who were baptized and justified by faith. With the contrast between death and resurrection, Paul presented the path that the Romans should truly take. The reason Paul preached these lessons was to help gentiles achieve salvation through the gospel, not by keeping the Law.

A supplementary explanation to the previous argument followed in relation to life. This is found in the declaration that Christ was raised from the dead and does not die again and that death no longer has dominion over him (6:9). Paul described two phenomena that occurred after Christ's resurrection. One is not to die again, and the other is that death cannot claim it again. This is believed to have developed based on Paul's previous narrative. After he had taught the Corinthians about the resurrection, he mentioned that death stings sin and the Law (1 Cor 15:56). This shows that the power of death is related with sin and death. However, in Rom(C), Paul argued that the age of death that began with Adam had ended and that the age of life had begun with Christ. With this, the core of the gospel, which makes one raise from death to life, was addressed once again. This was an instruction based on the theological interpretation of baptism. However, Jewish members would have had a hard time accepting Paul's teachings.

Paul drew a conclusion regarding the death and resurrection of Christ. It is said that Christ died to sin once and for all and that he lives to God (6:10). Paul drew a contrast between death and eternal life. Christ is described as the one dying to sin itself. It was written in Galatians that through the Law he was dead to the Law so that he might live to God (Gal 2:19). However, in Rom(C), Paul replaced the Law with sin that was a more fundamental factor in religious life. While Paul described Christ as dying for sinners in Rom(A) (5:8–10), Christ was described as the one dying for sin itself in Rom(C). With this, Christ was defined as the one who would eradicate sin itself, the source of producing sinners and death. Accordingly, he could be referred to as the one who lives toward God. God is paired with sin, and they are highlighted as beings that cannot coexist. Paul emphasized freedom from sin and a life with God. Jewish members who were accustomed to governing sin with the Law would not have found it easy to accept Paul's teaching that Christ was superior to it.

Finally, advice appeared on the path the Romans should take. This is found in the teaching that they should consider themselves dead to sin but alive to God in Christ Jesus (6:11). Here, as seen before, Paul applied the death and resurrection of Jesus Christ to the Romans. They were those who had been dead to sin but alive to God in Christ Jesus, just as he had done. With this kind of instruction, Paul taught that the Romans should become participants in the death of atonement and resurrection of salvation in Christ Jesus. This allowed them to enjoy the benefits of being spiritually united with Jesus Christ. This description once again shows that as time went by, Paul set up Jesus Christ as a model for the religious life of the Romans. Jewish members would not have accepted his instruction on account of their obedience to the Law.

In summary, Paul interpreted baptism as the way of union with Christ in the light of death and life. It was argued that the Romans should gain life by participating in the death and resurrection of Christ. This means living a life according to the core of the gospel. It is, however, dubious that his instruction on baptism could neutralize the efforts of Jewish members to achieve righteousness by observing the Law.

Dedication to God (6:12–15)

Paul wanted the Romans to be captured by God rather than by sin. This is the path for those who gained a new life through the death and resurrection of Christ. This advocates a life under grace that is following the gospel. Having presented two injunctions, Paul delivered the instruction to imitate Jesus Christ.

The first injunction was suggested with regard to sin. This is found in the exhortation not to allow sin to dominate the mortal bodies so as not to obey the lusts of the body (6:12). Here, "sin" seems to be personified for the first time, appearing as a force that dominates people's mortal bodies. In this way, sin is revealed not as a mind that commits transgression from an ethical perspective but an entity that leads the Romans to evil from a spiritual point of view. Once in Rom(B), Paul wrote that God has given people over to impurity in the lusts of their hearts in order to dishonor their bodies toward one another (1:24). However, in Rom(C), lust was mentioned to be reigned by sin. This shows that the concept of lust was developed in relation to spiritual issue in Rom(C) more than in Rom(B). With this, the Romans were exhorted not to be dominated by sin and led to death. This would have been an acceptable lesson for both Jewish and gentile members.

The second injunction was filed right after the first one. It is said that the Romans should not hand over their members to sin as weapons of unrighteousness (16:13a). Sin was personified in that the Romans could be handed over to it as weapons of unrighteousness. This means that they could be caught up in sin for unrighteousness. Sin was described as an entity dominating unrighteousness. Here, the weapon of unrighteousness probably refers to the ability to commit transgression. There seems to be an underlying lesson behind this: that when they tried to keep the Law, they could become more caught up in sin and result in transgression. This is in accordance with the teaching in Rom(B) that the Law convicts of sin (3:20). In any case, Paul's teachings would not have been viewed as desirable by Jewish members who pursued righteousness by observing the Law.

Paul then delivered a lesson about union with Christ Jesus in the form of positive command. This appears in the exhortation that having followed the one who have been raised from the dead, the Romans should present themselves to God as weapon of righteousness (6:13b). Paul wanted them to be presented to God as weapons of righteousness by following Christ Jesus raised from the dead. Ultimately, the weapons of righteousness play a role in leading people to life. Having written it from a perspective of spiritual struggle, Paul provided the Romans with an opportunity to make a choice between righteousness and unrighteousness.

Accordingly, the death and resurrection of Christ were important elements for Paul in helping them be the weapon of righteousness to defeat the sin and the Law. However, among them, especially Jewish members, would not accept what Paul preached and did not want to abandon the Law they had kept.

An explanation was made about the relationship between sin and grace. This appears in the declaration that sin will not have dominion over the Romans because they are not under the Law but under grace (6:14). Paul once again put the Law in contrast with grace, emphasizing that the Law absolutely falls short of grace. At the same time, he related sin to the Law. Anyway, Paul told the Romans that if they were under grace, sin would never have dominion over them. Only the grace of God will keep people from being caught up in sin and prevent them from heading for death. This declaration also contains a warning that Jewish members should not make efforts to be righteous by the works of the Law. However, they would not have accepted his lessons easily.

A rhetorical question appeared that closes the discussion on the relationship between sin and grace. It is said, "what then?" and it leads to the declaration that one cannot sin because he or she is not under the Law but under grace (6:15). Of course, the expected answer to this is "by no means." Paul taught that the Romans should not commit sin while being under grace rather than the Law. This is to repeat the previous lesson that the Law does not lead to the righteousness of God but only leads to the realization of sin, as written in Rom(B) (3:20). In this way, in Rom(C), having emphasized the grace of God and Christ Jesus, Paul presented it as the path to salvation that is the new life in Christ. Paul delivered this lesson to keep the Romans, especially Jewish members, away from attempting to be righteous by the observance of the Law.

In summary, Paul taught that the Romans should live following Christ Jesus, who was raised from the dead. This means living according to the gospel. Then, the Romans could enjoy God's grace by living in life. With this, Paul continued the argument that he emphasized at the beginning of Rom(C); the Romans had to defeat sin and live by grace.

The Servant of Sin or Righteousness (6:16–23)

Paul continued his discussion of death and eternal life in relation to the topic of whose servant a person was to be. The Romans had not to be slaves of sin but to be servants of God's righteousness. This is the way to live according to the gospel.

Paul addressed the issue of being servants of someone. This is found in the saying that if one gives himself or herself as someone's servant, he or she becomes the servant of the person he or she obeys (6:16a). For this purpose, Paul began with the phrase, "do you not know?" in order to get the consent of the Romans. In religious life, the issue of becoming someone's servant means to serve him or her as the Lord. For instance, Paul urged the Corinthians not to be servants of men but to be servants of Christ (1 Cor 7:22–23). In Galatians, the lesson was given to be sons of God rather than the servants of the Law (Gal 4:6–7). At the beginning of Rom(A), Paul defined himself as a servant of Jesus Christ (1:1). Then in Rom(C), he applied it to the Romans to be servants of Jesus Christ. Of course, the Romans would have wanted to be servants in a proper way. Paul's presentation of becoming someone's servant to the Romans reflects the situation that they did not go in the direction that Paul had wanted at the time.

A description of the consequences of becoming someone's servant followed. This is revealed in the statement that while living as a slave to sin leads to death, living as a servant to obedience leads to righteousness (6:16b). Paul here put sin in contrast with obedience and death in contrast with righteousness. Sin is inseparable from disobedience to God. Paul once again defined sin as a personified entity by stating that those who give themselves over to it become its slaves and end up in death. This reminds readers of Adam, who committed sin and brought death to descendants (5:14–15). On the other hand, the phrase "servant to obedience" makes readers think of Jesus Christ, who obeyed God. He brought righteousness and life to many people through his righteous deeds (5:18). In this way, the obedient servant is in contrast with Adam from a typological perspective. Accordingly, Paul proposed a new way to obtain righteousness: obedience to God through Jesus Christ. This contains Paul's hope that the Romans would attain righteousness by obeying God.

Paul presented his gratitude to God in relation to status. It is said that while the Romans had been originally slaves of sin, they obeyed the example of the teachings with their hearts, were freed from sin, and became servants of righteousness (6:17–18). Although Paul referred to the changed condition of the Romans, it is believed to point to the opportunities given to them. They had to keep the instructions given by Paul, so that they should be free from sin and become servants of righteousness.

Paul preached the gospel based on the death and resurrection of Jesus Christ to the Romans. This was the path that both Jewish and gentile members had to take for eternal life. With this dichotomous description, Paul presented the direction the Romans should choose. Of course, the final choice was up to them.

The Romans were exhorted to attain holiness. This appears in the statement that they had previously lived in unrighteousness through uncleanness and lawlessness, and that they must yield themselves as servants to righteousness and attain holiness (6:19). Having spoken in an imperative form here, Paul showed that the Romans had not yet attained a state of righteousness and holiness. Uncleanness and lawlessness are in opposite to holiness. While unrighteousness was dealt with as a serious topic in Rom(B) (1:18—3:31), holiness was an important value in the Jewish faith in general. Accordingly, in Rom(C), having kept Jewish members in mind, Paul emphasized that they should attain holiness. If so, this reflects the fact that although they kept the Law, they did not reach holiness and remained in unrighteousness due to uncleanness and lawlessness. With the negative evaluation of them, Paul showed that they had not yet properly lived following the Law.

Paul once again distinguished between sin and righteousness. This is revealed in the paradoxical statement that when the Romans were slaves of sin, they were free toward righteousness (6:20). Paul placed sin in opposite to righteousness and wrote about the relationship between them in a paradoxical way. It was emphasized that the Romans had to break away from the bondage of sin and reach righteousness. Paul once presented a life of obedience to God by imitating Jesus Christ as a way to escape from sin and achieve righteousness (5:18–19). This teaching is also valid here, as Paul encouraged the Romans, who were still caught up in the Law and sin that lead to death, to enjoy righteousness and grace that lead to life.

The consequences of being a slave to sin were mentioned. It is said that, having considered the fruit the Romans obtained while enslaved to sin, it was death (6:21). Paul made them think of the time when they were slaves of sin. At that time, they were trying to obtain righteousness by keeping the Law. According to Paul, it was considered that they had not yet completely escaped the state of being a slave to sin. In any case, Paul pointed out that it was truly shameful for them to be slaves of sin and claimed that the only fruit they ultimately achieved was death. In this way, Paul continued to emphasize death due to sin. This reflects the situation in which the Romans lived, contrary to the direction suggested by Paul. As a result, he could not help but criticize them.

In contrast, Paul envisioned the position the Romans should be in. This is found in the declaration that they are now free from sin and have become the servants of God, so they should obtain eternal life, the fruit of holiness (6:22). With this positive evaluation, Paul presented the state they should reach. This is to be liberated from sin and become a servant of God. As a result, they will receive eternal life. This life is given when one dies but be raised from death back to life in union with Christ Jesus (6:8–11). Therefore, they had to give up their sinful attitude of trying to achieve righteousness by keeping the Law, rather to be the people of God by the grace of God and Jesus Christ. Here, the words "fruit" and "eternal life" remind readers of the fruit of the tree of life in the garden of Eden (Gen 3:22). This shows that the contrast between sin and eternal life must be interpreted from an Adam-typological perspective. The fact that Paul continued to emphasize to the Romans that they had to be free from sin and bear the fruit of eternal life indicates that they did not live the life he had desired. If they had lived by his teachings, this comment would not have been necessary.

The final conclusion to the contrast between sin and grace was presented. This is seen in the statement that while the wages of sin is death, the gift of God is eternal life in Christ Jesus our Lord (6:23). Paul used the expression "wages of sin" following "fruits of sin"; on the contrary, the gift of God was presented as an alternative. Additionally, death is in contrast with life in Christ Jesus our Lord. Paul has been discussing the relationship between sin and grace in order to teach that the Romans should rise from death to eternal life. This means a life that leaps from the death inherited from Adam to the eternal life given by Christ. The fact that the extreme contrast between death and eternal life appeared in the last part shows that the Romans' life should be changed from the road to death to the path to eternal life according to the gospel. This was a topic Paul continued to address in Rom(C).

In summary, Paul argued that depending on whether one becomes a slave to sin or a servant to righteousness, the result is death or eternal life. The transformation from death to eternal life is given to those who live according to the gospel, summarized in the death and resurrection of Christ. Paul used continuously dichotomous descriptions from a typological perspective. It should be concluded that they had to restore the original nature of Adam before the fall.

2. THE LAW AND FAITH (7:1–25)

Paul dealt with the issue of death and life in relation to the Law. Having started at the beginning of Rom(C), Paul continued to deal with them as the core of the gospel. In the meantime, Paul showed a reserved stance on the Law in order to decide the direction the Romans should choose. The Adam-typological approach takes a key role for the gospel.

Limitations of the Law (7:1–6)

Paul dealt with the issue of death and life with the analogy to law. This presents a life that imitates the death and resurrection of Christ. In this respect, Paul presented the Romans with a way to live according to the core of the gospel.

First, the limitations of law is described. This is revealed in the explanation that for those who know the law, it only functions while the person is alive (7:1). Paul insisted that the law had limitations in terms of time and context. Here, the term "law" means legal provisions that are applied to people generally rather than the Law believed to have been given to Moses. In any case, Paul sought the consent of the Romans with the introductory phrase "do you not know?" In this way, he made a strong appeal to them, having conveyed that only the proposition they had known was in effect.

Paul explained the limitations of law using the legal relationship between husband and wife as an example. It is said that a woman who has a husband is bound to him by law while he is alive, but that if he dies, she is free from being bound to him (7:2). This kind of instruction was already mentioned to the Corinthians in relation to the state of marriage (1 Cor 7:39). Accordingly, Paul was able to describe the analogy of marriage in more detail by applying the bond of law to the Romans in Rom(C). This conveys the lesson that law can play a role or lose effectiveness depending on relationship among people. With this example, Paul tried to teach the Romans the limitations of law. This is believed to have been passed down as Paul's response to the Jewish members of the Roman church who kept insisting on the eternality of the Law after reading Rom(B). If my interpretation is acceptable, it shows that Paul wrote Rom(C) to explain their relationship with the Law.

The application of law continued. This appears in the statement that if a man's wife goes to another man while her husband is alive, she is called an adulteress, but that after her husband dies, she is free from that law and does not become an adulteress even if she goes to another man (7:3). Here, Paul used the relationship between husband and wife to explain that between the Law and the Romans against the backdrop of marriage as defined by law. Adultery was considered a fatal transgression among Jews against the backdrop of marital principle given in the garden of Eden and written in the seventh article of the Ten Commandments (Gen 2:24; Exod 20:14). Paul tried to point out the limitations of the Law while making a realistic interpretation based on the eternal principle established by God.

Paul applied the metaphor of a married couple to the Romans. This is revealed in the statement that they died to the Law through the body of Christ, so that they might belong to him who had been raised from the dead, in order that they might bear fruit to God (7:4). Paul compared the Romans to a woman, the Law to a former husband, and Christ to a new husband. This means that the Romans can go to another husband, that is, Christ, because their former husband, the Law, is no longer in effect. Paul insisted that the usefulness of the Law has come to an end. This shows Paul taking a step back from the negative view on the Law as described in Rom(A) (4:15) and Rom(B) (3:20). In addition, Paul argued that the Romans had to bear fruit for God, that is, eternal life. Here again, the Adam-typological description appears once again in terms of death and life. Based on the gospel consisted of the death and resurrection of Christ, Paul preached the lesson that the Romans should return to the state before the fall of the first human being lived in the garden of Eden. However, in spite of Paul's instruction, Jewish members might not have easily accepted his teachings because they were accustomed to the eternity of the Law. On the other hand, gentile believers would not have felt much pressure to accept his instruction.

Now, the religious decisions of the Romans were presented with a comparison between when they were bound by the Law and when they were free from it. First of all, the Romans were described as those having no choice but to face death because the sinful passions were at work in their members due to the Law when they were in the flesh (7:5). Paul pointed out the sinful passions caused by the Law when people were in the flesh and argued that it ultimately leads them to death. The sinful passions is considered a more religiously developed concept than the lust of heart used in Rom(B) (1:24) and then Rom(C) (6:12). In this way, Paul presented sin as something that actively leads people to death. Paul dealt with the themes of death and life in relation to sin.

Paul then mentioned life when free from the Law. It is said that having died to what bound, people have been free from the Law so that they could serve in the new way of the spirit, and not in the old way of the written code (7:6). Paul linked the path the Romans should follow with the spirit and put it in contrast with the old path based on the written code, that is, the Law. Here is implied a contrast between death by the Law and life by spirit. It should be noted that the spirit appeared here. Paul once mentioned the love of God given through the holy spirit in Rom(A) (5:5), and then the kingdom of God was defined as righteousness, peace, and joy in the holy spirit in Rom(B) (14:17). However, in Rom(C), the spirit was presented as a being that leads people to a new level of life. With this, Paul advised the Romans to escape from the Law and written codes that lead them to death. Rather, they had to live according to the spirit that leads to life. As such, the relationship between Paul and the Romans was still in a state of disagreement at the time of writing Rom(C).

To sum up, Paul wanted the Romans to break away from the Law and to be led by the spirit. This continues dealing with the major issue of Rom(C): that the Romans must choose between death and life. Paul encouraged them to live according to the gospel. However, Jewish members would have had difficulty following up Paul's theological developments because they were too accustomed to the permanence of the Law.

The Law and Sin (7:7–13)

Paul argued that the Law and sin lead people to death. Having passed its responsibility on to sin, Paul showed how to soften the view on the Law. Paul probably accepted the Romans' critique and adjusted his views on the Law. In any case, Paul thought that people who followed the Law were living against the gospel.

The reconsideration of the Law was shown with a rhetorical question. This is detected in the phrase "what shall we say then?" In response to the rhetorical question, he said, "Is the Law sin?" and then "it cannot be." He finally claimed that one does know sin through the Law (7:7a). Paul seemed to have acknowledged that he had described the Law too negatively in Rom(A) (4:15) and Rom(B) (3:20, 31). Nevertheless, having mentioned that people would not have known what sin was except through the Law here in Rom(C), Paul continued supporting the proposition that the Law convicts of sin as written in Rom(B). However, having faced the critique of the Romans, especially Jewish members, that his view on the Law was too negative, Paul seemed to have need to explain more in detail the relationship between the Law and sin.

Paul introduced an example of becoming aware of sin through the Law. It is said that a person would not have known about sin except through the Law because he or she would not have know lust if it did not said, "Do not covet" (7:7b). Paul added authority to the Law by quoting a verse from the Bible (Exod 20:17; Deut 5:21). Having been used in connection with human nature in Rom(B) (1:24), the word "lust" was used in connection with the role of the Law in Rom(C) (6:12). Then, it is said to announce the normal function of the Law (7:7b). The role of the Law should be noted here. When Paul previously emphasized that the reason the Law came in was to increase trespass (5:20), trespass refers to a concept that could be used interchangeably with sin. Here, the Law is defined as the one making people know that sin is sin. In this respect, the Romans had to recognize the virtuous function of the Law. With this, Paul shifted from a negative perspective on the Law until now to a reserved stance a little bit. This is probably the result of Paul accepting the critique of Jewish members. This view would have been acceptable to them.

Now the role of sin was presented in connection with commandments. It is said that having seized the opportunity afforded by the commandments, sin produced every kind of lust that is covetous desire (7:8a). Paul argued that the personified sin takes advantage of the commandments to work out all kinds of greed in people. This kind of description was not found in the writings of any religious person at the time. Having mentioned the word "commandment" instead of "written code," Paul used another expression for the Law. In this way, he sought to exempt it from the negative role. This is the first case that the Law was given a reserved view by saying that apart from the Law, sin is dead (7:8b). Paul developed the logic that if the Romans did not cling to the Law, there would be no reason for them to be caught up in sin. Paul had to assign a negative role to sin in order to silence the critique of the Romans against his negative view on the Law. However, it seems that Paul's argument was not persuasive to the Jewish members of the Roman church. This is because Paul showed a negative stance toward the commandments.

Paul made a self-confessional description of the role of the Law. It is said that once he was alive apart from the Law, but when the commandments came, sin sprang to life and he died (7:9). Paul described the state before receiving the gospel. By this, he emphasized that the Romans were in exactly this condition. Paul described sin as an entity taking on a villainous role. First, the expression that he was alive apart from the Law means that when Paul did not know the Law, he lived without knowing about sin itself. Since sin did not work at that time, people did not die but lived. At the same time, Paul confessed that when the commandments came, sin came to life and he died. This means that when he learned the provisions of the Law, that is, the commandments, sin came to life and made him know about sin that eventually led him to death. Paul probably thought that the sense of guilt that arises in people due to the commandments leads them to death. This is in line with the previous statement that sin took advantage of the opportunity given by the commandments and brought lust which led people to death (7:8). In any case, having placed responsibility on the commandments instead of the Law, Paul significantly reduced the intensity of critique against the Law. This interpretation is believed to have been delivered to comfort Jewish members who opposed Paul's negative teachings about the Law. However, they would not have accepted that the commandments were presented in a negative light instead of the Law.

A critique against the commandments was described. It is said, "The very commandment that was intended to bring life actually brought death" (7:10). Having made a contrast between life and death, Paul pointed out the dysfunction of commandments. This means that there is something wrong with a commandment that should lead people to life but leads to death. Paul stated it on the basis of the premise that this kind of result comes about because of the sin holding the commandments captive. By doing this, Paul wanted to convey the lesson that the gospel leads people from death to birth. This could be said to be a measure taken by Paul when the Romans criticized his negative view on the Law as reflected in Rom(A) and Rom(B).

Paul kept presenting the negative role of sin. This appears in his confession that having seized the opportunity afforded by the commandments, sin deceived him, and through the commandment put him to death (7:11). Paul made a revolutionary statement about the relationship between sin and the commandments. Paul previously stated that the "sinful passion" was at work among people (7:5) and that sin took advantage of the commandments to fulfill all kinds of greed within them (7:8). Accordingly, Paul was able to describe here the work of sin in relation to him. Having mentioned the commandments a second time in a negative light, Paul made a statement that seemed to grant indulgence to the Law. Moreover, having emphasized the powerful role of sin, he described himself as a victim of the commandments. In this way, it pointed out the uselessness of the commandments and at the same time implicitly presented a life according to the gospel. However, it is unclear whether Jewish members accepted Paul's interpretation that the commandments lead people to death.

A conclusion about the Law was drawn. This appears in the declaration that the Law is holy and the commandment is holy, righteous, and good (7:12). Paul declared that the Law is holy for the first time and that the commandment is also holy, righteous, and good. Here, holiness, righteousness, and goodness are religious values for Jews. Having given these kinds of value to the Law and commandments, Paul expressed a positive stance toward them. In this way, Paul took a step back from the negative view on the Law. This shows that he did not want his views on the Law and commandments to be misunderstood by the Romans, especially Jewish members. With this, Paul hoped to find a theological breakthrough that could persuade them. This is because they had to maintain good relationships in order to obtain support for the mission to Spain.

The logic that the commandments bring death due to sin appeared at last. It begins with the declaration that what is good cannot become death to Paul (7:13a). Paul argued that what is good, that is, the commandments, did not lead him to death. As a result, the negative stance toward the commandments was withdrawn. In addition, Paul declared that sin produced death in him through what was good in order that sin might be recognized as sin (7:13b). As described above, this is in line with the declaration that sin seized the opportunity afforded by the commandments to lead people to death. Having avoided the extreme statement that the Law leads people to death, Paul was able to place the fundamental responsibility for death on sin. Rather, it ultimately made him declare that the commandments make people sinful (7:13c). This means that the power of sin is so strong that even the commandments are used against it. The series of statements shows that even though the good commandments do lead people to death, such a result occurred because sin abused the commandments in that direction. Therefore, Paul had no choice but to describe sin as the cause of death. Meanwhile, having not mentioned the Law, Paul alleviated the responsibility of the Law. In this way, Paul tried to avoid the critique of Jewish members against his negative views on the Law. They may have affirmed the role of sin, but they would have had a hard time accepting Paul's argument about the role of commandments.

To sum up, Paul pointed out sin as the ultimate source that leads people to death. This kind of life occurred because of an attitude that does not originate from the gospel. In this way, the Law and commandments were exempted from responsibility. In this way, Paul tried to neutralize the critique of Jewish members; however, it is not clear whether they would have understood his argument and accepted it.

Life Under Sin (7:14–20)

Paul confessed about his life under sin. This symbolizes that he entered the path of death rather than life. Paul maintained the Adam-typological description with an association with an image of choosing evil rather than good he desired. This also shows the anguish between death and life.

The weakness of the "flesh" was mentioned for the first time. This appears in the statement that while the Law is spiritual, Paul himself was fleshly and sold as a slave to sin (7:14). Paul said for the first time that the Law is spiritual, recalling the holy aspect presented earlier (7:12). The spiritual Law is in contrast with the fleshly Paul. The contrast between "spiritual" and "fleshly" has already been treated several times to the Corinthians and Galatians (1 Cor 3:1–3; Gal 5:16, etc.). Accordingly, having applied the word "spiritual" to the Law in Rom(C), Paul attempted to alleviate the critique of Jewish members against his negative view on the Law expressed in Rom(A) and Rom(B). At the same time, he presented his own weakness, belonging to the flesh and being sold under sin, as a solution. In this way, Paul emphasized the need to be free from sin. It is necessary to take a look at the role of the flesh here. For instance, in Rom(B), Paul wrote that no "flesh" would be justified before God by the works of the Law, and that the Law convicts of sin (3:20). On the contrary, in Rom(C), it was described that the sinful passions resulted from the Law were at work in the members of human being while he or she was in the flesh (6:12). Then, having defined himself as "flesh," Paul confessed that he had been sold under sin. In this way, the "flesh" does not refer to the physical body but rather to the weak nature of humans that cannot help but be attracted by sin. This is a confession that sin has control over everyone in the flesh. Paul placed the responsibility for the death of mankind on sin not on the Law or commandments. This would have been a way to obtain consent not only from Jewish members but also from gentile members.

Paul described the condition under sin. This is found in the statement that having not understood what he did, Paul did not do what he had wanted to do, and he did what he had hated (7:15). Paul confessed that his life was not going the way he wanted. Here is a contrast between what he wanted and what he hated. With this, Paul confessed that he was living in sin, even though he did not want to commit it. This means that he lived such a life because he could not overcome sin. In this way, Paul argued that since no one could escape the influence of sin, the Romans were not different. This internal confession is contrary to what he confessed in Galatians that he lives for Christ who loved him (Gal 2:20). With it in Rom(C), Paul brought to mind the image of Eve standing before the tree of knowledge of good and evil. This represents cases where God's commands were knowingly violated. It seems that Paul used this event as a theological background to confess his internal conflict. If so, this can be also said to be an Adam-typological description. While the contrast with Adam was described in connection with the "one to come," now the relationship is applied to Paul himself. By doing this, he presented a state that sought to escape from sinful desires and seemed to have nothing to do with the Law. With regard to this, all members of the Roman church probably agreed with his internal confession.

The relationship between sin and the Law was treated again. This is seen in the statement that if Paul did what he did not want to do, he acknowledged that the Law is good (7:16). Paul expressed his thoughts in two stages. First of all, doing something he did not want means ultimately committing sin. Second, the Law ultimately plays a good role because sin is revealed immediately when viewed in the light of it. This shows that Paul retreated from his negative perspective on the Law as written in Rom(A) and Rom(B) and that he took a reserved stance in Rom(C). In doing so, he once again showed that sin was in an antithetical relationship with the Law. This is quite different from what Paul had claimed in Rom(B) that sin can be realized through the Law (3:20). This shows that the more Paul communicated with the Romans, the less negative his views on the Law became. It seems that there was a certain level of acceptance of their critique against his negative view on the Law. This was Paul's attempt to win their hearts.

Paul then placed the ultimate responsibility on sin. This is seen in the confession that it is not he who makes him do what he does not want to do but sin that dwells within him (7:17). Paul described sin as something that controls the subject of action. Sin was presented as the ultimate subject that causes people to do what they do not want to do. Thus, Paul acknowledged the fact that he, as a human being, had been also subject to sin. In similar manner, according to him, the Romans had been also caught up in sin. Accordingly, sin was highlighted as an entity that makes even the Law lead people in an evil direction. Therefore, the task of entangling the more powerful forces of sin was urgent for people.

Then, human nature was described. This appears in the confession that something good did not dwell in him, that is, his "flesh," and that although he wanted to do good, he did not do anything good (7:18). Paul lamented that nothing good dwells in the "flesh." As already told to the Corinthians and the Galatians, the "flesh" refers to the sinful nature of human beings that challenges and opposes God (1 Cor 3:1–3; Gal 5:16–21, etc.). Meanwhile, having stated that nothing good dwells in the flesh in Rom(C), Paul tried to deliver the instruction that the will to pursue good cannot exist in sinful nature. It is then confessed that although Paul had a desire to do good, he was unable to do it. This is a lament that there is no being or force within people that can control the sin that resides in human beings. This refers to a situation that as Paul did not do something according to his good will, so the Romans were in the same situation. This gave Romans a desire for a being who could overcome sin.

Paul reiterated his inability once again. This is seen in the saying that instead of doing the good that he wanted, he did evil that he did not want (7:19). Paul adopted two pairs of contrasts between what is desired and what is not desired, and between good and evil. The contrast between good and evil has already appeared from a perspective of general ethics (2:7–10; 12:17; 13:3–4), and Paul even vigorously exhorted the Romans to overcome evil with good in Rom(B) (12:21). However, having written the internal conflict between good and evil in Rom(C), Paul confessed that he was unable to overcome evil with good. The difference between the descriptions of good and evil in Rom(B) and Rom(C) shows that Paul's attitude toward them changed as time went by. Paul once again presented the direction the Romans should take by means of a dichotomous description. Although this seems impossible, it is living a life of doing good by relying on God who makes it possible (4:20–21). Having revealed the internal conflict, Paul attempted to align himself with the

Romans. With this, he wanted to make them accept the teachings about good, so that they could overcome evil and be led to eternal life.

Finally, sin appeared as the force that causes evil. It is said that if Paul did something he did not want to do, it is not he who caused him to do it but the sin that dwells within him (7:20). Paul pointed to sin as the ultimate force of evil stronger than himself. This has already been mentioned several times before and is stated here as the final conclusion. In any case, it is important to observe that sin is presented as the force that resides in everyone. The personified sin causes people to commit evil. This appears for the first time in Paul's theology as a new interpretation. Paul's confessional conclusion would have been enough to raise awareness of sin among all Romans. This may have been enough to shift their attention from the issue of observing the Law to that of sin.

In summary, Paul confessed the reality that he also committed evil due to sin from an Adam-typological perspective. Sin is an important topic addressed from the beginning of Rom(C). Paul also revealed weakness by confessing that he had been controlled by sin and implied that he had no choice but to face death. Paul ended up conveying the fact that it was difficult to live according to the gospel based on the death and resurrection of Christ. However, it is doubtful whether the Jewish members of the Roman church accepted this.

Sin and God (7:21 –25)

Paul described the internal conflict that arose within him. Extreme contrasts appear again for this purpose. This is a conclusion resulted from his own spiritual experience and a commitment to live according to the law of God, not the Law. This confession highlighted the fact that Paul was also a being who looked at life from death. He wanted to convey that the same is true for all members of the Roman church.

A new principle was presented with regard to good and evil. This appears in the statement that Paul found a law at work in that when he wanted to do good, evil was right there with him (7:21). Here, Paul seems to have used the word "law" to mean principle or rule. While people who do good or those who do evil were distinguished in Rom(B) (2:9–10), good and evil are described as fighting within a person in Rom(C). It seems that Paul learned this principle from his own experience. This was written to let the Romans know that they would be in the same situation.

In this respect, Paul made it known that he was weak in faith. His self-reflective confession was intended to acknowledge the fact that Jewish members would also find it difficult to live according to the gospel.

Then, Paul mentioned the conflict between good and evil in more detail. It is said that although he delighted in the law of God in his inner being, he saw another law at work in the members of his body waging war against the law of his mind and making him a prisoner of the law of sin (7:22–23). Having used several pairs of contrasts, Paul portrayed the struggle between good and evil in himself. First, the contrast between the inner being and the members of body was mentioned. The inner being probably refers to the human spirit, while the members of body refer to what was previously expressed as "flesh." They are different forces that oppose each other within human beings. Second, the contrast between the law of God and that of sin was dealt with. While the former represents the life God wants, the latter refers to the force that leads people to death. Paul heightened the fact that two different values exist and struggle within people. Third, a contrast appeared between joy and obsession. Despite Paul wanted to follow the law of God on his own with joy, he had to witness the reality of following the law of sin through obsession. This reveals the reality that things did not go as he wanted. In the end, Paul described himself struggling between good and evil and trying to overcome it. The confessional narration was made to present himself as an example to the Romans. However, it is doubtful whether there was anyone who experienced spiritual distress to the degree that Paul had.

The internal self-portrait of Paul was presented in more detail. This is revealed in the description that he was a miserable person who had to be rescued from the body of death (7:24). Paul was the first to write a self-confessional narrative. It is said that he wanted to do good but instead worried and suffered about doing evil. Therefore, Paul asked someone to rescue him from the body of death. This situation is different from his confidence, described in Galatians, that Christ is the one who rescues people from the evil age (Gal 1:4). While Paul objectively mentioned a savior to save people in Galatians, he showed himself looking for his own savior in Rom(C). Moreover, whereas Paul described Christ Jesus as a mediator praying for intercession at the right hand of God in Rom(A) (8:34), he did not mention anything about the mediator in a painful situation in Rom(C). Here it is revealed that Paul's theology changed over time. In any case, it is important that Paul presented death as a result of following the law of sin. Paul intended to say that the Romans were also in such a state and to let them know that they also needed to be delivered from death. In this way, Paul clearly showed through his self-reflective confession how difficult it is to live according to the gospel that one must be led to life from death.

Paul introduced Jesus Christ as a savior. This appears in the description of giving thanks to God through the Lord Jesus Christ (7:25a). Having mentioned the issue of his own salvation, Paul introduced Jesus Christ as a savior and thanked God for sending him. Whereas Jesus Christ was described in relation to salvation in Rom(A) (5:9–10), the righteousness of God that represents the state of salvation was mentioned in connection with the faith of Jesus Christ in Rom(B) (3:20–31). Accordingly, Paul was able to introduce Jesus Christ as a savior just after mentioning his own salvation in Rom(C). These descriptions show that as time passed, Paul increasingly presented Jesus Christ as the savior of all mankind. This is the core of the gospel that Paul wanted to convey. It is, however, unclear whether the Romans, especially those of Jewish origin, agreed on this because they seemed to look forward to righteousness by keeping the Law.

A conclusion has been presented with regard to Paul's stance on the Law. This is revealed in the confession that whereas he was serving the law of God with his heart, he was a slave to the law of sin in the flesh (7:25b). Here, while the mind corresponds to the inner being mentioned earlier, the "flesh" refers to the members of one's body. In any case, here too the mind and the law of God appear in contrast to the "flesh" and the law of sin. This means that the Law can be either the law of God or the law of sin according to one's attitude. To put it more specifically, when the Law is approached from the perspective of God, it becomes the law of God; on the other hand, when it is treated as a captive of sin, it becomes the law of sin. In this way, Paul taught the Romans to make a decision by presenting the question of whether they could give themselves to God or be caught up in sin. It is believed that this conclusion could have been reached after a long debate between Paul and the Romans about the Law. However, it seems that Jewish members would have had a hard time accepting Paul's argument, saying that the law of God was fulfilled by keeping the Law.

In summary, Paul himself declared that it was difficult to live according to the gospel. This was revealed through a confession of his internal conflict. In any case, he presented Christ as his savior and encouraged the Romans to also accept him. However, it is not clear whether they, who were adhered to the Law, accepted his advice.

3. CHRIST AND THE SPIRIT (8:1–30)

Paul continued the theme of death and life by relating it to Christ and the spirit. The contents of the gospel developed in connection with the spirit. This was written as a response to Paul's wish for a savior. In similar manner, Paul encouraged the Romans to participate in God's salvation found in Christ and the spirit.

The Law of the Spirit of Life (8:1–13)

Paul dealt with the themes of death and life by linking them to the spirit and the flesh. This shows Paul's effort to understand the gospel in relation to the spirit. Paul wanted that the Romans would be people led from death to life with Christ and the spirit.

The spiritual state that the Romans should pursue was presented. This appears in the declaration that there is absolutely no condemnation for those who are in Christ Jesus (8:1). Paul came up with a solution for his spiritual condition. Actually, he had to be condemned because he did not do good he wanted but did evil he did not want. However, he presented being in Christ as the way to salvation from condemnation. This is in contrast with the previous description that "one person" has led many people to the condemnation of God because of sin (5:18). The phrase "being in Christ" seems to mean following the life of Christ. Accordingly, the Romans had to live as people who come to life through the death and resurrection of Christ that constitutes the core of the gospel. In any case, while presenting the path to avoid the condemnation, they were urged not to cling to the Law but to adopt the new method given by Christ Jesus. However, because Jewish members were familiar with the Law, they would not have easily accepted Paul's new teachings.

Paul described a state in which people were not condemned. It is said that the "law of the spirit of life in Christ Jesus" has liberated people from the "law of sin and death" (8:2). Paul put the spirit of life in Christ Jesus in contrast with sin and death in relation to law. This means that the spirit of life brings salvation to people through Jesus Christ. In this way, Paul substituted the law of the spirit of life here for the law of God mentioned earlier (7:22). Moreover, the spirit, previously described as a being in contrast to the Law and "written code" (7:6), is introduced here as a being who brings about life. The one-sided teaching of Paul would have been quite uncomfortable to the Romans because they believed that the Law leads people to life. However, Paul explained life and Jesus Christ against the backdrop of Adam in the garden of Eden. The Adam-typological approach was used from the beginning of Rom(C) and was a good way to explain the intention of Paul. Having argued in this way, Paul taught the Romans that they should live according to the will of God expressed from the beginning of world, not according to the Law. This presented a principle that could be applied equally to both Jewish and gentile members.

God was introduced as the one having worked for the salvation of people. This is reflected in the declaration that God did what the Law could not do because of its weakness by the "flesh" (8:3a). Having put God in contrast with the Law with regard to ability, Paul tried to show what God had done for the Romans. This describes God as the one who liberates people from sin and death while the flesh is weak and acts as if caught in sin. Paul argued that God controls sin that neither the Law nor the flesh can handle. God did this according to the law of life in Christ. This is a soteriological role given to the spirit of life in Christ Jesus. Having mentioned in this way, Paul reduced the role of the Law and asked the Romans to accept the gospel that provided them with salvation from death.

Paul described what God had done for people. It is said that God sent his own Son in the likeness of sinful flesh and condemned him to sin (8:3b). Paul insisted that Christ Jesus the Son of God played the role of atoning figure. This reminds readers of Paul who said that God had sent his Son under the Law to atone those under it (Gal 4:4–5). Here the Law is mentioned in a negative light, saying that it cannot redeem people. On the other hand, in Rom(A), Paul insisted that Christ died for the ungodly, that is, sinners (5:6–8). His atoning role was clearly stated there. However, in Rom(C), it is stated that Christ Jesus came in the form of sinful flesh. Although his death is not mentioned here, Paul had already written about it in an earlier letter. Accordingly, Paul implied that because of the atoning death of Christ, the role of liberating people from sin and saving them from death was transferred from the Law to him. It would be shocking to Jewish members who tried to keep the Law. On the contrary, for the gentile members, it would have been quite a refreshing way of atonement. In this way, Paul presented the Romans with a way to be saved through the spirit of life in Christ Jesus apart from the Law.

The spirit of people was described in connection with the fulfilled requirement of the Law. This is found in the statement that the requirements of the Law are fulfilled to those who walk according to the spirit and not according to the flesh (8:4). Paul insisted that the spirit of God makes people fulfill the requirement of the Law that is the righteousness of God. This is a more positive instruction than what Paul said to the Galatians: that if one walks according to the spirit of God, he or she will not fulfill the desires of the flesh and are not under the Law (Gal 5:16–18). On the other hand, Paul insisted that the spirit makes people fulfill the requirement of the Law in Rom(C). This is reminiscent of previous statement to break away from the Law and serve with something new in the spirit (7:6). As a result, the Romans were advised to turn away from the path of seeking salvation by keeping the Law according to the flesh to that pursuing a life according to the spirit. Having put the spirit in contrast with the Law, Paul presented the spirit as a new tool for salvation. It is unclear how persuasive his teachings were to Jewish members.

Paul made a contrast between those who follow the flesh and those who follow the spirit. This is found in the description that while those who follow the flesh think about things of the flesh, those who follow the spirit think about things of the spirit (8:5). Paul developed the narrative to the point of contrasting the things of the flesh and those of the spirit. The contrast between those of the flesh and those of the spirit was already known to the Corinthians and the Galatians (1 Cor 3:1– 3; Gal 5:16– 24). Accordingly, in Rom(C), Paul was able to make a contrast among the objects of their thoughts and pursuits. It is important to note that all of these contrasted distinctions were raised in situations where Paul was being challenged or criticized. With them, Paul wanted Jewish members to go beyond the traditional viewpoint they espoused and leap to a new level by the spirit. However, it is not clear how responsive they were to this.

Different results were mentioned depending on one's attitude. It is said that while those who follow the flesh will be eventually led to death, those who follow the spirit will be led to life and peace (8:6). Of course, Paul kept using the contrast between death and eternal life; however, it is the first case that he connected them to the flesh and the spirit. Paul once presented Christ to the Corinthians as the life-giving spirit (1 Cor 15:45). It has been written in Galatians that people will reap eternal life from the spirit (Gal 6:8). Accordingly, in Rom(C), the spirit was developed into something that brings about life. The distinction between death and life was also developed by applying the death and resurrection of Christ, the core of the gospel, to the Romans. In this way, this dichotomous description was a useful tool to suggest the path the Romans should naturally choose. Of course, they had to follow the spirit and pursue life and peace. However, it is not clear whether they accepted Paul's proposal without resistance.

Paul elaborated on carnal thinking. This appears in the statement that the "flesh" is hostile to God; thus, it not only prevents people from submitting to the law of God but also makes them unable to do so (8:7). Paul defined the "flesh" as the sinful nature, that is, a force opposing God. The opposition of people to God was once mentioned in Rom(A). His Son was sent to die for sinner while being in a relationship of enmity with people (5:10). However, in Rom(C), Paul described the sinful nature as an enemy of God that prevents people from submitting to the law of God. Paul warned the Romans of the consequences if they did not live according to the spirit. This is presented to help them live according to the gospel. However, it seems that the Romans did not easily follow his teachings.

The final condemnation was made against the flesh. It is said that those who are in the flesh cannot please God (8:8). Paul placed those who live in the flesh at the antithesis of God. This has been used continuously since before. For instance, Paul once taught in Rom(B) that those who serve Christ please God and receive praise from men (14:18). However, in Rom(C), it developed into a declaration that those who are in the flesh cannot please God. Paul made a contrast between Christ and the flesh with regard to the issue of pleasing God. This was also given as a warning to the Romans to prevent them from living according to the flesh. Anyway, Paul taught them to be those who truly please God, emphasizing that they should follow the spirit, not the flesh.

Paul described the presence of the spirit. This appears in the statement that if the spirit of God had dwelled in the Romans, they would have not been in the flesh but in the spirit (8:9a). Paul once again put the spirit in contrast with the flesh. The contrast between the two was raised at a time when Paul had been challenged. For example, the Corinthians distinguished between the spiritual man and the fleshy man (1 Cor 3:1–3). In Galatians, the spirit was constantly contrasted with the flesh (Gal 3:3; 4:29; 5:16–24). Accordingly, in Rom(C), Paul simply defined that if the spirit of God had dwelled among the Romans, they would not have been in the flesh but in the spirit. Here the matter of living in the spirit comes to the fore, which reminds readers of abiding in Christ earlier. In this respect, Paul revealed the close relationship between Christ and the spirit.

Here the spirit of Christ was introduced for the first time. This appears in the declaration that anyone who does not have the spirit of Christ does not belong to him (8:9b). Paul clearly mentioned the "spirit of Christ." It is, however, unclear whether this refers to the spirit given by Christ or the spirit that makes one a kind of being with Christ. Having dealt with the spirit of Christ, Paul revealed the intention to make the Romans follow in the footsteps of Christ. This strategy has already been used in Rom(A) and Rom(B) when he described the identity and role of Jesus Christ at the ending part of main body of each letter (5:1–11; 3:21–26). Having used this kind of approach, Paul tried to make the Romans reach salvation through Christ Jesus, regardless of the Law.

Paul explained in more detail the person of Christ. This is found in the expression that if Christ is among the Romans, their bodies are dead because of sin but their spirits are alive because of righteousness (8:10). Paul created an extreme contrast between the mortal body and the living spirit. The issue of whether Christ was in someone or not turned into that of the death of body and the life in spirit. This contrast reminds readers of what Paul himself confessed earlier, that with his heart he serves the law of God, but with his flesh he serves the law of sin (7:25). With this kind of declaration, Paul taught that the Romans should follow in the footsteps of Christ. The category of people who should live like Christ was expanded to the Romans. It is interesting to see the contrast between the human body and the spirit. Paul once informed the Thessalonians that a person is composed of body, soul, and spirit (1 Thess 5:23), and presented the body of soul and that of spirit to the Corinthians (1 Cor 15:44). However, in Rom(C), Paul put the death of body because of sin in contrast with the life of spirit because of righteousness. In this way, having emphasized the contrast between death and eternal life, Paul tried to make the Romans to follow Christ whose death and resurrection constitutes the core of the gospel.

Finally, the spirit of God was introduced in connection with the resurrection of body. It is said that if the spirit of God, who raised Jesus from the dead, dwells among the Romans, then God, who raised Christ Jesus from the dead, will dwell within them and give life to their mortal bodies through the spirit (8:11). Paul argued that just as God raised Christ from the dead, he would also give life to the mortal bodies of the Romans through the spirit. It is important to note that God was defined twice as the one who had raised Jesus Christ from the dead. Paul emphasized the power of God in raising Jesus Christ from the dead and that the same thing would happen to the Romans. The resurrection of Christ from the dead appears frequently in Paul's letters and plays an important role in his theology (1:4; 4:24; 1 Thess 1:10; 1 Cor 6:14; 15:12, 20; 2 Cor 1:9; Gal 1:1).

At the same time, the fact that this was used again in Rom(C) shows that for Paul, God holds an important position in that he eventually gives life to the Romans. This means bearing the fruit of the gospel. As a result, the issue of death and life appeared from the beginning of Rom(C) has been discussed in various ways up to this point.

The identity of "debtor" was applied to the Romans. This appears when Paul called them "brothers" and defined them, including himself, as debtors (8:12a). Paul used the concept of debtor in a couple of places. It was once used to introduce himself as a debtor to both Greeks and barbarians, wise and foolish in Rom(A) (1:14). This probably means that he was called to ministry because of them. Then, Paul defined the gentiles as debtors to the Jerusalem church for spiritual grace (15:27). This means gratitude to the precedents in faith because of spiritual influence. At last, in Rom(C), the Romans were defined as debtors because they received life through Christ Jesus. Paul's description of the debtor would have made the Romans humble before God. There would not have been anyone among them who could refute Paul's teachings.

Paul argued that people should not live as their flesh leads. This is found in the saying that the Romans should not be indebted to the flesh to live according to it (8:12b). Paul said that one who is indebted to the flesh has no choice but to live as the flesh leads. It has already been mentioned earlier that the end of life led by the flesh is death. Thus, Paul emphasized that the Romans should not give in to the flesh. This reminds readers of the teaching that the Romans should not hand over their members of body to sin as weapons of unrighteousness (6:13). Paul taught that the Romans should make spiritual efforts to live a life free from the flesh.

The contrast between the flesh and the spirit was repeated in relation to death and eternal life. This appears in the statement that if people live according to the flesh, they will surely die, but if they put to death the deeds of the body by the spirit, they will live (8:13). Paul once again presented the Romans with a choice between the flesh and the spirit in terms of death and life. This was a request for them to turn from the path leading to death according to the flesh to the path leading to eternal life according to the spirit. While Paul had previously taught that sin leads people to death, here he described the flesh as the entity leading to death. If so, it turns out that sin and the flesh have a close relationship with death as a medium. Once Paul taught the Galatians to reject the lust of the flesh as opposed to the spirit (Gal 5:16–18). However, in Rom(C), "the misdeeds of the body" was used instead of "the lust of the flesh."

This is believed to provide confidence that the Romans can sufficiently regulate themselves from an ethical perspective. In other words, it was an instruction that if they lived in the spirit, they could have conducted their behavior properly. In relation to this, Paul previously lamented that he was doing what he had not wanted to do (7:19). This shows that he should have been able to control himself, but he was not able to do so. Accordingly, Paul taught the Romans to follow the path to life by controlling the deeds of the body with the spirit of God. Having delivered these lessons, Paul erased the issue of the Law from the eyes of the Romans.

In summary, Paul revealed the role of the spirit of God for eternal life. According to him, the Romans had to be free from sin and come to life through the spirit of God in Christ Jesus. To this end, having made the contrast between sin and grace, body and the spirit, and death and life, Paul emphasized that God, who raised Jesus Christ from the dead, would work in the same way on the Romans. In this way, Paul persistently insisted on the life according to the gospel.

The Children of God (8:14–23)

Paul gave various status to people who live in the spirit of God. This was expressed as the sons of God, children, adopted sons, etc. They are those who have been saved and enjoy life. This ultimately leads to glory.

The identity of those who live by the spirit of God was presented. It is said that those who are led by the spirit are sons of God (8:14). Paul argued that the Romans were made sons of God by the spirit with a meaning that they were given a life (8:6, 10–14). This is also the result of being united with Christ, the Son of God (6:3–6). The declaration of becoming sons of God by the spirit seems to be at the pinnacle of his previous discussion on the relationship between death by the flesh and eternal life by the spirit. This was a status given to the Romans who broke away from the Law and "written code" but began to serve with the new spirit. Paul gave them filial status from a spiritual perspective. By doing this, Paul tried to win over the hearts of the Romans.

Paul then presented a slightly reserved position regarding the filial relationship with God. This appears in the statement that the Romans did not receive the spirit of servants fearing their masters, but received the spirit of sonship and were able to call God "daddy" the Father (8:15). Paul described to the Romans how to obtain a filial relationship. Once the right to call God "daddy" was given to the Galatians because they had received his son's spirit (Gal 4:6). There is no friendlier expression than this to describe the relationship between God and human beings. However, in Rom(C), the term "spirit of sonship" appeared without any reference to the Son of God Jesus Christ. Although the status of adopted sons was granted to Romans, it means that they were qualified to participate in life with Christ. In any case, having become the adopted son of God, the Romans could be those who share the nature of Christ the Son of God, which can be represented by eternal life. As time passed, having organized the theology on becoming a divine son, Paul wanted them to become closer to Christ through the spirit, not through the Law.

The testimonial role of the spirit of God was mentioned in connection with the filial status of the Romans. This is found in the declaration that the spirit of God himself testifies with the spirits of people that they are children of God (8:16). Paul introduced the identity of children of God in relation to the spirit. This is an expression that gives more intimacy than the adopted sons of God. In Rom(A), Paul said that Christ, resurrected by the spirit of holiness, was declared to be the Son of God (1:4). Likewise, in Rom(C), those who received the spirit are defined as the children of God. Then, Paul declared that the spirit of God testifies together with the spirits of people. Having suggested "spirit" as the common element for the two, Paul emphasized the communication between them. This is an exhortation that the Romans should become the children of God by the spirit of God. Having presented it based on the spirit of God rather than the Law, Paul paved the way for even gentile members to become the children of God.

Paul mentioned the rights for inheritance. This is seen in the statement that by becoming an heir of God with Christ, one also suffers in order to receive glory (8:17). Paul mentioned the rights of the Romans to share the inheritance with Christ. The term "heir" has already been used to the Galatians with a saying that if they had been Christ's, they would have been Abraham's descendants and heirs according to the promise (Gal 3:29). However, in Rom(C), the heir was not related to Abraham but only to Christ. In this way, Paul defined the relationship of the Romans with God focusing on Christ. Having eliminated the connection with Abraham the forefather of Jews, Paul widened the door even to gentiles to be included into the heir of inheritance with Christ. Accordingly, they were given the mission to endure both suffering and glory with Christ as heirs. Suffering and glory were mentioned against the backdrop of

Christ's death and resurrection. They were presented as elements that people who live in the world according to the gospel must bear. Only then, they become heirs of God's promise together with Christ.

A contrast appears between suffering and glory. It is said that the present suffering cannot be compared to the glory that will be revealed (8:18). Paul emphasized that the Romans had to endure because the glory that would be revealed in the future far exceeds the present suffering. In this context, suffering and glory were definitely condensed expressions with the death and life of Christ. Paul said that suffering cannot be compared to glory. It means a transformation from a life that sought to be righteous by keeping the Law to a life that seeks to resemble Christ in the spirit of God. If they succeed in such work, they would enjoy salvation and eternal life, that is, the glory that will be revealed in the future. Having presented this alternative, Paul encouraged all Romans to be the heirs of promise by the spirit.

Paul extended the scope of those to be saved to include the creatures of world. This is revealed in the statement that the creature has waited for the sons of God to appear (8:19). Paul turned his eyes toward creatures. This implies that all creatures were to be governed by the sons of God and become like them. In other words, the sons of God led by the spirit should rule creatures according to his providence. This means that all creation wants to enjoy life with them. Paul presented a new instruction on the duties of those who have become sons of God in the spirit. This probably reflects the situation in which nature at that time was in a state of being degenerated into all kinds of idols, as recorded in Rom(B) (1:19–24). Having described in this way, Paul presented the sonship to restore nature in its original shape and to deal properly with creation in the spirit.

The reason that all creatures look forward to the appearance of the sons of God was explained. It is written that the creature's submission to frustration is not due to its own will but only due to the being that causes it to submit (8:20). Paul took the position that creatures should not enter the path of destruction; rather, he hinted at the existence that causes it to do so. However, there is no specific mention of those that lead creatures into futility, but it is likely that it is sin itself. If so, the nothingness to which the creature submits means death. The reason Paul even mentioned the destruction of creatures was to teach that it is important to know which force a person is captured by. He strongly insisted that the Romans had to choose to live according to the spirit of God because being caught up in sin inevitably leads to death not only for people but also for creatures.

Paul insisted that creatures were willing to submit to the children of God. It is said that creatures also seek to be liberated from slavery to corruption and attain the glorious freedom of God's children (8:21). Paul asserted that the creatures also wanted to turn from the path leading to death to the path of glory that the sons of God had sought to reach. The ultimate glory desired by those who are led by the spirit of God in Christ is salvation leading to eternal life. In this respect, all beings had to move in a direction that produces correct and beneficial results. This seems to be based on the premise that creatures should not be linked to idolatry. Paul delivered this lesson because the Romans had already been given the duty to lead creatures to life. By doing this, Paul expanded the scope of faith beyond the rule of Law to the management of creation. Of course, it is doubtful whether his teachings were effective for the Romans.

The miserable state of creatures was described. This appears in the description that all creatures groan and suffer together (8:22). Paul dealt with the sighing and weeping of creatures probably because there were critiques from Romans about his mention of creatures written in Rom(B). There, people were described as those worshiping and serving creatures by turning God's truth into lies (1:25). Having received this instruction, the Romans would have questioned how to treat creatures. Accordingly, in Rom(C), Paul pointed out that creatures had been suffering because they had been worshiped in the form of idols and were being used in the wrong direction by sin. Thus, creatures needed the help of God's children living according to the spirit of God. The argument is that creatures have unintentionally become victims that obscure the glory of God by people. Accordingly, creatures must be liberated from their slavery to corruption and attain the glorious shape of nature itself. For this purpose, Paul insisted that the children of God had a mission to work hard for the created world. Accordingly, it taught them not to be confined under the tradition of the Law but to carry out the will of God that works more broadly.

The redemption of body is dealt with for the first time. This is found in the description that they, as recipients of the firstfruits of the spirit, groan inwardly as they wait for adoption, that is, the redemption of body (8:23). Paul described the sons of God as the firstfruits of the spirit. This reminds readers of how he referred to the resurrection of Christ as the "firstfruits" (1 Cor 15:23). Accordingly, in Rom(C), Paul defined the sons of God through the spirit as firstfruits, which refers to those who have received life. Nevertheless, it is stated that they had no choice but to groan inwardly. This is the claim that the adopted sons who have received eternal life by the spirit of God are those waiting for the redemption of their bodies. Since Paul probably equated the firstfruits of the spirit with resurrection, it refers to the redemption of the body. Paul already used the word "redemption" to the Corinthians with righteousness and holiness in terms of God's wisdom (1 Cor 1:30). Then, it was used to refer to righteousness obtained in Christ that is another expression of salvation in Rom(B) (3:24). However, in Rom(C), Paul used it for the salvation of the body, meaning that the body should be liberated from death, that is, eternal life. This is contrasted with the previously mentioned body of death (7:24). These changes show that the idea of redemption became increasingly associated with life through resurrection. It seems to be mentioned against the backdrop of the garden of Eden, where the sons of God should return and get eternal life that would be given from the tree of life in it. Having described Christ from an Adam-typological perspective at the beginning of Rom(C), Paul was able to apply it to the sons of God who had to take after Christ Jesus. However, it is questionable whether these extreme teachings of Paul would have been accepted by Jewish members.

In summary, Paul continued to discuss life that presupposes resurrection. The redemption of creation was a task that the children of God who received the spirit of God had to handle. This reaches its peak in connection with the theme of death and eternal life dealt with in Rom(C). This is the application of the core of the gospel, based on the death and resurrection of Christ, to people. It is believed that Paul had all creatures in the world in mind and proposed a mission to all people, including gentiles.

The Salvation of God's Children (8:24–30)

Paul dealt with the salvation of God's children. This is expressed in various ways, starting with the mentioning of hope and ending with the use of "glorified." Paul wanted the Romans to attain eternal life through resurrection mentioned frequently in Rom(C)

Paul treated the issue of salvation. This is found in the saying that mentions the salvation of the Romans by hope and defines the hope that appears is not hope (8:24). Paul identified the redemption of body as salvation obtained by hope. If so, salvation means to be the adopted sons of God through the redemption of body in the spirit. It is necessary to pay more attention to invisible hope. In Rom(A), Paul linked hope with the love of God and presented the death and resurrection of Christ for sinners as a way of salvation (5:5–10). Here, of course, his resurrection is described as a prerequisite for salvation. Accordingly, it seems in Rom (C) that Paul ultimately presented resurrection by linking invisible hope with salvation. This also means the redemption of body. In the end, Paul seems to have defined life as an invisible hope while presenting it as salvation through resurrection. He has consistently dealt with it in Rom(C).

An exhortation was given to wait patiently for hope. This appears in the instruction that the Romans had to wait with patience because they had hoped for what they could not see (8:25). Having pointed out that salvation was something invisible to the eyes, Paul taught the Romans that they should wait patiently for it. As already treated above in Rom(A), the issue of hope was described in connection with the love of God revealed through the death of Christ and the salvation through his resurrection (5:5–10). However, in Rom(C), the contents of hope are related to the issue of being adopted sons of God and the redemption of body. They are expressions of salvation. It is unclear whether Paul's teachings were persuasive enough to Jewish members who had been accustomed to visible evidence, for instance, circumcision regulated by the Law.

Paul described the role that the spirit of God plays for people. It is said that the spirit of God helps people because of their weaknesses (8:26a). Whereas Paul mentioned weakness in faith in Rom(A) (4:19; 5:6; 14:1), he applied the issue of weakness to the relationship between the spirit of God and the Romans. This means that the spirit of God helps the weak from a spiritual perspective. Then, how the spirit of God helps people with their weaknesses is to be explained. This means that the spirit of God personally intercedes for people with groaning that cannot be uttered because they do not know what to pray for (8:26b). Paul assumed that if a person is weak in faith, he or she does not know what to pray for. The answer to this is that the spirit of God intercedes for the person with indescribable groaning at times. The word "groan" was previously used in connection with the suffering of creatures and the redemption of people (8:22–23). However, here, the spirit of God is described as groaning for people to help them. In this way, Paul further strengthened the role that the spirit of God plays for people in weakness. Although these teachings were new to the Romans, they would have been easy to accept. Because these teachings are not in the Law, they could have been accepted without much difficulty by Jewish members.

It is necessary to pay attention to the spirit of God introduced as a mediator. This is reflected in the expression that the spirit of God personally intercedes for people with groanings that cannot be uttered. Paul said that the spirit of God plays the role of mediator. This reminds readers of Christ Jesus interceding for people at the right hand of God as written in Rom(A) (8:34). The theme of intercession appears in common in both places. However, there are differences in that while Christ Jesus was described as a mediator in Rom(A), the spirit of God takes on the role in Rom(C). Although the term "intercede" appears in a slightly different form, it does not seem to be a big difference. Christ's intercession at the right hand of God is somewhat different from what the spirit does for people with groaning. The differences show that Paul transferred the role of mediator for people from Christ Jesus to the spirit of God. In this way, Paul developed the theology of mediator as time went by.

The relationship between God and the spirit was described. This is found in the description that the one who searches people knows the thoughts of the spirit (8:27a). It is God who searches the hearts of people. God's knowledge of the thoughts of the spirit indicates that they were in communication. Paul once gave similar teachings to the Corinthians, claiming that the spirit of God penetrates even the deep things of God (1 Cor 2:11). However, in Rom(C), God was introduced as the one who searches people and knows the thoughts of the spirit. In the two documents, the roles of God and the spirit are described interchangeably—at any rate, God and the spirit working closely with people. By doing this, Paul wanted to instill confidence in the Romans that God knows and guides everything through the spirit.

Then, how the spirit works for people was dealt with. This appears in the statement that the spirit intercedes for people according to the will of God (8:27b). It is to be noted that the spirit praying for man with indescribable groaning is followed by praying according to the will of God. This conveyed the lesson that the Romans should follow the guidance of the spirit. In addition, it is also noteworthy that while Paul had simply declared that Christ plays the role of mediator in Rom(A), he described how the spirit intercedes for people in various ways in Rom(C). This shows that the role of mediator became centered on the spirit over time. In this way, Paul developed the issue of mediator theologically step by step.

It is necessary to study the will of God. In Rom(A), Paul connected the desire to go to Rome with the will of God (1:10; 15:32). It is narrated from a first-person perspective in relation to his plan. Later in Rom(B), the teachings of the Law were presented as the will of God from a standpoint of criticizing Jews (2:18). This was connected to the issue of the other party Paul was dealing with. However, in Rom(C), Paul mentioned the will of God as something that the spirit must look into. The will of God is objectively related to the spirit as a third party. In this way, the issue of the will of God was interpreted more and more from a spiritual perspective as Paul sent letters to the Romans. By doing this, Paul taught them to live according to the spirit, who conveys God's will, rather than being bound by the Law.

Now Paul has come to a conclusion. It is said, "In all things God works for the good of those who love him, who have been called according to his purpose" (8:28). Paul defined the Romans as those who loved God and were called according to his purpose. It is important to note that instead of "God's love for people" found in Rom(A) (5:8), "those who love God" appeared in Rom(C). The difference conveys an instruction that the Romans' attitude should be changed by showing their love for God through faith. Paul called on the Romans to submit to God's purpose. Those who love God and those who are called according to his purpose must be treated on the same level. Those who are called by God and love him are those who must achieve good through cooperation. Having emphasized unity like this, Paul conveyed the message that all members of the Roman church should be one. Accordingly, Paul implied that both Jewish and gentile members were called by God into his people.

Paul presented the second thing that the Romans needed to know. This means that those whom God foreknew he also predestined to be conformed to the image of his Son (8:29a). Paul described the status of the Romans in two ways. Having mentioned those whom God foreknew, Paul suggested the concepts of foreknowledge and election. In addition, being conformed to the image of the Son means resemblance of him. Having previously pointed out that one must have the spirit of Christ, Paul presented the person of Christ (8:9). This was presented as a way to become united with Christ. However, the expression "image of the Son of God" should be noted because Paul insisted to the Galatians that the image of Christ should be formed in them (Gal 4:19). The image of the Son of God is mentioned for the first time in Rom(C). The reference to "image" brings to mind the statement that in the beginning God created human beings according to his own image (Gen 1:27). It is believed that Paul associated the Romans with the image of the Son of God who had been raised from the dead with power through the spirit of holiness (1:4). In any case, Paul tried to deliver the lesson from a typological perspective on the beginning of world that all people should become children of God destined to live forever according to the will of God.

The Son of God was described in more detail. He is the firstborn among many brothers (8:29b). Paul introduced the Son of God as a representative of many brothers. Among them, Jesus Christ is the firstborn, the first to become the Son of God, and is thus an example for all brothers. With this kind of description, Paul connected Jesus Christ with the Romans centering on the identity of the Son of God. This shows Paul's attempt to embrace the Romans around Jesus Christ, the Son of God. In Rom(C), toward the end of the main text, Paul took the form of preaching about Jesus Christ, as he did in Rom(A) and Rom(B). With this, the gospel he preached came to the fore.

Then, a description of brothers appeared. They are those whom God predestined, called, justified, and glorified (8:30). Paul listed the spiritual stages that would be given to the Romans. This informs them to grow spiritually. A similar statement was already told to the Corinthians, when Paul said that they were washed, sanctified, and justified in the name of the Lord Jesus Christ and the spirit of God (1 Cor 6:11). However, Rom(C), Paul went beyond the stage of justification even to that of glorification. This verse conveys the lesson that the Romans should be those who truly serve God. Paul wanted them to change from observing the Law to growing in faith to be more like Jesus Christ. Of course, this is the way for all people, including gentiles, to enjoy eternal life.

To sum up, this part can be said to be the theological conclusion of Rom(C). Paul wanted the Romans to be those who attain salvation through the mediation of the spirit. In addition, the lesson was given that the Romans should live as those who received the image of the Son of God risen from the dead. This was a request for all Romans, and there would have been no reason for them not to accept it. It is important to note that this presupposed that believers from gentile backgrounds were also included.

4. THE ETHICS OF SAINTS (13:8–10; 15:1–13)

Paul dealt with the ethics that the Romans had to follow. This deals with living by the love of Jesus Christ in relation to the Law. In this way, he proposed a life of mutual support while taking a reserved stance on the Law. The unity of the Romans was also emphasized from an ethical perspective.

A Life of Love (13:8–10)

Paul presented a lesson about love for neighbors to fulfill the Law. Having mentioned those who love God, Paul applied it to neighbors. The influence of love on the Law was also mentioned.

The lesson of love was imparted to the Romans. This appears in the teaching to owe no debt except the debt of love (13:8a). Paul mentioned the issue of loving and being loved through the expression "no debt except the debt of love." The issue of debtors already appeared in Rom(A) (1:14; 15:27) and then was used in Rom(C) (8:12). Accordingly, having mentioned the debt of love here, Paul presented the ethical life of the Romans. The teaching to serve one another with love was already delivered to the Galatians (Gal 5:13). While Paul mentioned the issue of loving brothers in Rom(A) (12:10), he expanded the category to loving neighbors in Rom(C). In this way, the Romans were permitted to form relationships through a debt of love. This reflects the fact that Paul tried to restore intimacy with them, especially Jewish members.

Paul then redefined the relationship between love and the Law. It is said that those who love others have fulfilled the Law (13:8b). Paul took a conservative stance toward the Law in Rom(C). The concept that the Law is fulfilled through love for one's neighbor was once mentioned in Galatians (Gal 5:14). There, it was described what happens when one loves someone as himself or herself. However, in Rom(C), loving others was simply presented as a way to fulfill the Law. This seems to show that the intensity of love has weakened. At any rate, this shows Paul's intention to end the controversy over the Law. If so, it seems that Paul took a reserved stance on the Law as he faced critiques of the Jewish members of the Roman church over time.

The commandments to be acted upon with love were presented. This is found in the statement that the Romans should not commit adultery, murder, theft, or covetousness but love their neighbor as themselves

(13:9). Paul took the four prohibitions from the Ten Commandments, which Jews were familiar with. The provision to love one's neighbor is the highest commandment in the Law and the way to fulfill all other commandments (Lev 19:18). In this way, love of one's neighbor occupies a superior position over other commandments. Paul once used the word "commandment" with a negative sense of meaning because the commandments are described as being abused by sin (7:8–10). On the other hand, this time, he took a reserved stance with a statement that the commandments are all included in love for neighbors. In this way, Paul showed that it is important from what perspective the commandments should be approached.

Paul made a conclusive statement regarding the relationship between love and the Law. It is said that love does not do evil to neighbors and fulfills the Law (13:10). Paul presented love as a way to fulfill the Law. This is related to the proposition that the commandment to love one's neighbor as oneself allows one to keep all the commandments. In addition, it is necessary to look at Paul's logic about love. In Rom(A), God's love for people was emphasized in the way God sent the Son to die for sinners (5:8). It was emphasized that no one and nothing can separate the Romans from the love of Jesus Christ and God (8:35, 39). Accordingly, Paul taught in Rom(C) that they should love God (8:29) and then love their neighbors (13:10). Paul changed the description of the Romans from those loved by God in Rom(A) to those who had to love God and neighbors in Rom(C). This reflects the change from a friendly relationship with them to an uneasy one. It is believed that Paul adopted this change of position while keeping criticism, especially from Jewish believers, in check.

In summary, Paul emphasized love for neighbors. To this end, he mentioned twice that love for one's neighbor fulfills the Law. The love for neighbors puts into practice the core of the gospel based on the death and resurrection of Christ. Love for one's neighbors seems to have been used as a stepping stone for missionary work toward gentiles.

Mutual Edification (15:1–13)

Paul presented a code of conduct for neighbors beyond the scope of church members. This is a request to become one with each other based for the mutual edification. With this, Paul taught the Romans to embrace even gentiles with love for neighbors. This was a way to build a justification for the mission to gentiles.

The relationship between the strong and the weak was addressed. This is expressed in the teaching that the strong must bear the weaknesses of the weak and not please themselves (15:1). Paul presented an alternative to prevent the Romans from judging or criticizing one another. This means carrying each other's burdens. Whereas Paul taught the Romans to accept those who were weak in faith and not to make an evaluation on them in Rom(A) (14:1), he did not limit the relationship between the strong and the weak to the matter of faith in Rom(C). Although Paul did not clearly state by what criteria the strong was distinguished from the weak, they seemed to be closely related to the human composition of the Roman church. In other words, it seems to refer to the relationship between Jewish members, who were the major group of the Roman church, and gentile members, who were the minority. Accordingly, Paul advised Jewish members to take charge of gentile members in their religious activity. This is in line with the instruction on love for one's neighbors. In addition, Paul said that the Romans had not to live a life that pleased only themselves. This is presented by Paul as a warning lesson. With these lessons, Paul revealed the willingness to embrace not only Jews but also gentiles with love. This is a kind of work to establish the preliminary justification for the mission to gentiles.

Paul taught how the Romans should live a life that did not please themselves. This appears in the teaching to please one's neighbors for good and for the purpose of edification (15:2). Paul taught the Romans that loving their neighbors was the way to please them. While the term "good" was mentioned in relation to one's own matters in Rom(A) (12:9) and in Rom(B) (12:21; 14:16), it was mentioned in relation to one's neighbors in Rom(C). In particular, the issue of neighbors continued the teaching about loving them (13:10). In this way, Paul paid attention to love and joy for neighbors. Whereas the issue of edification appeared in parallel with peace in Rom(B) (14:19), it was described as the final goal in Rom(C). Paul suggested that the Romans should live a life of doing good and edifying others with love as a way to fulfill the Law. This presents a better virtue than keeping the Law.

Paul presented Christ as an example. This is revealed in the statement that he did not please himself (15:3). Christ was described as the one living a life that pleased others. To prove this, Paul quoted a verse from the Bible (Ps 69:9); however, it is not considered sufficient to define such a life of Christ. In any case, having introduced Christ as the one who died for sinners in Rom(A) (5:8–10), Paul maintained that tone in Rom(C). This once again conveys the lesson that the Romans had to live following Christ.

Hope was heightened for the religious life. Having described the purpose of quoting the Bible, it is emphasized to have hope through patience or the comfort of the Scriptures (15:4). Paul said that if people must persevere for hope, they must receive comfort from the Scriptures. While patience and hope had already been mentioned in Rom(A) (5:3–4), they were organized in their own way by mentioning them again in Rom(C). According to Paul, people must have hope and live in patience and comfort because that is the way of taking upon himself the weakness of the weak. The Romans had to take upon themselves the weaknesses of their neighbors and live a life of loving them. Paul revealed the wish that the Romans go beyond the scope of the Law.

Paul described what the Romans should have for the glory of God. This appears in the statement that the God of patience and comfort will make the Romans imitate Christ Jesus and come together with one mind, so that they may glorify God, the Father of the Lord Jesus Christ (15:5–6). Having suggested patience and comfort as God's character, Paul related them to the things given through the Scriptures earlier. In addition, it is stated that what God wanted from the Romans was to live according to Christ Jesus and agreed with one another. This is similar to how Christ did not live a life that pleased him. The Romans also had to live following him. The purpose for which this was given is that the Romans, with one mind, would glorify God the Father of the Lord Jesus Christ. Paul's emphasis on their unity shows that they have not yet become one. Accordingly, he wanted them to cooperate and live a life of goodness.

Now what the Romans had to do was written down. This is found in the teaching that just as Christ received people to glorify God, the Romans had to also receive one another (15:7). Paul once again insisted that the Romans had to follow Christ. This is a lesson about unity by accepting one another just as Christ accepted them. Paul wanted the strong to bear the weaknesses of the weak and to please their neighbors for their goodness and edification. This is all about fulfilling the Law through the act of loving one's neighbors. Paul advised the Romans to live a life of love following Christ based on the gospel. Gentiles cannot be excluded here.

Paul argued that gentiles should be embraced into the people of God. This is revealed in the statement that Christ became a follower of circumcision for the sake of God's truth, confirming the promises given to the ancestors and allowing gentiles to glorify God for his mercy (15:8–9a). This verse can be said to be an enlargement of the subject presented in the previous verses. Paul first explained the reason that Christ was circumcised, claiming that it was to confirm the promises given to the ancestors. The claim that Christ came into the world according to the promise given to the ancestors was already told to the Galatians (Gal 3:16). Accordingly, Paul argued in Rom(C) that God's truth was proven by the coming of Christ into the world according to the promise. This was written to provide justification for the Romans to live according to Christ. Second, Paul expressed the opinion that gentiles could also become the people of God on account of God's mercy. This is something already told to the Galatians (Gal 3:8). Accordingly, Paul was able to argue in Rom(C) that gentiles could be incorporated into the people of God. Meanwhile, Paul implied that Christ had come under the Law as a follower of circumcision. This shows that Paul took a reserved view on the Law and that he tried to show the intention to be united with the Romans, especially Jewish members, in Christ.

Paul cited several verses from the Bible to justify involving gentiles into the people of God (15:9b–12). They are, "Therefore I will praise you among the Gentiles; I will sing hymns to your name" (Ps 18:49); "Rejoice, O Gentiles, with his people" (Deut 32:43); "Praise the Lord, all you Gentiles, and sing praise to him, all you people" (Ps 117:1); and "The root of Jesse will spring up, one who will arise to rule over the nations; the Gentiles will hope in him" (Isa 11:10). They mention terms such as "gentiles," that is, "nations." They also mention how to give thanks, praise, and hope to God. Paul quoted them in order to assert that the gentiles were also accepted by God. Furthermore, Christ was defined as the "root of Jesse," which is consistent with the description that he was born "of the lineage of David according to the flesh," as written in Rom(A) (1:3). Paul went on to say that the gentiles also looked to the Davidic savior. This means that God had long revealed the intention to make gentiles his people. Whereas Paul established the scheme of "Jews was first and then Greeks" in Rom(A) (1:16). And then it was reused with an implication of equality between them in Rom(B) (2:9–10). Paul began to argue for the equality between Jews and Greeks/gentiles (3:9, 29–30). However, in Rom(C), there is an emphasis on gentiles as it is claimed that they could also become the people of God. In a sense, even the priority of gentiles to Jews is implied here. In this way, the more letters Paul wrote to the

Roman church, the more he revealed the tendency to emphasize the mission to gentiles.

Paul's wish was finally conveyed to the Romans. This appears in the declaration of confidence that the God of hope will fill them with all joy and peace in faith and give them hope overflowing with the power of the holy spirit (15:13). Paul emphasized "hope" by using it twice. Hope was defined as something that came from God to the Romans by the power of the holy spirit. It was previously described that salvation is achieved through hope (8:24), and they are also used in connection with the spirit of God. Then, when Paul used the word "hope," he wanted that the Romans would truly become the people of God. This includes both Jewish and gentile members of the Roman church.

In summary, Paul wanted the Romans to have an attitude of embracing their neighbors beyond the scope of church members. This includes missions not only to gentiles within the Roman church but also to those outside the church. With this, he hoped that salvation would come to them as well, making them the people of God. In this way, Paul emphasized the interest in the mission to gentiles as he concluded Rom(C). However, it is unclear whether the Jewish members of the Roman church followed Paul's teachings and opened their hearts to gentiles.

5. CLOSING PART (16:17–20)

At the end of Rom(C), Paul declared a blessing along with exhortation. However, having considered that the content of his exhortation was quite harsh, it is revealed that the power of those who criticized him among the Romans was quite strong. Still, Paul gave his blessing, revealing the end of a letter.

Paul's exhortation reflects the fact that the Romans were in a critical situation. This appears as an invitation to watch out for those who cause conflict or create obstacles contrary to the lessons they have learned, and even to recommend that they should leave such people (16:17). While Paul revealed that he had given various teachings to the Romans, he also hinted at the situation in which people who went against him caused conflict or created obstacles among them. This refers to a situation in which the Romans responded his instructions delivered in the previous letters differently. This aspect already appeared among the Galatians (Gal 5:12). Accordingly, in Rom(C), Paul suggested a break with those who were disrupting the church. They were probably some Jewish members who continuously criticized Paul. On the contrary, he was able to give this advice probably because of his confidence in the gospel he had preached.

A critique against those who should leave the church was described. They are defined as those who do not serve our Lord Jesus Christ but only serve their own bellies and who deceive the hearts of the innocent with subtle and flattering words (16:18). Having used two sets of contrasts, Paul depicted the situation the Romans found in themselves. First, while there were those who served our Lord Jesus Christ, there were also those who only served their own bellies. Here, a person who serves our Lord Jesus Christ means living as his servant, and a person who only serves his own belly refers to one living for his or her own benefit. Second, Paul put a contrast between the innocent people and those who deceive their minds with subtle and flattering words. Paul once criticized those who had misled the Galatians and the Corinthians with flashy words (Gal 5:10; 2 Cor 11:6). Accordingly, in Rom(C), Paul reacted sensitively to those who had cast doubts and raised objections to the gospel he had preached in Rom(A) and Rom(B). The theme of deceiving the hearts of the innocent with subtle and flattering words is reminiscent of the serpent who deceived Eve and then Adam by dictating flashy words (Gen 3:1–5). The Adam-typology seems to be used for the exhortation of the Romans. In consequence, the Romans were advised to turn away from such people. In this way, it is revealed that the Romans were divided on sides due to Paul's teachings.

At the same time, Paul also praised the Romans. It begins with the statement that he was happy because everyone heard their obedience (16:19a). When Paul mentioned their obedience, he hinted at the possibility that their faith became known to other churches in gentile areas. This description also appears in Rom(A) (1:8). They were those who needed to get away from those who only filled their own stomachs and deceived others. Paul then advised the Romans to be wise in what is good and foolish in what is evil (16:19b). This conveys the fact that choices can be made through the contrast between good and evil. Although Paul lamented that he had wanted to do good but did evil (7:19), he wanted the Romans to live by doing good. These teachings also remind readers of the instruction to do good and build up people (15:2; cf. 8:28). Moreover, as mentioned earlier, the contrast between good and evil is reminiscent of the tree of knowledge of good and evil. The typological allusion to Adam and Eve in the garden of Eden is implied in the contrast.

Then, an eschatological exhortation was given to the Romans. It is said that the God of peace will soon crush Satan under the feet of the Romans (16:20a). Paul mentioned Satan to the Romans for the first time. This seems to refer to the forces behind them leading to the direction of opposing him. Paul mentioned Satan to the Corinthians, alluding to the apostles of the Jerusalem church (2 Cor 11:15). However, when Paul used the term "Satan" in Rom(C), it is believed that he was referring to those who opposed the gospel among the Romans. In any case, the expression that Satan will be crushed under their feet reminds readers of the curse God gave to the serpent in the garden of Eden (Gen 3:15). This kind of association with Adam and Eve is a theme that appears from the beginning of Rom(C). In any case, the expression that the Romans will crush Satan under their feet conveys the immediate eschatological judgment. With this, Paul asked the Romans to reject those who had expressed negative views on the gospel. At the same time, he was confident of God's final victory over the evil power.

Finally, Paul gave words of greeting to the Romans. This is a blessing that the grace of our Lord Jesus be with them (16:20b). Paul ended Rom(C) with a blessing as he had done in the case of Rom(A) (16:24) and Rom(B) (15:33). Having often mentioned peace and grace in other letters, Paul mentioned the grace of our Lord Jesus only here in Rom(C). This reflects the fact that the relationship between Paul and the Romans was not good enough to bless them with unlimited love. In any case, as time passed, Paul focused more on the Lord Jesus in his writing.

To sum up, Paul was aware that conflict arose among the Romans due to differences in their positions toward him. This suggests that those who had criticized him were strong enough for the term "Satan" to be adopted. Accordingly, Paul warned that there would be eschatological judgment on those who did not follow Christ that he had delivered. This response also shows that Paul had a strong dedication to the mission he wanted to accomplish.

6. CONCLUSION.

Paul sent the third letter Rom(C) to the Romans. This is what Paul wrote in response to the people who criticized his statement in Rom(B) that the Law convicts of sin. Thus, Paul focused on the explanation of relationship between the Law and sin in Rom(C). The main idea is that sin took advantage afforded by the commandments and had led people to death. In this way, Paul avoided mentioning the Law directly and described it as being completed by loving neighbors at the concluding part. In Rom(C), Paul seems to have taken a reserved stance on the Law in order to win the hearts of the Romans. However, it seems that his expectations were ultimately unsatisfied.

In Rom(C), the conflict that Paul had with Romans is reflected. This is supported by the fact that dichotomous contrasts were heavily used. A representative example is the contrast between death and eternal life. In connection with this, contrasts such as between sin and grace and between the flesh and the spirit are used. This shows that Paul attempted to clearly form a battle line while simplifying the logic. Paul dramatically put his views in contrast with those of his opponents, trying to get them to agree with him. The dichotomous contrast was already shown in Galatians written at the time when the gentiles' challenge reached its peak.

The gospel played a central role in Paul's logic in Rom(C). This means that the core of the gospel, summarized in the death and resurrection of Christ, lies behind most of the narrative. Although this description was weakened in Rom(B) due to criticism of Jewish members, Paul emphasized it again in Rom(C). This is clearly reflected in the theme that the Romans had to move from the path of death to that of eternal life. Paul developed this kind of logic and applied it to love for neighbors based on God's love and became the basis for fulfilling the Law.

Paul expressed his opinion using the Adam-typology. This was to establish Adam as the ancestor of mankind beyond Abraham and to argue that not only Jews but also gentiles could become the people of God without any distinction. Accordingly, Paul used it explicitly with a reference to the "one to come" at the beginning of Rom(C) but also used it implicitly at the end. Accordingly, Paul argued for the legitimacy of mission to gentiles. Although Paul did not express outwardly, he expected the Romans to participate in the mission with financial support.

A strong willingness for the mission to gentiles was formed. This is revealed in the fact that the strength of contrast with Jews have gradually reduced in Rom(C). Rather, Paul's will to complete the mission to gentiles was further strengthened as he emphasized that God already told for them as revealed in the Bible. This position would not have been welcome to Jewish members who made up the majority of the Roman church. Nevertheless, Paul tried to persuade them and carry out this plan.

The exact location and time for the writing of Rom(C) has been unknown. Having considered the traffic situation at the time, it only suggests the possibility that Rom(C) was written about six months later than Rom(B). Unlike Rom(A) and Rom(B), there is no mention of Jerusalem in Rom(C). It seems to have been written while Paul was heading for Rome after finishing work in Jerusalem. If so, it appears that Paul wrote it in late 56 CE.

IV

Rom(D)

Paul sent the fourth letter, Rom(D). This dealt with the theme that because Jews had abandoned God's will, gentiles were given the opportunity to become the people of God. Accordingly, Paul taught that gentiles should not be arrogant in front of Jews; rather, they should be careful and humble before God. However, he said that God had not exclusively abandoned Jews. Nevertheless, Paul's gentile-oriented narrative cannot be denied. In Rom(D), Paul treated the relationship between Jews and gentiles in terms of salvation.

Rom(D) was written as Paul's response to the reaction of the Jewish members of the Roman church who had read Rom(C). It seems that they stopped criticizing Paul against his view on the Law because he had showed the reserved stance on it there. However, his argument that gentiles should be included into the people of God seemed to have offended Jewish members. Accordingly, they asked Paul for an explanation, and he had no choice but to reveal his opinion in Rom(D). This is unique in that it is described as belonging to the mystery of God. In any case, Paul never gave up the mission to gentiles.

Paul used a couple of metaphors in Rom(D). This is shown in the parable of the earthenware vessel and that of the olive tree. It seems that Paul used to adopt metaphor for the explanation of something he could not explain well. In contrast with Paul's use of few metaphors in the previous letters, metaphor was used to describe God's plan with regard to Jews and gentiles in Rom(D). However, it is not clear whether this narrative was effective for the Romans, especially those of Jewish origin.

Rom(D) can be divided into six sections. First, Paul's passion for his fellow countrymen was described as the introduction to the letter (9:1–5). Second, a discussion of God's election was dealt with (9:6–29). Third, God's plan of salvation was discussed in general (9:30—10:21). Fourth, God's mystery for the salvation of Jews and gentiles was mentioned (11:1—12:2). Fifth, the ethics of saints were presented (13:11-14). Sixth, the closing part was written (15:14-21; 16:25-27).

1. PAUL'S PASSION FOR JEWS (9:1-5).

Paul revealed the passion for his fellow Jews. This was about the descendants of God by promise rather than about his own people from the perspective of lineage. Paul would have had no choice but to mention the issue of the salvation of his own people in order to win the hearts of the Jewish members of the Roman church.

The beginning part of Rom(D) seems to have disappeared when it was compiled into the present form of Romans. The sender, the recipient, and greetings would have been recorded here. However, the compiler had no choice but to discard them because the beginning part of Rom(A) was already used. Accordingly, the current text seems to present the introduction to Rom(D). Paul here changed the subject to a new one, showing that it was independent of the previous letters. This is important in that it summarizes what Paul wanted to talk about in the following texts.

Paul defended himself from the beginning. It is said that he spoke of the truth in Christ and did not lie (9:1). Paul appealed to the Romans that he had been honest and sincere. It was once said to the Galatians that he had not lied before God (Gal 1:20) and claimed to the Corinthians that God knew that he had not lied (2 Cor 11:31). Paul said in Rom(B) that all people are liars, but only God is true (3:4). It is believed to be probably used for insincerity of Jewish members. However, in Rom(D), Paul not only said that he did not lie but also added that he told the truth. This implies that Paul wanted to address an important topic. On the other hand, it can be inferred that there were times when the Romans accused Paul of being a liar after reading Rom(C). This created a situation in which Paul had no choice but to defend himself. The fact that this statement appears at the beginning of Rom(D) implies that the debate between Paul and the Romans was serious.

Then, Paul expressed his sad feelings. This is revealed in the statements that he had great anxiety and constant pain in his heart and that his conscience testifies to this in the holy spirit (9:2). It should be noted that the holy spirit is connected with the issue of witness. The role of the spirit of God was once described as the one interceding for people with groaning in Rom(C) (8:27). Accordingly, in Rom(D), it could be said that one's conscience testifies in the holy spirit. In this way, Paul used the best expressions to inform the Romans, especially Jewish members, of his concern about them. Paul talked about the encounter with an important issue made him anger and painful. Here, it is important to identify what Paul claims to be true in the midst of his anxiety and pain. Having implied that his plan was not accepted by the Romans, Paul revealed the desire to carry out the mission to the end.

The reason for Paul's anxiety and pain was revealed. It is said that even though he had been cursed and cut off from Christ, he had something to convey to his brothers, that is, Jews (9:3). Paul stated that he could run the risk of his spiritual and religious life for them. The word "curse" was used to the Corinthians and the Galatians who had challenged him (1 Cor 12:3; 16:22; Gal 1:8–9; 3:13). And in Rom(B), it was used in relation to those who had persecuted the Romans (12:14; cf. 3:14). Then, in Rom(D), Paul applied it to himself in a context intended to bring benefit to fellow Jews. To this extent, it refers to their salvation. Just as Paul insisted in Rom(A) that Christ died for the salvation of sinners (5:6–10), he declared in Rom(D) that he would be cursed for his fellow Jews. While Paul took a critical stance toward Jews in Rom(B) (3:10), he showed himself to be filled with concern and worry about them in Rom(D). The difference shows that spiritual affection for Jewish members arose during his interactions with them. This was a strategic action taken for the mission to gentiles, which he believed was entrusted to him by God.

Now Paul introduced the content that caused him to be in pain and anxiety. For this purpose, the things that God gave to Jews were first described (9:4–5). Having defined Jews as Israelites, Paul said that they had been adopted as sons, that they had the divine glory and covenants, received the Law, the worship, and promises, that their ancestors were theirs, and that Christ was born of them in the flesh. The word "Israelites" refer to those of the saved people of God. Additionally, the presence of worship and promises shows that they were topics applied to Jews. Above all, the expression that the ancestors were theirs also means that God had been with Jews for generations. Lastly, according to Paul, the birth of Christ from them means that they were originally the objects of salvation. Although things given to Jews were also listed in Rom(B) (2:17–20), they were presented as a prerequisite for criticizing them. On the contrary, what was given to Jews in Rom(D) was beneficial to them. This reflects the fact that over time, Paul became concerned about the Jewish members of the Roman church who had criticized him. In addition, he developed affection to lead them on the right path from a spiritual point of view. In this way, having talked about his pain and anxiety, Paul described the grace that his brothers, his physical countrymen, had received from God.

In summary, Paul prioritized the concern and passion for fellow Jews. Here, the privileges that they received from God are listed. However, they were only listed to convey the fact that Jews had not enjoyed what they should have done. This was a preliminary step to change from a position of respect toward them to a position of criticizing them.

2. THE ELECTION OF GOD (9:6–29)

Paul discussed the issue of God's election. This means that God has chosen the people according to his will. Paul dealt with the issue of God's election based on people, events, and lessons from the Bible. It seems that his emphasis on the mission to gentiles in Rom(C) was provocative to the Jewish members of the Roman church.

Isaac and Jacob (9:6–13)

Paul first dealt with the case of Isaac and Jacob for the election of God. It is said that the election was done in accordance with God's promise and will. Paul revealed that the Romans were contesting his teachings and asserting their lineage privileges.

The authority of God's words was mentioned first. This is presupposed in the statement that the words of God do not appear to have been nullified (9:6a). Paul emphasized that the promise of God has been alive. It was once said in Rom(B) that the words of God have been entrusted to Jews (3:2). This reflects the privileges given to Jews. This kind of statement appears again in Rom(D). Paul used such a strong tone because his relationship with the Romans was not good enough to speak in a positive mode. In other words, this statement reflects the situation that they were reluctant to accept Paul's previous teachings. Accordingly, it is anticipated that the contents of the Rom(D) would develop in a direction that will cause considerable controversy.

Paul introduced the words of God for the definition of Israel. This is reflected in the statement that not all who are born of Israel are Israelites and not all of Abraham's seed are his children, but only those who are born of Isaac will be called his seed (9:6b–7). Having borrowed these verses from the Bible, Paul described the formation of God's people. Paul once wrote about the children and people of God with a comparison between Abraham's two sons, Ishmael and Isaac, in Galatians (Gal 3:16; 4:21—5:1). However, only Isaac was mentioned in Rom(D). Paul tried to prevent the Romans from accessing the issue of Abraham's seed from a physical perspective. This means that only through a legitimate son Isaac can they be recognized as Abraham's descendants. With these words, Paul first tried to gain the consent of the Jewish members of the Roman church.

A more specific interpretation was presented regarding the descendants of Abraham. It is said that the children of the flesh are not the children of God, but the children of promise are considered the seed of Abraham (9:8). Having emphasized God's promise and excluded the children of the flesh, Paul eliminated Ishmael from the category of God's promised descendants. In regard to becoming the children of God, the promise comes to the fore. Paul emphasized the promise of God to the Galatians about Christ (Gal 3:13–22). However, in Rom(D), the promise was mentioned in relation to the issue of all people becoming the children of God. This interpretation of Paul leaves room for the possibility that among Jewish members who consider themselves descendants of promise, there may be some who do not fall into this category. By doing this, Paul opened up the possibility for gentiles to become the children of God. This saying would have made Jewish members shocked.

Paul described the promise given to Abraham more clearly. This refers to the promise of God that Sarah would have a son at this time following year (9:9). Paul used this story to emphasize that Isaac was the son born by promise. In fact, Abraham was so old at the time that it was almost impossible for this promise to come true (Gen 18:10). However, God made the impossible possible and kept the promise as written in Rom(A) (4:18–21). Paul used Abraham's story because he wanted to let Jewish members know that God could also make gentiles his people beyond the Jewish lineage. This defines God as the one who makes the impossible possible. Having based on paradoxical logic, Paul made Jewish members shocked with regard to the election of God.

The scope of the promise has become narrower. This is found in the description that while Rebecca became pregnant and had not yet given birth to children, the promise was given to the person whom God had called (9:10–11). Paul mentioned that the descendants that God had promised to Abraham would be born through Rebecca, Isaac's wife, and that even though they had not done anything good or evil before they were born, God chose one baby only according to his will (Gen 25:19–26). This repeats the lesson that Abraham's descendants were determined not by lineage but by God's promise. Paul emphasized that the election of God was based on promise. This is also a preparatory work to unfold the logic that even gentiles could be elected by God as his people.

Paul talked about the reversal of birth order. It is said that God told Rebecca, "The older will serve the younger" (9:12; cf. Gen 25:23). Here another verse was cited, saying that God loved Jacob but hated Esau (9:13; cf. Mal 1:2–3). Having paid attention to the issue of reversal, Paul insisted that lineage order cannot take precedence. This conveys a lesson that Jews, who regarded themselves as descendants of legitimate children, may end up serving gentiles, who were considered lesser in terms of faith. Having emphasized the sovereign election of God, Paul conveyed a lesson that the promises given to Jews could be made available to gentiles. In the end, Paul raised a counterargument to Jews' claim of privileges based on lineage. Paul presented the principle of "Jews first and then Greeks" in Rom(A) (1:16) and then mentioned equality between Jews and gentiles in Rom(B) (2:9–10; 3:29–30). Subsequently, in Rom(C), interest in gentiles was amplified (15:9–12). Finally, in Rom(D), Paul even hinted at a reversal between Jews and gentiles. Accordingly, it was painful for Paul that his own people, Jews, might have been abandoned by God. The logic that gentiles could be elected was underlying here. This kind of instruction was shocking to Jewish members. Thus, Jewish members should rely solely on God's election, not their lineage.

In summary, Paul emphasized the promise of God with regard to the true descendants of Abraham, that is, the people of God. It seems that having emphasized the election of God according to the promise, Paul might offend the Jewish members of the Roman church. According to him, the status of Jews and gentiles could be reversed. This made readers anticipate that God's will for gentiles will be treated in the following texts.

Moses and Pharaoh (9:14–18)

Paul presented the case of Moses and Pharaoh to explain the election of God. It has been written to prevent the Romans from raising objections to God's will. Special mention was made of the events that took place among the gentiles. This description was also intended to open the way for gentiles to become the people of God.

An introductory phrase was presented in order to talk about the election of God. It is said that there can be no unrighteousness with God (9:14). With this expression, Paul presented the view that God was right when he had chosen Isaac and Jacob and defined only those who had come down through them as the descendants of Abraham. This is something that God did voluntarily, so no one could raise an objection. With these expressions, Paul revealed the intention to continue to describe God's omnipotent election. Even if the Jewish members of the Roman church agreed with God's election itself, they would disagreed with whether it included gentiles.

Paul cited a verse that had been passed down to Moses. It is said that God will have mercy on those whom he will have mercy on and will have pity on those who will have pity on (9:15). Having quoted this verse from Exodus, Paul wanted to convey the intention of God to show himself to Moses (Exod 33:19). This was cited to emphasize the election of God in order to show that no one can object to his will. The underlying intention here is that just as Paul did not object to the belief that Jews had been chosen, the Romans should not object even if God makes a different choice in the future. This implies that the Romans should not interfere with the mission to gentiles that Paul wanted to carry out according to the will of God.

In response, Paul immediately explained why he quoted a verse from the Bible. This is found in the statement that this is not because of those who want, nor because of those who run, but because of God who is merciful (9:16). With this saying, Paul conveyed that there was no place for human intentions to be involved. The saying that it is not because of someone who wants it excludes human intention. In addition, the fact that it is not caused by a person running also excludes human effort. Paul said that the question of whether or not one is chosen depends solely on the will of God. This statement is based on the premise that no one among the Romans should object to God's election of gentiles. With this, Paul took preliminary steps to request the Romans to support the mission to gentiles that should be carried out immediately. However, it is not clear whether Jewish members agreed to this.

Paul once again quoted a verse from the Bible to strengthen his teaching. It is said that God appointed Pharaoh, so that through him God might show his power and spread his name throughout the earth (9:17). Having quoted it from Exodus, Paul emphasized the fact that Moses chose Pharaoh to show the power of God (Exod 9:16). God used Pharaoh, representing gentiles at that time, as a tool for what he had wanted to do. Paul heightened the fact that God is the one who chooses even those who oppose him and uses them for his name. This also conveys to the Romans an instruction that God can choose any type of person for his work. Paul wanted to show that he had been entrusted the mission to gentiles by God and that the Romans should provide support for this purpose.

The conclusion is presented here. This is found in the saying that God has mercy on those he chooses and sometimes uses those he chooses in a stubborn way (9:18). With this description, Paul made a contrast between Moses and Pharaoh. Whereas Moses worked with God's mercy, Pharaoh became hardened before God. Having mentioned them, Paul presented an extreme contrast between those who respond to God's election and those who reject it. This contrast made the Romans choose what kind of person they should be before God. In addition to this, it is necessary to think about the situation between Paul and the Romans. As shown before, the fact that Paul emphasized God's election in Rom(D) reflects the fact that the Romans had raised questions about this after reading Rom(C) in which the election of gentiles were described (15:9–12). Accordingly, when Paul sent Rom(D), he had to say that such a choice belongs entirely to God and is not guaranteed by lineage. Paul's argument was correct according to his logic. However, it was difficult to be accepted by Jewish members who had been obsessed with the tradition of their election for a long time.

To sum up, Paul emphasized the omnipotent election of God with the story of Moses and Pharaoh. Having described them, he wanted to show that the matter of becoming God's people depends not on lineage but on his election. Accordingly, the premise was laid here to assert that both Jews and gentiles can become the people of God according to his will. It seems that Paul expected the Romans to join him in the mission to gentiles. However, Jewish members would have been indifferent to reality.

Jews and Gentiles (9:19-29)

Paul taught the election of God with an analogy of potter. The main theme is that God chooses people according to his will. Paul opened the way for the election of gentiles that no one could dispute.

The election of God was highlighted once again with two rhetorical questions. This appears in the description that people cannot point out God's faults or oppose him (9:19). Paul believed that God is perfect and that he is not someone with whom people can argue. His belief reflects the fact that there were some Romans who challenged him against his insistence on the election of gentiles. There were some who had cast doubts and raised questions about the legitimacy of mission to gentiles. Thus, he had to give them an answer that the Romans should obey as God elects his people.

Accordingly, Paul taught the Romans to obey the will of God with rhetorical questions. It has been written that a person cannot dare to question God and that a created object cannot ask its creator why he or she was made like this (9:20). Paul emphasized the sovereign will of God for the election of his people. The fact that the election of God was mentioned several times indicates that it was such an important topic. Paul wrote little about the issue of God's election in Rom(A), Rom(B), and Rom(C). The fact that this issue was specifically mentioned in Rom(D) shows his obsession with the mission to gentiles. This claim would have brought about opposition from Jewish members.

The parable of potter was given as an example. This appears in the saying that the potter has the authority to make out of clay vessels, one for noble use and the other for ignoble use (9:21). Paul highlighted the contrast between vessels to be used honorably and those to be used ignominiously. This parable comes from Jeremiah (Jer 18:4) and conveys the meaning that a potter can make a vessel as he pleases. With this, Paul delivered the instruction that God can choose people according to his will. This once again conveys the implication that Jews cannot blame God for electing gentiles. Jewish members would have had no choice but to agree to some extent with Paul's claims.

Paul conveyed the interpretation of the two types of vessels with rhetorical questions. This is seen in the contrast between vessels of wrath and those of mercy (9:22-23). Paul defined the vessels of wrath as those whom God elected to destroy in order to let them know his power, while he defined the vessels of mercy as those whom God prepared to let them know the riches of his glory. God had poured out his wrath on those who did not live according to his will, so that they would know his power. When Paul used the word "wrath," the Romans would have been alert to his teaching because they had already learned enough about it in Rom(B) (1:18—2:11). Therefore, the Romans, especially Jewish members, received an instruction that they had to obey God's will in order to avoid the wrath. On the other hand, God also chose people to make known the abundance of his glory. The vessels of mercy refer to those who have been elected by God to receive his glory in abundance. In this way, Paul taught the Romans that it was important to join this class.

The vessel of mercy was interpreted specifically. This refers not only to Jews but also to those called by God among gentiles (9:24). Paul focused on the issue of being elected by God or not, rather than the racial distinction between Jews and gentiles. This clearly presented a path for gentiles to become God's people. As a result, the relationship with God was important not only for Jews but also for gentiles. Since the election of God was entirely dependent on his sovereign will, both Jews and gentiles had to obey him. Having dealt with this issue, Paul presented the justification for the mission to gentiles. This logic has a power that no one in the Roman church can reject.

Paul cited a verse from the Bible to emphasize the election of God. This is found in the citation from Hosea that God will call those who are not his people and love those he did not love (9:25; Hos 2:23). Paul then quoted another verse, which says that even though they are not the people of God, they will be called sons of the living God (9:26; Hos 1:10). These two verses were quoted to support the argument that God chooses those who were not his people as his beloved people and sons. Having quoted them, Paul insisted that the gentiles had been called the people and the adopted sons of God. These quotations show a focus on the gentiles immediately after presenting the parable of the vessels. Having used the writings of Hosea the prophet, Paul seemed to have tried to claim that the teachings he was preaching were the gospel (cf. 1:2).

A verse was also cited from Isaiah. It is said that although the number of the children of Israel is like the sand of the sea, only a remnant will be saved, and that the Lord will fulfill his word on the earth and quickly put it into effect (9:27–28; Isa 10:22–23). Paul insisted that not all Jews would be saved; rather, only those who are elected by God will be saved. Paul applied this principle to the Romans, having argued that among them, Jewish members could not obtain the status of God's people even due to their lineage. With this, Paul tried to support the proposition that God calls his people even among gentiles. Then, another message was provided in that the time of salvation is near. This is a teaching to the Romans, especially those of Jewish origin, not to be conceited but to wait more humbly before God for election. With this, Paul warned some of the Romans who had cast doubts on his mission to gentiles. Although the Jewish members of the Roman church knew about the passages quoted above, they probably resented Paul applying those to them.

Paul once again quoted some words from Isaiah. It is said that if the Lord Almighty had not left mankind with seed, they would have become like Sodom and Gomorrah (9:29; Isa 1:9). Paul presented Sodom and Gomorrah as synonyms for the judgment carried out by God. This was written to inform that because of God's grace, the Romans had survived rather than being destroyed like the people of Sodom and Gomorrah. This shows that Paul emphasized God's grace and election. Accordingly, the Romans should not be arrogant but should live as people who have been chosen by God. Having argued for it, Paul conveyed to the Romans, especially those of Jewish origin, that their previous traditions regarding their status as God's people had not been always preserved. This shows that Paul received strong claims from the Romans that they were the people of God after reading Rom(C). Accordingly, he delivered this teaching in Rom(D) with the hope that they would know the will of God and be reborn as his chosen people.

In summary, Paul emphasized the will of God by quoting several verses from the Bible. They focus on the prophecy that gentiles can be elected as the people of God. At the same time, Paul quietly demanded that the Romans, especially Jewish members, give up their privileges. This was ultimately a measure to justify the mission to gentiles he had to carry out. However, it is unclear whether Jewish members obediently abandoned their religious traditions and accepted Paul's new interpretation.

3. THE WAY OF SALVATION (9:30—10:21)

Paul discussed the issue of salvation. It was claimed that God calls not only Jews but also gentiles as his people. To this end, Paul presented faith in the core of the gospel as a condition for salvation. This opened the way for gentiles to become the saved people of God without any restrictions.

Righteousness by Faith (9:30–33)

Paul again mentioned the issue of righteousness by faith. Having mentioned that Jews were unable to achieve it but gentiles acquired it, Paul suggested a reversal between the two groups of people. Once again the contrast between faith and the works of the Law appears in order to aim at the mission to gentiles. This is considered a basic work to deal with the path to salvation.

The issue of reversal between Jews and gentiles was presented. This is found in the contrast between the righteousness obtained by the gentiles through faith and Israel's failure to fulfill the Law (9:30–31). Paul used the contrast to focus on the election of gentiles by God. First, it is necessary to look at what Paul described about gentiles. He told that they obtained righteousness even though they did not follow the Law (9:30). In relation to this, the reversal between Israel and gentiles is an important theme in Rom(D). Having listed the theological foundation for the reversal between the two with the story of Jacob and Esau, Paul put an emphasis on the election of people by his will and a person's faith. Even though Paul faced severe resistance from Jewish members regarding God's election of gentiles, Paul did not abandon his belief in their inclusion into the people of God without keeping the law of righteousness. Accordingly, in Rom(D), Paul could not help but emphasize the righteousness of God by faith. Second, the fate of Jews was mentioned in the statement that Israel, who followed the law of righteousness, did not reach it (9:31). Although he acknowledged that the Law leads to righteousness, Paul argued that Jews' attempt to obtain righteousness by keeping it had failed. This shows Paul's efforts to lead them in the direction of having faith. However, Paul's attempt would have been difficult to obtain the consent of Jewish members who did not want to give up their privilege.

A verse was cited from the Bible in relation to the stumbling stones. It is said that God will place stumbling blocks and rocks in Zion, so that those who believe in him would not be put to shame (9:33; Isa 28:16). The stumbling blocks in Zion makes readers think of Christ. With an allusion to Christ, Paul taught that if Jews did not have faith in God, who sent Jesus Christ to Israel, not only they would not be justified but also would actually be put to shame. Conversely, the above quote provides the lesson that gentiles can be justified by faith in God as Christ did. This shows that Paul continuously emphasized faith to the Romans, so that the gentiles could be included into the people of God.

In summary, Paul was heartbroken because Jews could not reach the goal due to the works of the Law. On the other hand, having presented a path to salvation, Paul emphasized that gentiles reached righteousness by faith. With this, Paul began to describe gentiles more favorably than Jews. This is given as a result of God's election.

Paul's Desire for the Salvation of Israel (10:1–7)

Paul expressed the desire for Israel to be saved. The righteousness is not achieved through the methods pursued by Jews but is revealed through the faith of Christ. Paul described salvation centered on Christ, who became the end of the Law. Paul's desire for the salvation of Israel makes it possible to conclude that Jewish members did not reach Paul's standard.

The attachment to Jews was revealed. This is found in the statement that Paul's desire for Israel was their salvation (10:1). This is in line with what he exclaimed at the beginning of Rom(D), hoping that he would be cursed and cut off from Christ for the sake of his brothers, his relatives in the flesh (9:3). The wish was for God to save Israel, Jews. Paul made this statement so that the Jewish members of the Roman church could be saved. Paul, who criticized the stubbornness of Jews in Rom(B), expressed his earnest hope for their salvation in Rom(D).

Paul made an evaluation of Jewish members in relation to faith. It is insisted that they were zealous for God but did not follow correct knowledge (10:2). Paul had both positive and negative sides to them. Paul often spoke to the Corinthians about knowledge, which meant both the principles of world (1 Cor 13:2, 8) and the theological interpretation of the creation of universe (1 Cor 8:6). However, in Rom(D), knowledge was described in relation to the method of salvation for Jews. Having used the word "knowledge" from a soteriological perspective, Paul truly wanted to lead Jewish members to salvation from his own perspective. Although Jews had knowledge that they would be saved if they diligently followed the Law, Paul pointed out that it was not correct. In this way, Paul made them to be alert.

The incorrect knowledge of Jews was also mentioned. It is said that because they sought to establish their own righteousness, they did not submit to the righteousness of God (10:3). Paul used the expression for the first time that Jews had sought to establish their own righteousness. Having used it, Paul strongly criticized the wrong attitude of the Romans, especially Jewish members. This reminds readers of previous statement that Jews pursued the law of righteousness (9:30–31). It was to establish a justification for the proclamation of the gospel to gentiles. Anyway, no matter what, he wanted to help Jewish members gain righteousness following the will of God. This shows that Jewish members did not accept the direction suggested by Paul.

Paul mentioned Christ in connection with the righteousness of God. It is said that Christ became the end of the Law to bring about righteousness for everyone who believes in God (10:4). Paul described the role of Christ in relation to righteousness. This tendency has already been attempted in previous letters. In Rom(A), Paul wrote that people were justified by the blood of Christ (5:9). Subsequently, in Rom(B), Christ Jesus was defined as the righteousness of God revealed outside of the Law (3:21). In Rom(C), Paul also declared that those who had been predestined to be conformed to the image of the Son of God were justified (8:29–30). Having based on the description of Christ, Paul stated in Rom(D) that Christ is the end of the Law to achieve righteousness for those who have faith in God. The connection between the Law and Christ appears here for the first time. This shows that Paul took a reserved stance on the Law in Rom(D) as he had done in Rom(C) (7:12, 14; 13:8, 10). This was an effort to improve his relationship with the Romans by accepting their critiques against his negative view on the Law and by suggesting Christ as the way to salvation.

Then, the relationship of the Law to righteousness was described. It is revealed in what Moses had said: one who practices the righteousness that is by the Law must live by that righteousness (10:5). Paul cited a verse from Leviticus (Lev 18:5), which was already used in Galatians to make an extreme critique that the Law was given for transgression (Gal 3:12). On the other hand, in Rom(D), having stated in the preceding verse that Christ was the end of the Law to achieve righteousness for all believers, Paul immediately mentioned righteousness that is by the Law. This shows a position that recognizes the Law to some extent. In particular, the practice of righteousness that is by the Law was mentioned instead of the works of the Law. However, it seems that Paul quoted the verse based on the premise that people cannot keep all the articles of the Laws. His reserved stance on the Law shown in Rom(C) continued here so that Paul could win the hearts of Jewish members in any way possible. However, an interpretation is underlying here in that righteousness can never be achieved by keeping the Law.

Paul personified righteousness that is by faith. This is found in the presentation of what righteousness that is by faith said (10:6a). Whereas Paul once personified sin in Rom(C) (7:8), he personified righteousness that is by faith in Rom(D). Although this is in contrast with the righteousness that is by the Law mentioned just before, it shows a position of comparative advantage for righteousness that is by faith. Paul emphasized it and seemed to have used this method of expression to make the Romans to pay attention to the gospel focusing on faith in God.

The contents of righteousness by faith were listed in the form of contrast. It is stated that no one should say, "Will a man ascend to heaven?" because this is to bring Christ down and that no one should say, "Will a man descend into the abyss?" because this is to bring Christ up from the dead (10:6b-7). Paul sought to explain righteousness by faith with a pair of paralleled sayings. The former was taken from Deuteronomy (Deut 30:12-13), where God's command was replaced by Christ. Paul substituted "to bring Christ down" for the expression that someone should bring God's command down to people to hear them. This was possible because Christ Jesus was depicted as the one at the right hand of God in Rom(A) (8:34). Anyway, Paul said that even if a person ascends to heaven, he or she cannot bring Christ down with him or her. As recorded in Rom(A), only God, who gave his Son for sinners, can send Christ back to the world (5:8). In the latter case, the term "sea" in Deuteronomy was replaced by "abyss" in Rom(D). Paul thought that it was more impossible to bring Christ back from the bottomless pit than to bring God's command across the sea. This description was possible because Paul had already used the expression several times that God raised Jesus Christ from the dead. This means that no one but God can raise Christ from the bottomless pit. In the above parallel, Paul replaced God's commands by Christ. As his coming and resurrection are mentioned, righteousness by faith in God is presented as being given by not rebelling against what God has done. As a result, Paul increasingly focused on Christ and emphasized righteousness by faith. Likewise, in Rom(D), Paul insisted on righteousness by faith in God and emphasized the fact that God's will cannot be changed by man. This also suggests that the door to missions to gentiles was opened.

In summary, Paul argued that Jewish members should follow Christ and attain righteousness by faith in God. This is essential because it is only in accordance with what God wants. Accordingly, Paul desperately wanted Jewish members to participate in salvation. It is, however, doubtful whether his teachings, which were so focused on Christ, were accepted by them.

Confession as the Way to Salvation (10:8–13)

Paul described how to be saved. The salvation resulted from acknowledging Jesus as Lord and believing that God raised him from the dead. Paul consistently described the core of the gospel in connection with salvation. As a result, the passion for the mission to gentiles did not subside.

Paul's interpretation of what had been said earlier about righteousness by faith was presented. This begins with the introductory phrase, "Then what do you say?" and states that the word is near to man in his mouth and in his heart, that is, the word of faith (10:8). Paul changed a passage from Deuteronomy to suit his own purposes (Deut 30:14). "Moses' command" was changed to "word" in order to convey the meaning that God's words have been close to people (cf. 9:6). At the same time, Paul wanted to claim that they were the words of faith that he had preached. This means that the teachings he delivered were closer to what God had wanted to convey than the commands of Moses or the Law. In the end, he taught the Romans that since he had delivered the words of God, which went beyond the Law of Moses, they had to keep them. Ultimately, the underlying meaning here is that the gospel of Jesus Christ preached by Paul was the words of God.

Paul presented a way to salvation. This appears in the declaration that if a person confesses with his or her mouth Jesus as Lord and believes that God raised him from the dead, he or she will be saved (10:9). Paul listed two elements for salvation. One is to acknowledge Jesus as Lord, and the other is to believe that God raised him from the dead. Paul presented a way to salvation by combining the two elements for the first time. This was done based on the recognition of God's omnipotence. Paul once declared to the Corinthians that they could confess Jesus as Lord with the spirit (1 Cor 12:3). However, this was not related to the issue of salvation. On the other hand, in Rom(D), Paul described the confession in connection with the issue of salvation. Then, it is necessary to discuss the theme of raising Jesus Christ from the dead related to salvation. Paul already claimed it in Rom(A) (5:10). In Rom(C), it has been argued that the Romans should also gain new life by imitating Christ who rose from the dead (6:3–11). Here, new life means a state of salvation. Accordingly, in Rom(D), it was possible for Paul to insist that one must believe in God who had raised him from the dead to be saved. In this way, the death and resurrection of Christ were important in Paul's theology from a soteriological perspective. They constitute the core of the gospel, which Paul strongly preached to the Romans. This is to accept the character of God who makes the impossible possible, as recorded in Rom(A) (4:17–22). Paul's argument centered on the Lord Jesus seems to have contained elements that were difficult for Jewish members to accept.

The explanation of how to achieve salvation has been further supplemented. This is found in the explanation that a person believes with his or her heart, resulting in righteousness, and confesses with his or her mouth, resulting in salvation (10:10). Here Paul attempted two sets of parallels. The first one appears between believing with the heart and confessing with the mouth, and the second one is between righteousness and salvation. Having presented the theme of reaching righteousness by faith in God in Rom(A) (1:17; 4:13), Paul placed righteousness in a close relationship with salvation (5:8). Accordingly, in Rom(D), it was able to be stated that believing with one's heart leads him or her to righteousness. Here righteousness is inseparable from salvation. Then, having mentioned the word "confess" twice in a row, Paul presented it as a way to express one's belief in what he or she believes. However, Jewish members should have felt burdened by the fact that the path to salvation was presented centered around Christ, not the Law.

Paul quoted a verse from the Bible to support his insistence. It is said that anyone who believes in God will not be put to shame (10:11; Isa 28:16). Paul linked belief in God with "not being put to shame." The word "shame" was once used in relation to issues of faith (9:33). Having used the word "everyone" here, Paul opened up the possibility that not only Jews but also gentiles could be saved if they had faith. In this way, Paul consistently insisted that faith in God was an essential element for salvation.

The opportunity for salvation was described as being the same for everyone. This is first confirmed by the declaration of no discrimination to Jews or Greeks (10:12a). Paul argued that both Jews and Greeks could achieve salvation equally. This shows a difference from the expression "Jews first, then Greeks" with discrimination in Rom(A) (1:16) and then that without discrimination in Rom(B) (2:9–10). However, after raising interest in the nations in Rom(C) (15:9–12), the attention to gentiles was getting bigger in Rom(D) (9:30–33). Accordingly, the expression "Jews or Greeks" could be used in the context of no distinction between them.

In this way, the more letters Paul sent to the Roman church, the more he emphasized the equal opportunity for salvation given to Jews and Greeks. Paul's claim would have made the Jewish members, who made up the majority of the Roman church, shocked.

Paul insisted that God does not discriminate. This is because God is the one Lord and is rich to all who call on him (10:12b). Paul emphasized that God is so rich that he calls all people without discrimination. This means that salvation comes without discrimination to those who call on God, whether Jews or Greeks. Having emphasized the wealth of God, Paul revealed the intention to embrace countless gentiles as the people of God. Regarding this, even when Paul wrote Rom(D), he tried to make both Jews and Greeks accept the gospel in order that they would be the saved people of God.

Here, a method of salvation is presented. This appears in the instruction that everyone who calls on the name of the Lord will be saved (10:13). Paul presented the element of calling on the name of the Lord as an essential premise for salvation. This teaching appears for the first time in Rom(D) in addition to the previous elements, confessing and believing, related with salvation (10:9). While Paul focused on God's efforts to save people in Rom(A) (5:6–10), he emphasized man's efforts toward God in Rom(D). This is a change in perspective that began to appear in Rom(C). Anyway, Paul presented a method for the salvation of gentiles. In any case, Paul tried to elicit the testimony of the Romans, especially Jewish members. This description can be said to be Paul's attempt to instill faith of Jesus Christ among the Romans as time passed.

In summary, Paul emphasized the fact that gentiles, along with Jews, were able to be saved people of God. This is achieved through faith and confession in the death and resurrection of Christ, which is the core of the gospel. However, Jewish members would not have easily accepted Paul's teachings because it would have been difficult for them to abandon the traditions they had upheld.

The Way of Faith (10:14–21)

Paul emphasized that the path to salvation is open to gentiles beyond Jews. This was suggested that the words of Christ had already been preached to them. In this way, Paul attempted to write a narrative that would gradually open the door to gentiles.

Four rhetorical questions appear in succession. They are as follows: "For how shall they call on him in whom they have not believed?"; "How shall they believe in him of whom they have not heard?"; "How shall they hear without someone preaching to them?"; and "How shall they preach unless they have been sent?" (10:14–15a). Having written them, Paul mentioned the steps leading up to calling on the Lord. This means that one cannot call on whom he or she does not believe, no one can believe in the one of whom he or she has not heard, one cannot hear without preaching, and no one can preach without being sent. Paul insisted that God sent Jesus Christ as well as Paul. While the obedience to the gospel was emphasized in the previous letters, hearing the message of Jesus Christ sent by God and calling on his name were presented as the way leading to salvation in Rom(D). In this way, Paul emphasized that everyone is in a position to call on God to be saved.

A series of verses were quoted from the Bible. First, it is said that the feet of a person who spreads good news are beautiful (10:15b; Isa 52:7). Paul quoted it to emphasize the role of preaching good news. While the gospel was defined as the prophecies of prophets about the Son of God in Rom(A) (1:2), the one who preached the gospel was praised here in Rom(D). Having quoted this, Paul presented himself as a servant sent by God to spread good news, that is, the gospel. However, there would not have been many Romans who easily accepted Paul's confidence in the gospel. Otherwise, there would have been no need for Paul to write four letters.

Paul dealt with a daunting reality. This appears in the statement that not all people obeyed the gospel, along with a quotation, "Who has believed our message?" (10:16; Isa. 53:1). Paul pointed out that the prophet Isaiah had received God's command and proclaimed it; however, Israelites did not accept it. This implies that it was the case even at the time when Paul preached the gospel. This also allows readers to understand the relationship between Paul and the Romans. If Paul had been welcomed by them even through letters, there would have been no need to write four letters. The fact that he had to respond to the continued questions and critiques meant that his claims were not accepted. In any case, it is important to note that just as Paul had quoted several verses from the Bible in order to emphasize the mission to gentiles in Rom(C) (15:9–12), the same tendency appeared in Rom(D). In this way, Paul relied on the Bible to assert the legitimacy of preaching the gospel to gentiles.

A conclusion was made regarding faith. It has been written, "Consequently, faith comes from hearing the message, and message is heard through the words of Christ" (10:17). Paul emphasized faith that begins with hearing the words of Christ. This kind of pattern was already shown to the Galatians in connection with the spirit (Gal 3:1–5). It is important that Christ is emphasized here. However, since the expression of "words of Christ" was used for the first here, it is not clear exactly what it means. The words of Christ could means either what Christ said or what was said about Christ. The latter should be preferred here, since Paul had not described anything that Christ preached directly. If so, this would mean the gospel. It can be said that although the Romans had to accept the gospel, it seems that reality have gone against Paul's expectations.

Paul insisted that everyone hear the word. This is revealed by the rhetorical question of whether they had not heard; the expected answer was, "Yes, we have heard" (10:18a). Paul claimed that everyone in the world heard the message. To support this, he quoted a verse from the Bible: "Their voice has gone out into all the earth, and their words to the ends of the earth" (10:18b; Joel 2:32). Paul clearly claimed not only that he had preached the gospel to the Romans but also that the gospel had been already widely known to people all over the world. This was written for the purpose of preventing the Romans from making excuses for not having heard the message of God's will. With these descriptions, Paul showed that the Romans did not fully accept the gospel he had preached.

An attempt was made to leave Jews without excuse. This is found in the rhetorical question that asks whether Israel did not know (10:19a). Paul asked Jewish members directly. This requires an answer that they absolutely knew. At the same time, Paul quoted the words of Moses written in Deuteronomy: "I will make you envious by those who are not a nation; I will make you angry by a nation that has no understanding" (10:19b; Deut 32:21). This means that God would give grace to the Israelites through gentiles who had not been God's people to the point of making them jealous. Having quoted this verse, Paul emphasized the necessity of spreading the gospel to gentiles. According to Paul's logic, his missionary work to gentiles ultimately provides a clue that opens the way to salvation for Jews. Paul excused himself to the Romans for trying to preach the gospel to gentiles as far as Spain.

Paul once again cited a verse from the Bible to support his claim. This was quoted from the writing of Isaiah for the validity of the mission to gentiles and critique against Jews (10:20–21). First, it tells that God revealed himself to those who had not sought him and appeared to those who had not asked for him (Isa 65:1). Paul wanted to say that

God sought and found all people in the world beyond Jews. Something like this was described in Rom(B), where it was said that God reveals his divinity in creation (1:20). However, it is said in Rom(D), God reveals himself directly to people. Paul insisted that when he had preached the gospel to gentiles, they found God and believed in him. Thus, Jews could not make any excuse. It is said that God has stretched out his hands all day long to people who disobeyed and spoke contrary (Isa 65:2). With this quotation, Paul criticized Jews for not accepting the words of God. It is to say that Jewish members did not properly accept the gospel. At the same time, it provided them with the legitimacy of mission to gentiles.

In summary, Paul presented the argument that because God has revealed himself to all people in the world, they should believe in him. To them belong Jews as well as gentiles. By doing this, Paul presented the justification for the mission to gentiles. Rather, he emphasized that the missions to gentiles should be carried out to a degree that would make Jews jealous.

4. THE MYSTERY OF GOD (11:1 — 12:2)

Paul described the plan that God had for Jews and gentiles. It was gentiles that made Jews jealous of them and have a desire for salvation. With this, Paul insisted that although God's plan for the salvation of Jews was weak, it was still maintained. This narrative conveys the fact that both Jews and gentiles were under God's plan of salvation. Having defined it as God's mystery, Paul confessed his faith in God.

Jews (11:1–12)

Paul described God as not completely abandoning Jews. It was ordained that the door was widely open for the salvation of gentiles merely for strategic purposes. Accordingly, Paul asked Jewish members to become God's chosen remnants.

God's plan for the salvation of Jews was addressed with a rhetorical question. This appears in the form of "Did God reject his people?" and the expected answer is "by no means!" (11:1a). Paul argued that God had not abandoned his people. In addition, in order to strengthen his argument, Paul announced that he was an Israelite, a descendant of Abraham, and a Jew from the tribe of Benjamin (11:1b). In other words, having put an emphasis on his Jewishness, Paul did not want Jews to be kicked out of God's people. Once to the Corinthians did Paul identify himself as a Hebrew, an Israelite, and a descendant of Abraham, and then defined himself as a servant of Christ (2 Cor 11:22-23). This was made in his defense against the challenge of some Corinthians sponsored by Cephas, a representative sent by the Jerusalem church (1 Cor 1:12). Similarly, in the case of Rom(D), when Paul had been criticized by Jewish members against the mission to gentiles, he tried to gain their consent by introducing his identity. It was used to be a powerful weapon in religious terms. Nevertheless, Paul did not have any negative attitude or antipathy toward his fellow countrymen, Jews. Rather, Paul expressed the desire for them to be saved.

Paul spoke of God's consistency of caring for Jews. This is found in the statement that God did not abandon his people, whom he foreknew (11:2a). Having stated God's maintenance of Jews as his people twice, Paul strengthened the view that Jews had been never abandoned by God from his people. It is necessary to examine the process by which Paul's interest in Jews and gentiles changed. In Rom(A), Paul opened the door to gentiles by emphasizing that Abraham had been given the promise at the time of uncircumcision (4:10-11). Then, in Rom(B), the role of the Law in distinguishing between circumcision and uncircumcision was broken down, and equality between Jews and gentiles was presented (2:25-29). Above all, in Rom(C), it is stated that Christ became a follower of circumcision to confirm the promises given to the ancestors and to ensure that gentiles also receive God's mercy (15:8-9). With this, the status of gentiles came to the fore. On the other hand, in Rom(D), the earnest desire for the salvation of Jews was revealed (10:1, etc.). This shows that they are far from salvation. In any case, Paul did not want to let go of God's interest and love for his fellow Jews. This was also written with the hope that Jewish members would change from a critical position to a friendly one toward him.

With regard to the care of God, an incident of Elijah was introduced. This is the incident in which Elijah accused Israel to God; since Ahab, the king of Israel, had killed the prophets and tore down the altars of the Lord, Elijah said that although he himself survived, his life was in danger (11:2b-3; 1 Kgs 19:10). Having mentioned this incident, Paul seemed to confess that he was left alone. There were too few people who had been on his side among the Romans. Having made this statement, Paul intended to make Jewish members alert. The premise was laid here that God was with Paul just as he had been with Elijah the prophet. Having identified himself from a prophetic perspective, Paul tried to convey an instruction that God wanted to take care of the Romans through him.

Then, God's answer was introduced. It is said that God reserved for himself seven thousand people who had not bowed the knee to Baal (11:4). Having quoted what God said to Elijah on Mount Horeb (1 Kgs 19:18), Paul emphasized God's sovereign will. This shows that God worked, contrary to Elijah's thoughts. Moreover, the use of "seven thousand" suggests the fulfilled number of the people of God. With this kind of description, Paul left a task for Jewish members to be one of those reserved by God. Having mentioned the incident of Elijah, Paul hoped that Jewish members would conform to God's will rather than Jewish tradition. However, it is unclear whether they accepted his request.

Paul presented the interpretation of Elijah's incident. It is said, "So too, at the present time there is a remnant chosen by grace" (11:5). Paul wanted to say that in his time, as in the time of Elijah, there were remnants chosen by the grace of God. Having mentioned the remnant who were chosen by grace, Paul said that even among Jews according to their lineage, there were some who would attain salvation. It is important here to mention that God chose by grace. In Rom(A), Paul emphasized that people must have faith in order to belong to the grace of becoming heirs of God (4:16; 5:2). And then it is said in Rom(B) that one must have faith in order to be freely justified by God's grace. The redemption in Jesus has been pointed out as the grace of God (3:24). While the word "grace" was used most often in Rom(C), it refers to reigning as king and enjoying eternal life (5:17, 21). However, in Rom(D), Paul described God's grace in relation to the issue of election. With this, Paul taught that being chosen as one left behind by God is possible only through the grace of God. This is an argument that Jewish members should also fall into the category of being chosen by the grace of God.

The nature of grace is described. This appears in the statement that if it is by grace, it is not by works; otherwise, grace is not grace (11:6). Paul presented becoming one of God's remnants as grace. The grace was put in contrast with works. In Rom(A), Paul made a contrast between grace and wages (4:4) and described it as enjoying peace with God on account of righteousness by faith (5:1–2). Then, in Rom(B), grace was in parallel with the redemption in Christ Jesus (3:24). Moreover, in Rom(C), the grace of God and Jesus Christ was presented as what makes people righteous (5:16) and stood in opposition to sin and the Law (6:1, 14–15).

Finally, in Rom(D), being chosen by God was referred to as grace. All of them are connected to being saved people of God. With this kind of description, Paul taught that even Jewish members had become the people of God by grace, not by their works of the Law. This means that the path to salvation is open to both Jews and gentiles.

Paul continued to evaluate Jews. This is found in the statement that Israel did not get what they sought, but the elect did, and the rest became foolish (11:7). Paul pointed out that while Jews thought they had been the people of God, they had not been in reality. Paul would like to say that there were some people who had been elected among Jews but not many as they expected. This means that if they should have thought to become the people of God by lineage, it looks foolish. Having written in this way, Paul implicitly presented the logic that among the wise gentiles, there were those who became the people of God while being thankful for the election. As more letters were sent to the Roman church, Paul tried to convey the lesson that the door was widely open to gentiles.

Then, a verse was cited from the Bible to support Paul's argument. It is said that God has given people to this day a spirit of confusion, eyes that cannot see, and ears that cannot hear (11:8). Paul quoted this verse from Isaiah in order to publicize the reality of Jewish members (Isa 29:10). Contrary to the general expectation, God did not allow Jews to recognize him. This is quite different from what was stated in Rom(B): that people did not recognize God's divinity implanted in creation (1:19–23). In Rom(D), Paul quoted the writings of Isaiah and stated that God revealed himself, but people did not accept it (10:20–21). Accordingly, having relied on the quoted verse from Isaiah, Paul changed the statement to say that God did not allow people to recognize himself. It was to portray the stubbornness of the Israelites. In this way, Paul maintained a more critical stance toward Jews than before. Ultimately, this was written to warn them, so that they should also be careful. In this way, in Rom(D), Paul tried to imply that the door was open to gentiles beyond Jews. Jewish members must have been shocked by this.

Various verses were quoted from David. It is said that the Jewish people's table would become a snare, a trap, a stumbling block, and a retribution, that their eyes would be dimmed so that they could not see, and that their backs would always be bent (11:9–10). These verses were quoted in order to describe David's desire for God to avenge his enemies (Ps 69:22–23). It seems that Paul applied these quotations to Jewish members in order to teach that God did not automatically make them his people simply according to their bloodline. This was written to imply that the door was open to gentiles. In Rom(D), Paul continued to subtly strengthen the interest in the mission to gentiles.

Finally, Paul reached to a conclusion. This is found in the description that Jews would not stumble until they stumble, but through their stumble, salvation would come to gentiles, making Israel jealous (11:11). Paul developed paradoxical logic for the salvation of Jews. It was claimed to arouse their jealousy toward gentiles. For this, Paul once again used a rhetorical question to teach this point: "Will they stumble until they stumble?" Of course, the answer to this was "it can't be done." Paul pointed out that although Jews had made mistakes, they had not stumbled to the point of falling. This was a fatal critique against them. At the same time, Paul claimed that God had planned for gentiles to be saved because of Jews, to make them jealous, and to make them truly strive to be saved. The same content was also conveyed through the words of Moses (10:19). This shows Paul's efforts to convince Jewish members of the reason he tried to preach the gospel to gentiles. In this respect, Paul's logic was completely paradoxical. Having judged from this, it appears that Paul had an uneasy relationship with Jewish members at the time he wrote Rom(D).

Paul stated the conclusion more clearly. It is said that Jews' fall would become the abundance of the world, and their failure would become the abundance of gentiles, so they would also become fullness (11:12). Here, Paul emphasized the mission to gentiles with parallelism. Jews' fall and their failure as well as the abundance of the world and that of gentiles run parallel to each other. These parallels convey the legitimacy of Paul's attempt to spread the gospel to gentiles, so that many of them might accept the gospel and become the true people of God. Paul tried to say that such a result would also affect Jews and enable them to fully become the people of God. As a result, it was stated that Jews would actually benefit from gentiles. This was also Paul's way of stimulating Jewish members to participate in the mission to gentiles.

To sum up, Paul emphasized that even among Jews, salvation is achieved only by the grace of God. However, it has been argued that because most Jews were foolish and abandoned God's choice, the privileges passed to the gentiles. Paul's interpretation is that this made the Jews jealous and let them return to God. In relation to this, Jewish members would have been resistant to his instruction that downgraded their religious position.

Gentiles (11:13–24)

Paul mentioned God's plan for gentiles. To explain this, the analogy of a wild olive tree grafted onto a true olive tree was presented. At the same time, Paul taught the gentiles to be humble before God. With this, Paul revealed the reason that he was engaged in the mission to gentiles.

It was declared that the door had been open to gentiles. This appears in the description that Paul began to speak to gentiles and declared his apostolic office with pride (11:13). Paul told for the first time to the Romans that he had been an apostle for gentiles. His identity as an apostle for them was given when he had received the revelation about the Son of God as passed down to the Galatians (Gal 1:16). References to the apostleship used to appear at the time of being challenged by some gentiles sponsored by the apostles of the Jerusalem church, as implied in 1 Corinthians, 2 Corinthians, and Galatians (1 Cor 1:1; 9:1; 2 Cor 1:1; Gal 1:1). On the other hand, the title "apostle" was rarely used or emphasized toward the Thessalonians and Philippians who had accepted the gospel and supported Paul (cf. 1 Thess 2:7; Phil 4:15). Accordingly, in Rom(D), having emphasized the apostleship once again, Paul further insisted the importance of mission to gentiles in spite of challenges from Jewish members against it. At the same time, he also implied that he did not receive support from Jewish members. They didn't seem to be very open to him.

Paul described what he had to do as an apostle for gentiles. This is found in the wish to make his own fellow Jews jealous and hope that some of them would be saved (11:14). Paul mentioned this kind of goal from the beginning of Rom(D). This reflects the fact that Jewish members did not yet show a favorable stance toward Paul. Nevertheless, Paul showed love for the fellow Jews. This shows that Paul maintained the desire for their salvation. However, it is not clear whether Jewish members accepted this theological interpretation of Paul.

Paul's endless love and concern for Jews was expressed. This appears in the statement that if the rejection of Jews was the reconciliation of the world, their acceptance would be life from the dead (11:15). Paul expressed how difficult it was for Jews to accept the gospel. If the gospel was not preached to Jews but only to gentiles, there would be no fighting and could be peace in the world. This may be right from a human perspective; however, from a spiritual perspective, it was not right because Jews were also those God had wanted to save. Therefore, Paul insisted that Jews' acceptance of the gospel and achievement of salvation was tantamount to life from the dead. This is given as a result of following the core of the gospel, which is based on the death and resurrection of Christ. Having argued in this way, Paul tried to avoid the misunderstanding that he had only done his best for the mission to gentiles and revealed that he had had a great interest in the salvation of his fellow Jews too.

Paul offered an analogy to support his claim. This is found in the description that since the flour of the first ripe grain offered in sacrifice is holy, so are the loaves of bread; and since the roots are holy, so are the branches (11:16). Paul approached the first analogy from a priestly perspective. Here, the metaphor of loaves of bread and that of the branch are paralleled around the word "holy." Paul emphasized the essence through the parallelism between flour and roots, and loaves of bread and branches. As the flour and the loaves of bread made from the first ripe grain are no different from each other, so the roots and the branches are no different from each other. Paul compared the flour and roots to Jews, while he linked the loaves of bread and branches to gentiles. In this way, Paul not only presented the importance of Jews but also emphasized the inclusion of gentiles into the people of God. This is a teaching that God will give up on neither Jews nor gentiles. In this way, Paul argued that Jews had to take responsibility for the mission to gentiles. However, it is not clear how many Jewish members responded to his insistence.

Then, a metaphor of the olive tree followed the analogy of root and branches. This is described in the analogy that several branches of the true olive tree were broken off and those of the wild olive tree were grafted in their place, receiving the sap of the roots to grow (11:17). Paul adopted a metaphor for what he wanted to convey by giving an example of horticultural techniques used at the time. This is about the combination of things that are similar but different. Paul pointed out that the wild olive tree branches grow by receiving the sap of the true olive tree rising from the roots. This satisfies the analogy that since the roots are holy, so are the branches. Although the identity of the object compared to the true and wild olive trees has not yet been revealed, readers can roughly learn about it from the context. While the roots of the true olive tree would refer to Jews who had the identity of God's people, the branches of the wild olive tree would refer to gentiles. The branches of the wild olive tree are usually grafted onto the true olive trees in order to bear more fruits. It is possible that Paul used the metaphor with the expectation that more gentiles would be included into the people of God than Jews. As shown before, Paul revealed the intention to bear fruit through the gospel from Jews to gentiles. However, it was difficult for Jewish members, who had identified themselves as the people of God, to accept this metaphor because they themselves did not open their minds to gentiles.

Paul conveyed a warning expressed in metaphor. This is found in the saying that the branches of the wild olive tree grafted in should not boast over those of the true olive tree (11:18). Paul taught that gentiles, who were compared to the grafted branches of the wild olive tree, had to know their original position and how to maintain it. This is a teaching that gentiles who received the gospel should not boast in front of Jews who had been originally elected as the people of God. Gentiles were entering the position of God's people originally occupied by Jews. This is in line with what Paul taught in Rom(A): that those of gentile churches had to repay materially for the spiritual grace they received from the Jerusalem church (15:27). In this way, while Paul preached about the relationship between Jews and gentiles, he could not hide his concern for gentiles. This may have sounded illogical because it required Jewish members to give up their privileges.

A specific warning was issued to gentiles. This appears in the saying that the branches of the true olive tree were broken off so that the branches of the wild olive tree could be grafted in (11:19). The issue here is that the grafted branches of the wild olive tree revealed their opinion. In other words, it is not the view of God who elected gentiles but the view of the gentiles who were compared to the grafted branches of the wild olive tree. Paul presented here two types of olive trees that share the same essence but have different characteristics. In the case of the earthenware vessel metaphor, a clear distinction was made between those of mercy and those of wrath. However, in the case of the olive tree, there was a distinction between the two, but there was room for mutual influence. Accordingly, Paul delivered an instruction that the gentiles had to realize for themselves that they could also be incorporated into the position of God's people occupied by the Jews. This is wrong as it shows arrogance and does not properly understand the essence. Paul used metaphors to warn gentiles not to be arrogant because God loved them. Paul did not want gentiles to fall away from the category of God's people in order to complete the mission entrusted to him.

Paul continued to issue the warning to gentiles. This is revealed in the statement that while Jews compared to the true olive trees had been broken off, gentiles compared to the branches of the wild olive tree were grafted in. It is because the former had not believed but the latter stood in faith; thus, gentiles should not have a high mind but rather be afraid of God's will (11:20). While Paul acknowledged the original plan of God for Jews, he also did his altered plan for gentiles. Since this was done according to the sovereign will of God, Paul emphasized that gentiles should be humble and not arrogant even before Jews. Having emphasized this attitude, Paul tried to encourage gentiles to remain in the God's plan of salvation for a long time. Since he had been entrusted with the mission to gentiles, he suggested ways to keep them as the people of God for as long as possible. However, this claim must have sounded quite unpleasant to Jewish believers.

The reasons that gentiles should be humble were listed one after another. This is because God did not spare the natural branches, so he could not spare the grafted ones (11:21). Paul warned that because God did not spare Jews, he may not spare gentiles, either. It is to be noted that Paul used the plural form for the original branches and the singular form for the grafted branch. It seems that Paul still wanted to show that the number of Jews, who were originally the people of God, was greater than the number of gentiles who were called to be his people. Otherwise, it seems that they wanted to show that only a small number of people accepted the gospel because the gentile mission was in its early stages at the time. At any way, the salvation of gentiles was due to God's special grace compared to that of Jews. With this, Paul showed considerable interest in gentiles while writing Rom(D).

Paul presented the character of God and warned about the identity of God's people. This appears in the declaration that while God is stern to those who fall and kind to those who rely on him, so the Romans should not become a person who is cut off (11:22). Paul highlighted the fact that God responds according to the personality of the object. This is in line with Rom(C) in that those who love God are defined as those called according to his purpose (8:28). This provided a reason for both Jews and gentiles diligently to rely on God's kindness. As Paul induced the Romans to make a decision with dichotomous descriptions in Rom(C), this tendency also appeared in connection with God's response in Rom(D). However, Jewish members would have been repulsed by Paul's attitude of forcing a choice on them.

Another advice for gentiles appeared. This is revealed in the statement that gentiles will also be grafted in if they do not remain in faith because God has the power to graft in (11:23). Paul gave a warning message to gentiles. In other words, the logic is that what happened to Jews could also happen to gentiles. This logic appeared for the first time in Rom(D). This is confirmed by the fact that the expression "unless you remain in disbelief" reveals a considerably relaxed stance toward them. Paul encouraged gentile members to have a clear identity as the people of God. However, the expression that one must actively believe to be grafted is not used. This shows that no coercive attitude was taken against them. It seems that Paul did not want to provoke Jewish members by not describing God's excessive favor toward gentiles.

Paul gave a final warning to the gentile members of the Roman church. It is said, "If you were cut out of an olive tree that is wild by nature, and contrary to nature were grafted into a cultivated olive tree, how much more readily will these, the natural branches, be grafted into their own olive tree!" (11:24). Having written this metaphor, Paul advised gentiles not to be arrogant even in front of Jews. It is because when gentiles become arrogant, they would be cut off to be thrown away and the original olive tree branches would be grafted in. Accordingly, gentiles had to always live humbly before God and Jews. Paul wrote these words because he did not want to offend Jewish members while empowering the gentile members. Rather, he expected their help so that he could continue to carry out the mission to gentiles.

In summary, Paul compared gentiles to branches of a wild olive tree that had been grafted in. Although they became the people of God by his grace, they were encouraged to be humble before God and Jews. Otherwise, Paul argued, eschatological judgment would come upon them as well. Nevertheless, Jewish members could not possibly have accepted Paul's teaching that they had been replaced by gentile members.

The Mystery of God (11:25–36)

Paul finally made a summary regarding the relationship between Jews and gentiles. This is about God's extraordinary plan of salvation for them. Paul declared that the salvation of the Jews would be limited until the number of gentiles was fulfilled, which he introduced as the mystery of God.

The mystery of God was presented to the Romans seeking wisdom. It is said, "Israel has experienced a hardening in part until the full number of Gentiles has come in" (11:25). Having defined the Romans as wise people, Paul claimed that he did not want them to be ignorant of the mystery of God. The word "mystery" along with the title "minister of Christ" was used by Paul to the Corinthians (1 Cor 4:1). It is, however, noteworthy in Rom(D) that the word "mystery" was used in association with the full number of gentiles, that is, becoming the people of God. Having written the extraordinary plan of God, Paul revealed a preferential stance toward gentiles. This is because Jewish members kept casting doubts on Paul, while gentile members accepted him with favorable stance. In addition, having made this kind of claim, Paul was able to further strengthen the reason that he had been involved in the mission to gentiles.

The salvation of Jews was dealt with. This is revealed in the statement that all Israel will be saved (11:26a). Paul was confident that Israel would be saved after the number of gentiles would be full. Their salvation was a topic that could not help but be addressed by Paul, who was a diaspora Jew. Whereas the salvation of Jews is dealt with in Rom(D), the salvation of gentiles is presupposed. While mentioning the salvation of Jews, Paul tried to carry out the mission to gentiles without losing favor with the Romans. In any case, it remained unclear how much Jewish members would trust Paul, who presented this plan as a mystery of God.

Paul cited two verses from the Bible to prove the salvation of Jews. First, it is said, "The deliverer will come from Zion; he will turn godlessness away from Jacob" (11:26b). Paul quoted this verse from Isaiah (Isa 59:20). It seems to have been written when Jews returned from captivity in Babylon and prayed for the speedy recovery of Israel. Paul seemed to have quoted this verse while thinking of Jesus Christ, who came to save Jews. In addition, Paul also quoted another verse that says, "And this is my covenant with them when I take away their sins" (11:27). This was also quoted from Isaiah (Isa 27:9). The covenant here seems to be that all Israel would be saved. Having cited these verses, Paul expressed the belief that God would one day save Jews. This reflects the efforts that Paul tried to gain favor with Jewish members. They probably agreed to some extent with Paul's theology.

In addition, the position of Jews was described in relationship with gentiles. This is found in the description that according to the gospel, Jews were enemies because of gentiles, but according to election, they were loved because of their ancestors (11:28). Paul revealed the preference for Jews and once again taught gentiles to be careful and humble before God. Jews were again declared to be the chosen people of God because of their ancestry, which was Paul's basic thought about them. As a Jew, it was natural that Paul also believed in this faith. This shows that Paul tried not to lose the friendship with the Jewish and the gentile members of the Roman church at the time of writing Rom(D).

Paul wanted to instill confidence in the Romans about God's plan as he had interpreted it. It is stated that there is no regret for God's gifts and calling (11:29). Paul used the word "gifts" in the plural form, meaning something spiritual given by God. Moreover, having put gifts in parallel to calling, Paul identified God's sovereign calling as gifts. Having called his people by giving gifts, God had set up the plan for gentiles. Having emphasized this kind of character, Paul wanted that the Romans would trust him in the mission to gentiles to be complete.

Once again, God's mercy toward gentiles was mentioned. This appears in the statement that gentiles had previously disobeyed God, but now they have received mercy because of Jews' disobedience (11:30). Paul argued that on account of Jews' disobedience, gentiles had been given the opportunity to become the people of God. This is in contrast with the previous statement that Jews were loved and chosen by God because of their ancestors. At any rate, having used two pairs of contrasts, Paul insisted that God began to show mercy to gentiles because of the disobedience of Israel, that is, Jews. This reveals the intention to make gentile members spiritually humble and not arrogant. Perhaps they took a stance of caution themselves. However, these teachings would have been perceived as humiliating by Jewish members.

At the same time, Paul did not forget God's love for Jews. This is found in the statement that Jews had also become disobedient in order that they also receive mercy as a result of God's mercy to gentiles (11:31). This kind of description reminds readers of Paul's hope written in the previous declaration that God might somehow arouse his own people, Jews, to envy on account of gentiles and save some of them (11:14). The difference is that Paul here described God's mercy toward Jews more than that expressed in the previous statement. This tone began when Moses' words were quoted earlier (10:19). At any rate, Paul did not give up the hope on Jews. Although he was primarily interested in the mission to gentiles, he also had an ultimate love for Jews. In this respect, this text can be said to be a conclusion about two groups, gentiles and Jews.

Now the paradox of God was introduced. This is revealed in the statement that God wanted to show mercy to all people by imprisoning them in disobedience (11:32). Paul explained that God caused all people, Jews and gentiles alike, to disobey without exception, and then said that God ultimately wanted to show mercy to them. This is reminiscent of what Paul said in Rom(B) that there is no one righteous except Jesus Christ as the righteousness of God (3:10–24). This was something God had planned. Having argued in this way, Paul tried to show that neither Jews nor gentiles can be saved without God's mercy. The paradoxical description could be a way to introduce the mystery of God.

Paul finally marveled at the mystery of God. This appears in three sets of expressions (11:33). First, the riches of God's wisdom and knowledge are deep; second, his judgments are unfathomable; and third, his ways are unsearchable. Whereas Paul once referred to the mystery of God in the earlier text (11:25), it is identified here as the riches of his wisdom and knowledge, judgment, and ways. Of course, this means that God did not give up on Jews by waiting until the number of gentiles would be filled due to disobedience of Jews. Having argued in this way, Paul strongly encouraged the Romans to rely on the mystery of God. Accordingly, Paul was able to argue that they should receive the teachings he preached. The Romans had to choose their religious position wisely.

Paul expressed his admiration for God. This is revealed in the rhetorical questions (11:34–35). First, who knew the heart of the Lord?; second, who was his counselor?; and third, who would give to the Lord first and receive a reward? Paul revealed the admiration for the mystery of God that not everyone can know. God is the one who moves according to his own will, the one who carries out his plans, and the one who gives what he has. This may have been Paul's response to the gentiles who showed a rather favorable attitude toward him. This was also a call to trust the teachings delivered by Paul himself. Accordingly, Paul encouraged both Jewish and gentile members remain within God's plan of salvation.

Finally, glory to God was asked for. This is revealed in the statement that all things come from the Lord and through him return to the Lord, so to him shall be the glory forever and ever (11:35). Paul presented God as the source and purpose of all creation. This shows a thoroughly God-centered theology. Paul had already written to the Corinthians that all things come from God and people exist for him (1 Cor 8:6). This was also a lesson to the Corinthians, who were gentiles, against the backdrop of Greek tradition of Monad from a philosophical perspective. On the other hand, in Rom(D), Paul was able to continue to describe God as the creator from a Jewish point of view to the Romans. This is based on the premise that everything will go according to God's plan. Paul ultimately declared that everything exists to bring glory to God. This made conclusion to the section of God's mystery by declaring that to God will be glory forever and ever.

In summary, as Paul presented the mystery of God, he emphasized that both Jews and gentiles should accept what he had preached. Having defined the salvation of Jews after the fulfilled number of gentiles as the mystery of God, it reaches the theological peak in Rom(D). It is, however, questionable how persuasive the content that Paul presented as the mystery of God was to the Jewish members of the Roman church.

Offering to God (12:1–2)

Paul first mentioned spiritual life to the Romans. This means that they should perform spiritual worship by offering their bodies as holy living sacrifices. Paul continued to write from a priestly perspective on the life of the Romans.

This part follows the previous one in various ways. First, the conjunction "therefore" was used in order to show their connection (12:1a). Second, having used the second person plural "you," Paul showed that this part is a follow-up to the previous one (11:28, 30–31). Third, the phrase "all of God's mercy" is reminiscent of the "compassion" mentioned earlier (11:30–32). In any case, Paul showed a softened attitude by expressing that he had encouraged the Romans with all of God's mercy. This reflects the fact that Paul approached them with caution. Having shown this kind of approach, Paul wanted to win the hearts of the Romans.

Paul advised the Romans from a priestly perspective. This appears in the statement that they had to offer their bodies as living sacrifices, holy and pleasing to God, because this was spiritual worship they had to offer (12:1b). Paul presented his role as if he were acting as a priest. The priestly perspective appeared in the mention of first-ripe grain flour offered for sacrifice (11:16). A holy "living sacrifice" reminds readers of the worship mentioned earlier (9:4). In this way, Paul developed the concept of worship. Accordingly, Paul taught that the Romans should offer spiritual worship beyond that of Jews offered on altar of the temple in Jerusalem. This also shows that Paul used an analogy, which was used to convey things that were difficult to explain. Paul embraced the Romans with the instruction from a priestly perspective.

Then the exhortation follows. It is said, "Do not conform any longer to the pattern of this world, but be transformed by the renewing of your mind. Then you will be able to test and approve what God's will is–his good, pleasing and perfect will" (12:2). The term "generation," which was translated into "this world" here, is mentioned several times in the Pauline epistles, usually in the context against God (Phil 2:15; 1 Cor 1:20; 2:8; Gal 1:4). Accordingly, even in Rom(D), "this generation" is presented as someone who should not be imitated. The Romans were advised to be transformed by renewing their "mind," which had been already used in a negative context in Rom(B) (1:28). And then, in Rom(C), Paul mentioned the heart in contrast to the flesh (7:23, 25). Paul then mentioned the mind of God in Rom(D) in order to encourage the Romans to be transformed by renewing their hearts (11:34). In light of this, being transformed by renewing one's mind means that the Romans should turn away from the life they had lived according to the flesh. That is why the Romans should pursue God's good, pleasing, and perfect will. God's will seems to mean that both Jews and gentiles will become his people. Accordingly, it can be said that the Romans were encouraged to live for the completion of God's will to make all his people. This was a model lesson that could have been accepted without much difficulty by Jewish members while pursuing their own religious values.

In summary, Paul called for devotion from the Romans. This means a life that dedicates everything to the will of God. Paul suggested from a priestly perspective that they would live according to God's plan. This also shows that in the final part of the main body of Rom(D), Paul delivered the most standard lesson to the Romans who pursued religious values.

5. THE ETHICS OF SAINTS (13:11–14)

Paul advised the Romans to prepare for the time of salvation. It was presented in a combative atmosphere from an eschatological perspective. Having compared the salvation to putting on clothes by the Lord Jesus Christ, Paul continued the theme of salvation in Rom(D). This part is quite short because Paul did not have much to write about their ethics due to the weakened relationship with the Romans at the time of writing Rom(D).

The time of salvation was mentioned. This is written assuming that the Romans know the time (13:11a). Paul already expressed his earnest desire for the salvation of Israel (9:27; 10:1; 11:14, 26) and also explained that salvation for gentiles was on the way in Rom(D) (11:11). He also said of how to receive salvation (10:9–10, 13). In this way, Paul frequently dealt with the issue of salvation to both Jewish and the gentile members. Accordingly, he seemed to be able to say here that they had known about the time of salvation. This refers to the time when they become the people of God. These teachings were something the Romans could accept without difficulty because this was already well known even within Judaism.

Paul expressed the time of salvation metaphorically. This appears in the expression that it was already time to wake up from sleep (13:11b). Paul described the time of salvation using short metaphor. It seems to be a method that has been widely known at the time. Paul once told the Thessalonians to know that the day of the Lord would come like a thief (1 Thess 5:2). However, in Rom(D), Paul changed a negative description related to a thief to a general description related to waking up. This means that the time of eschatological judgment and salvation was closer than before. According to Paul, the Romans had to take the attitude of preparing for salvation. The expression of "It is time to wake up from sleep" shows that the Romans were not yet awaken from spiritual sleep. Paul especially had to sound the alarm to Jewish members because they did not want to accept the gospel he had preached.

The time of salvation was mentioned in more detail. This is found in the statement that salvation was closer than when the Romans had first believed (13:11c). Paul did not specifically mention when they first came to faith. However, this could mean that their spiritual situation was getting worse than when the Roman church had been first established by Priscilla and Aquila. Since they were connected to the Corinthian church, they would have known about the time of salvation that Paul preached to the Corinthians. Paul told them that the end times were shortened (1 Cor 7:29). Accordingly, the couple returned to Rome, established a church, and conveyed this message to the Romans. Accordingly, Paul had to use an impending eschatological perspective to raise awareness among the Romans.

A solemn expression was used for the time of salvation. This appears as an expression to put off the works of darkness and put on the armor of light, as the night is deep and the day is near (13:12). First of all, the contrast between night and day appears centered around the verb "come closer." This developed into the contrast between the work of darkness and the armor of light. This is to be interpreted in relation to the question of the Romans regarding salvation. Accordingly, the work of night and darkness signifies a state of not being saved, while the armor of day and light refers to a state of being saved. Paul expressed a quite combative mood with the phrase "armor of light." This reminds readers of wearing the "helmet of hope" told to the Thessalonians in relation to salvation with the contrast between day and night (1 Thess 5:7–8). Afterwards, the phrase "weapons of righteousness" was used in Rom(C) (6:13). Accordingly, Paul attempted a militant expression in Rom(D), which seems to reflect the situation that the spiritual conflict with the Romans was quite heightened at the time of its writing.

The conditions for salvation were described. They are presented as provisions that one must walk modestly as one walks during the day, not be debauched or drunken, not lewd or lascivious, and not quarrelsome or jealous (13:13). Having suggested these provisions, Paul made a contrast between what would be done during the day and what should not be done at night. Debauchery, drunkenness, lewdness, lasciviousness, quarreling, and jealousy are the actions that belong to the night, that is, darkness. According to Paul, people who do these things cannot be saved. On the other hand, those who walk neatly as they do during the day are those who will be saved because they live uprightly in an ethical sense. Of course, they are actions that both the Law and conscience teach. Having suggested this kind of instruction, Paul taught that in addition to believing in God, living ethically upright lives is required for salvation.

Paul made a final conclusion. It is said that the Romans should clothe themselves with the Lord Jesus Christ and not make provisions for the flesh in its lust (13:14). Paul used an analogy between Christ Jesus and clothes. It was originally used in connection with baptism in Galatians (Gal 3:27). However, when Paul dealt with baptism in Rom(C), he did not mention the matter of being clothed. Rather, the expression of being clothed with Christ Jesus was used in relation to salvation in Rom(D). It would mean putting on the armor of light and walking neatly as in the day. This is in contrast to pursuing the work of the flesh for the sake of lust. Paul used the word "lust" in Rom(B) (1:24) and Rom(C) (7:7–8). Subsequently, interest in lust increased as it was used in Rom(D), meaning the unchanging and undying nature of human being. Paul defined it as the work of the flesh in contrast with the path leading to salvation. This description reveals that, towards the end of Rom(D), Paul once again seriously discussed the ethical life centered on salvation.

In summary, Paul described the ethical life of saints at the end of Rom(D). This also depicts the spiritual state of the Romans by describing the militant aspects from an eschatological perspective. Moreover, a life centered on salvation was presented. Whether Jews or gentiles, the Romans would not have opposed these teachings.

6. CLOSING PART (15:14-21; 16:25-27)

Paul finished writing Rom(D). Here, it is emphasized that he was a worker for gentiles, and the revelation of the gospel is highlighted. Until the end, Paul had the self-consciousness that he was an apostle for gentiles. At the same time, an ode to glory appears as the end of the letter.

Minister for Gentiles (15:14-21)

Paul described his role in his own way. Having emphasized the fact that he had worked hard as an apostle for gentiles, Paul expressed the intention to continue working on the mission to gentiles. This revealed his zeal to fulfill the mission to gentiles entrusted by God.

Paul first expressed the trust in the Romans. This is shown in the expression of them as being full of goodness, full of all knowledge, and able to admonish one another (15:14). Paul presented three reasons for his trust in them. The word "goodness" was used for edification of others, and "knowledge" was adopted for the expression of trust. The word "knowledge" was already used in connection with the Law in Rom(B) (2:20) and then linked to the mystery of God in Rom(D) (10:2; 11:33). Then, the expression of being filled with all knowledge means the acknowledgement of the mystery of God. Finally, encouraging one another refers to consideration of their conditions. In this way, Paul showed the trust in the Romans and tried to improve the relationship with them. This description of trust in the Romans would have gladdened their hearts.

The reason for writing Rom(D) was explained. This appears in the expression that Paul wrote more boldly to the Romans in order to remind them again of the grace God given to him (15:15). Paul emphasized that he wrote boldly. This was an attempt to draw the attention of the Romans once again. Paul once presented an important information at the end of Galatians, saying that he wrote it himself (Gal 6:11). Of course, the cases in Galatians and Rom(D) are different; however, there is something in common in that Paul tried to make known what he wanted to emphasize. Here, Paul emphasized the fact that God's grace was given to him. This informed the Romans that he had written in Rom(D) with authority and demanded them to accept the contents written in it.

Paul then recorded the purpose for which grace had been given to him. This is found in the statement that he had to become a minister of Christ Jesus for gentiles and to serve as a priest of the gospel of God, and that his offering of gentiles as a sacrifice was to make them sanctified and acceptable in the holy spirit (15:16). Here again the priestly perspective appears. Paul's work for the gentiles appears several times in Rom(D). This is the story that God had him preach the gospel to gentiles until Jews would become jealous and work until their number would be reached. And the fact that Paul intended to offer up gentiles as a sacrifice as a priest of the gospel of God reminds readers of his previous recommendation to offer them up as a holy living sacrifice (12:1–2). In this way, Paul strongly taught the Romans to offer themselves to God as worthy sacrifices. This may have been his final struggle to ask them to live as the people of God. However, it is not clear whether the Romans, especially those of Jewish origin, responded positively to his request.

Paul then boasted about his ministry. It is because he did the work of God in Christ Jesus (15:17). Paul was filled with pride in working for God because of Christ Jesus. This statement is quite different from those in the previous letters in which he declared that he would not boast about himself. (1 Cor 1:31; 2 Cor 11:30; Gal 6:14). However, in Rom(D), he was proud of himself on having done God's work in Christ. It is important that Christ Jesus and God were mentioned together here. This is believed to be a measure to reveal one's spiritual authority to the Romans. As a result, Paul did not give up his wish to have them participate in the mission to gentiles.

Nevertheless, Paul did not want to boast. All that he could say was that Christ had worked through him to bring the gentiles to obedience (15:18). Paul once considered himself an apostle for gentiles. This identity appeared for the first time in Galatians (Gal 1:15–16). After turning his back on the apostles of the Jerusalem church due to the debate over the gentile table in Antioch, he defined himself as an apostle for gentiles. The more the gentiles sponsored by the apostles of the Jerusalem church challenged him, the more Paul emphasized the apostleship. In the case of the Roman church, which did not have their support, it seems that Paul increasingly emphasized his role for gentiles as he received doubts and critiques from Jewish members. So it seems that he revealed his apostleship for gentiles publicly in Rom(D). In any case, whenever Paul encountered difficulties related to his apostolate, he would claim that he had received the mission from God for gentiles. In this way, he defended his work to Jewish members and encouraged gentile members to keep the teachings he had preached.

References related to the apostolate continued. This appears in the statement that Paul's mission was accomplished through words and deeds, the power of signs and wonders, and the power of the spirit of God (15:19a). Having emphasized the apostleship, Paul paid attention to the spirit and power (cf. 1 Cor 2:4, etc.). He had no choice but to make claim in this way because he was not actually appointed as an apostle for gentiles by the apostles of the Jerusalem church; however, it did not pose any problem to the Romans because the Roman church had no direct connection with the Jerusalem church. Accordingly, based on the work of God revealed to him, Paul emphasized that he was an apostle for gentiles and demanded the Romans to participate in the mission to gentiles with financial support.

Then, Paul mentioned the area that he had worked. This is manifested in the statement that he preached the gospel of Christ widely from Jerusalem all the way to Illyricum across the region of Macedonia (15:19b). Illyricon was located across the Adriatic Sea from the eastern coast of the Italia Peninsula, where Rome was located. Paul revealed the desire to go to Rome by mentioning Illyricum. Since he was close to Rome, he made an unspoken request to be invited to Rome and help him go further to Spain. In this way, Paul recognized what he had wanted to do for the mission to gentiles entrusted by God and tried to carry it out to the end.

The principle for the mission to gentiles was solid for Paul. This is found in the expression that he tried not to preach the gospel where the name of Christ had been called because he did not want to build on someone else's foundation (15:20). When Paul mentioned Christ and the foundation, they remind readers of the metaphor of building a house on the foundation of Christ as told to the Corinthians (1 Cor 3:10–15). However, when it came to Rom(D), it was written in the direction of not building on the foundation laid by others. This presents the principle of not preaching the gospel in places where others have already preached. The Roman church was established based on the teachings of Jesus from a Jewish perspective that Priscilla and Aquila learned from Paul; however, they did not yet heard of the gospel that he had developed after the challenge of some gentiles sponsored by the apostles of the Jerusalem church. Accordingly, Paul wanted to preach the new contents of the gospel to the

Romans and head to Spain. Having said in this way, Paul hinted that he would not stay in Rome for long period. The only reason he wanted to go there was to benefit them with the gospel and receive financial support in return for the mission even to Spain. This is what Paul said in order to avoid putting too much burden on the Romans. Paul had to clearly state that the closer he got to Rome, the less burden he would place on the Romans.

Paul then cited a verse from the Bible to confirm his intention. It is said that those who have not received the message of the Lord will see, and those who have not heard will understand (15:21). Paul quoted it from Isaiah, revealing the passion to spread the words of God to gentiles (Isa 52:15). The expression that people who have not heard will see and that those who have not heard will realize is shown to be at odds with each other. This means that people will experience things on a new level due to the gospel that Paul will preach further. In this way, Paul strongly requested the Romans to accept him, saying that they would experience a new dimension of religion through the gospel.

In summary, Paul revealed the belief that he was an apostle for gentiles. Accordingly, he expressed the wish to go to Spain via Rome and conveyed to the Romans the desire to spread the gospel. The confidence that the mission had been entrusted by God was emphasized. However, it has been unknown to what extent the Romans would have recognized the authority that Paul claimed.

The Mysterious Gospel (16:25–27)

The ending of Rom(D) presents a different picture from that of the previous three letters. Rather than greetings with a blessing at the end, it ends with an explanation of the gospel and a hymn of glory to God. However, without this, Rom(D) cannot be completed properly.

Paul presented God as the one who had built up the Romans. This is achieved through the gospel of Paul, the proclamation of Jesus Christ, and the revelation of mysteries that have been hidden for ages (16:25). Paul created a parallel between his own gospel and the proclamation of Jesus Christ. In Rom(A) Paul once defined the gospel as the prophecies that God made the prophets proclaim about the Son (1:2). However, here in Rom(D), he made a parallelism between the gospel and proclamation. At the same time, the gospel and proclamation were paralleled with the revelation of a mystery that had been hidden for ages. This heightens the authority of the gospel Paul preached. This was content worthy of being included in Rom(D) regarding the gospel that had been conveyed to the Romans.

Now an explanation appeared for a mystery that has been hidden for ages. This has been revealed through the writings of the prophets, according to the command of the eternal God, so that all nations might believe and obey (16:26). Paul emphasized that God's promise was fulfilled, revealing that the mystery was fulfilled through Jesus Christ. Having given authority to the Bible, he gave meaning to the mission to gentiles. The reason he wanted to go to Rome was to go on a missionary trip to Spain, which was considered the western end of the Roman Empire. With this description, Paul revealed his wish that the Romans would accept his gospel and provide financial support.

Paul finally gave glory to God. This only appears in the expression that to the wise God be the glory through Jesus Christ forever and ever (16:27). Paul said that God was wise enough to be glorified. God's wise nature has already been mentioned once before (11:33). However, here again, such character could be described because God had kept the revelation of mysteries hidden for eternity, then delivered it through prophets and revealed it to Paul. Moreover, the expression "forever and ever" was also previously used in Rom(D) (9:5; 11:36). This strengthened the justification that glory should be given to God. In this respect, Paul showed a narrative centered on God until the end of Rom(D). Although this is not in the form of a blessing unlike the cases of previous three letters, it is considered an appropriate content as the ending of a letter.

To sum up, while defining the gospel, he emphasized that he was a minister for it. At the same time, its mystery was emphasized. This shows that Paul persuaded the Romans to the end to accept the gospel he had preached.

7. CONCLUSION

Paul wrote the fourth letter, Rom(D). While emphasizing the salvation of gentiles, he did not ignore that of Jews. He attributed this to God's election and emphasized a life of obedience to it. Therefore, no one should be arrogant before God; rather, they should be grateful for the grace of salvation. To this end, Paul said that the mystery of God would make Jews jealous until the number of gentiles would be fulfilled. In this way, the salvation of Jews and gentiles was treated as an important topic.

It seems that the situation at the time of writing Rom(D) was reflected in its own way. This refers to a situation in which Paul no longer criticized the Law and sought to embrace all whether they were of Jewish and gentile backgrounds. However, Paul could not hide the fact that he emphasized the election of gentiles by God. Having persuaded the Romans, Paul wanted to receive financial support from them so that he could go to Spain and preach the gospel. In this respect, Paul gave them appropriate teachings for what he had wanted.

Paul seems to have increased the dependence on the Bible in Rom(D). This appears not only in quotations but also in the use of analogies. As a result, it appears that he used them as a means of delivering the mystery of God. To my judgment, the more space was devoted to the Bible, the more powerfully it could appeal to them. However, this attempt seems to have created a discrepancy because it differed from the viewpoint that Jews had understood up to that time.

Paul added a priestly perspective to the prophetic one. This shows that he went beyond the self-consciousness of being a worker sent by God and began to have the belief that he was a person responsible for the spiritual fate of the Romans. This tendency appears for the first time in Rom(A) in which his apostolate was heightened. It was understandable to both Jews and gentiles who were familiar with sacrifices at the time. In this way, Paul further strengthened his spiritual authority.

The exact location where Paul wrote Rom(D) has not been known. It is only assumed that it was written while he was heading from Jerusalem to Rome. This is because, unlike the cases in Rom(A) and Rom(B), Paul did not mention Jerusalem in Rom(D) as he had not done in Rom(C). If so, it seems that Rom(D) was written while getting closer to Rome in early 57 CE.

Epilogue

UNFORTUNATELY, ROMANS HAS BEEN understood as a book for the Christian doctrine. However, along with the basic gospel, Paul included what he wanted to request from the Romans. In this respect, Romans should be a letter aimed at solving practical problems. However, this appears to have been lost when Romans was formed in its current form by the middle of the second century CE, when the New Testament began to be formed. In this respect, it is necessary to understand the compilation of Romans for the correct understanding of what Paul really wanted to say. Otherwise, Romans will be regarded as a book of doctrine.

It seems that Paul sent four letters to the Roman church. This is, of course, an inference based on traces of editing, but it is quite possible. When the four letters are listed according to their chronological order, they show the relationship Paul had with the Romans and reveal how he developed the theological thoughts in response to the changing circumstances. As we trace them, we enter into the historical situation that Paul had with the Roman church in reality.

When examining the four letters mentioned above in their chronological order of being written, the following historical situation is reconstructed. Paul wanted financial support of the Romans for the mission to Spain in return for preaching the gospel to them. However, they seemed to have thought differently. Even though Priscilla and Aquila had learned about the Jewish Jesus from Paul in Corinth or Ephesus and returned to Rome to establish a church, they did not know much about the gospel as appeared in Galatians that Paul wrote during the period of the most severe challenge against the gospel under the sponsorship of the Jerusalem church. Moreover, although many members of the Roman church did not know about Paul directly, they were able to cast doubts about him due to news from other churches. Thus, it seems that they were reluctant to help him after they had read the first letter, Rom(A). Accordingly, Paul sent three more letters to persuade them, but not everything worked out as he had expected. This also reflects the fact that the Romans did not agree with Paul. As a result, the relationship with the Romans seemed to have become increasingly deteriorated.

Each of the four letters compiled into the current form of Romans has its own characteristics. The first letter Rom(A) contains a desire to be welcomed, an intention to preach the gospel, and a wish to receive financial support for the mission to Spain in return. This is a letter whose content is based on faith in God and the gospel summarized in the death and resurrection of Christ. However, the negative view on the role of the Law mentioned here seemed to have provoked the Romans, especially Jewish members. This made them raise questions about it. Accordingly, while writing Rom(B) in response, Paul emphasized God's wrath due to unrighteousness and continued describing the negative view on the Law. At the same time, he began to suggest equal qualification between gentiles and Jews. When Jewish members criticized Paul after reading it, he took a reserved stance on the Law and emphasized the mission to gentiles in Rom(C). However, the Romans seemed to have been reluctant to the mission to gentiles as the debate over the Law subsided. Paul had no choice but to emphasize the need for the salvation of gentiles in Rom(D). This would not have been accepted by them either. This is a reconstructed history that Paul had with the Romans.

It seems that Paul went to Rome. From the description that he was imprisoned by protesters and that a relative of Caesar was mentioned, it can be known that Paul actually did not perform well in Rome. Although it is recorded in Acts that Paul was welcomed upon arrival in Rome, this is most likely a fabricated account by a later author of Luke and Acts. It seems to be the fact that the Romans hesitated to invite Paul to Rome. This reflects the historical fact that he failed to go to Spain, which was his final destination. Once again, it shows that no matter how much it is God's work, Paul did not achieve everything in the way he wanted.

The reasons that Romans was compiled into its current form should be studied. It seems that an editor probably compiled Rom(A), Rom(B), Rom(C), and Rom(D) into the current form of Romans in the New Testament. If the compiling process is revealed, the intention will be clearly identified. However, surprisingly, there are fewer scholars who have seriously studied the compilation of Romans. Although many books have been written about Romans, they are short of revealing how it had been edited and compiled. Accordingly, research on this should be continued in the future. At any rate, the differences and changes found among texts provide a basis for revealing how and why Romans was compiled. The relationship between Paul and the Romans seems to have worsened as he wrote more letters. Then, although Paul attempted to restore it, the results did not seem to be successful. Accordingly, it seems that there arose a need to hide such a relationship during a time when Christianity was flourishing in spite of persecution by the Roman emperors in the early second century CE. Accordingly, the editor seemed to have erased that historical situation by combining the four letters into one.

The Christian faith seems to have undergone transformation two times. The first occurred when the Jesus presented in Q was defined as Christ by Paul. As a result, the historical Jesus was united with the Christ of faith. Then, Jesus Christ took on an important position in Christian faith. The second occurred as Paul's letters were compiled into the present form in the New Testament. I would say that Paul's seven authentic epistles can be divided into sixteen short letters. The seven epistles are Romans, 1 Corinthians, 2 Corinthians, Galatians, 1 Thessalonians, Philippians, and Philemon. Having placed them in the chronological order of being written, they reveal the series of processes that Paul had experienced with the churches in gentile regions. However, since they were compiled into the present form of epistles in the New Testament, the historical circumstances in which each letter was written can no longer be revealed. As a result, the historical letters were transformed into doctrinal epistles. Despite it is difficult to excavate Paul's intentions, I have traced the process of forming Paul's theology in order to restore it. In this way, once a transformation into Jesus Christ was taken place by Paul, but on another occasion, Paul's letters suffered a transformation.

Then, it is necessary to take a look at the reason that Paul's authentic sixteen short letters were compiled into the seven epistles as listed in the New Testament. It is necessary to consider that Acts, which includes information about Paul, was formed in the early second century. Without doubt, there is a big difference in regard to Paul's life as describe in his sixteen letters and Acts. The biggest difference is found in the description of his relationship with the apostles of the Jerusalem church. As reflected well in Galatians, Paul turned his back on them after he had engaged in a theological debate over the gentile table at Antioch. Accordingly, the apostles of the Jerusalem church sent representatives to the gentile churches that Paul had established under the leadership of Barnabas and asked them to reject him. Accordingly, whereas the Corinthian and Galatian churches challenged him under their sponsorship, the Thessalonian and Philippian churches supported him. Likewise, the Jerusalem church had experienced a lot of friction with Paul's gentile churches until it was destroyed by the Roman army in 70 CE. The reconstructed history of Paul would have been in conflict with the beautiful and harmonious picture of churches described in Acts. Whereas the persecution from external Jews was reflected in Acts, the internal conflict and struggle that occurred in the process of forming Christianity was reflected in the authentic epistles of Paul. Accordingly, it is believed that those who collected the New Testament in the early to mid-second century eliminated the images of conflict and struggle by combining Paul's sixteen letters into seven epistles. Four letters sent to the Roman church were also subject to compilation, so that they might not be able to reveal the controversial relationship between Paul and the Romans.

Here I would like to emphasize the importance of reconstructing Paul's life in his relationship with the Romans. The relationship with the Roman church is also clearly revealed when Romans is divided into its original letters. Only then will each verse of Romans reveal its true meaning. If this work is overlooked, the meaning that reflects the compiler's intention will eventually be derived. If so, Paul would be seen as the one having made a contradictory statement himself. Anyone who is aware of these problems will agree with my argument.

I do not believe that my research, based on redactional and compositional criticisms, is always correct. However, attempts to understand and interpret anew will not stop. This is to pursue the true faith of Christianity and is by no means an attempt to destroy it. With this, I would like to present the correct path for Christianity today. It may be difficult to overturn the theological mess created by the church fathers in the second century CE. Having defined the New Testament as the words of God, they have given too much authority to it. Thus, letting go of this is not an easy task. Unfortunately, even today, there are many people who go too far in putting a theological interpretation on the Bible. Nevertheless, I will continue to reveal the truth according to the spirit that God has given me.

Bibliography

Barth, Karl. *The Epistle to the Romans*. Philadelphia: Mulenburg, 1949.
Beker, Johan Christiaan. *Paul and the Apostle: The Triumph of God in Life and Thought*. Philadelphia: Fortress, 1980.
Brown, Raymond Edward. *An Introduction to the New Testament*. New Haven: Yale University Press, 2010.
Bultmann, Rudolf. *The Theology of the New Testament II*. New York: Charles Scribner's Sons, 1951.
Dodd, C. H. *The Epistle of Paul to the Romans*. New York: Ray Long and R. R. Smith, 1932.
Fitzmyer, Joseph A. *Romans: A New Translation with Introduction and Commentary*. The Anchor Bible 33. New York: Doubleday, 1993.
Hurd, John C. Jr. *The Origin of I Corinthians*. London: SPCK, 1965.
Jacobson, Arland D. *The First Gospel*. Sonoma, CA: Polebridge, 1992.
———. "The Literary Unity of Q." *Journal of Biblical Literature* 101 (1982) 365–89.
Kinoshita, J. "Romans–Two Writings Combined." *Novum Testamentum* 7 (1965) 258–77.
Knox, John. "Chapters in a Life of Paul." In *Colloquy on New Testament Studies: A Time for Reappraisal and Fresh Approaches*, edited by Bruce Corley, 339–64. Macon, GA: Mercer University Press, 1983.
Lovejoy, Arthur O. *The Great Chain of Being: A Study of the History of an Idea*. New York: Harper & Row, 1960.
Lüdemann, Gerd. *Paul the Founder of Christianity*. Amherst, NY: Prometheus, 2002, [Kindle].
Ra, Yoseop. *Paul, the Founder of Christianity*. Eugene, OR: Resource, 2021.
———. *Paul's Six Letters for the Corinthians*. Seoul: Pubple, 2018.
———. *Q, the First Writing About Jesus*. Eugene, OR: Wipf and Stock, 2016.
Sanday, W., and A. C. Headlam, *The Epistle to the Romans*. ICC. New York: Charles Scribner's Sons. 1975.
Schmithals, W. *Der Römerbrief als historisches Problem*. Gütersloh: Gütersloh Verlaghaus, 1975.
Thrall, William Flint, and Addison Hibbard. *A Handbook to Literature*. Revised by C. Hugh Holman. New York: Odyssey, 1962.
Wilson, Daniel J. "Lovejoy's *The Great Chain of Being* After Fifty Years." *Journal of the History of Ideas* 48.2 (1987) 187–206

Scriptural Index

Genesis
1:27	88
2:17	87
2:20–24	88
2:24	155
3:1–5	187
3:1–6	87, 120
3:1–19	138
3:15	19, 188
3:22	153
3:22–25	143
3:25	123
15:6	44
17:5	50
18:10	195
25:19–26	196
25:23	196

Exodus
9:16	198
20:14	155
20:17	157
33:19	197

Leviticus
18:5	204
19:18	182
24:20	90

Deuteronomy
5:21	157
10:16	101
30:6	101
30:12–13	205
30:14	206
32:21	210
32:25	119
32:43	185

1 Kings
19:10	212
19:18	213

Psalm
2:7	33, 34
5:9	106
10:7	107
14:1–3	106
18:49	185
32:1–2	45, 112
36:1	107
44:22	60
62;12	93
69:9	183
69:22–23	214
117:1	185
140:3	106

Proverbs
24:12	93
25:21–22	119

Isaiah

1:9	201
10:22–23	200
11:10	185
27:9	221
28:16	202, 207
45:23	68
51:4	103
52:5	99
52:15	231
52:7	209
53:1	209
59:7–8	107
65:1	210
65:2	211

Jeremiah

1:5	32
18:4	199

Hoses

1:10	200
2:23	42

Joel

2:32	210

Habakkuk

2:4	42

Malachi

1:2–3	196

Acts

17:5–9	78
18:1–3	73
18:26	73
19:23	78

Romans

1:1	31, 32, 34, 35, 128, 151
1:1–7	8, 31
1:1–15	10
1:1–17	9, 10, 13, 15, 20, 22
1:1—5:11	10
1:1—8:39	12
1:1—12:2	15, 20
1:2	10, 32, 39, 40, 56, 109, 200, 209, 231
1:2–4	146
1:3	34, 45, 185
1:3–4	33
1:4	15, 53, 101, 146, 170, 173
1:5	33, 37, 38, 62
1:6	34, 35
1:7	9, 34, 35, 54, 64
1:8	36, 37, 129, 187
1:8–15	22, 31, 36
1:8–17	8, 83
1:9	36
1:9–17	4, 5
1:10	36, 179
1:11	37, 63, 71, 111
1:12	37
1:13	37, 38, 69//
1:13–15	18
1:14	38, 71, 171, 181
1:14–16	12
1:15	9, 39
1:16	41, 41, 43, 101, 114, 185, 196
1:16–17	22, 31, 39, 94
1:17	41, 42, 104, 207
1:18	83, 88, 91, 92
1:18–23	4, 83, 104
1:18—2:5	92
1:18—2:11	6, 9, 14, 25, 82, 118, 119, 200
1:18—3:31	5, 9, 10, 11, 13, 16, 18, 152
1:19	84
1:19–20	120
1:19–23	214
1:19–24	174
1:20	84, 90, 138, 211
1:21	85
1:21–22	88
1:22–23	86

SCRIPTURAL INDEX

1:24	87, 88, 89, 149, 155, 157, 227	2:29	101, 102, 122
1:24–32	86, 91, 92	3:1	102
1:25	87, 175	3:1–6	9
1:26	87, 88	3:1–8	102
1:26–27	87	3:2	103, 194
1:28	88, 225	3:3	103
1:29–31	88	3:4	103, 192
1:32	89, 91, 98	3:5	103, 104
2:1	90, 91, 92, 98, 105, 125	3:6	104
2:1–11	90, 95	3:7	122
2:2	91, 108	3:8	104, 105, 120, 129
2:3	92, 98	3:9	105, 108, 110, 114, 137, 138, 185
2:4	92, 112	3:9–20	105
2:5	92	3:10	193
2:6	93	3:10–12	106
2:7–8	93	3:10–24	223
2:7–9	16	3:13	106
2:7–10	120, 122, 162	3:14	107, 117, 193
2:9–10	94, 101, 104, 105, 114, 129, 138, 163, 185, 196, 207	3:15–17	107
		3:18	107
		3:19	107
		3:20	11, 16, 108, 110, 115, 131, 137, 139, 142, 143, 145, 149, 150, 155, 156, 160, 161
2:10	133		
2:11	95		
2:12	96, 106, 108		
2:12–13	96		
2:12—3:20	9, 25, 82, 95	3:20–31	165
2:12—3:31	6	3:21	109, 204
2:13	96, 97	3:21–31	8, 25, 82, 109
2:16	96, 97	3:21–26	109, 170
2:17–20	97, 194	3:22	109, 114
2:17–24	97	3:22–24	140
2:17—3:8	12	3:23	110, 138
2:18	179	3:24	110, 112, 176, 213, 214
2:20	99, 228		
2:21	98	3:25	111, 112, 146, 147
2:21–23	9, 98	3:26	112, 117
2:23	118	3:27	113
2:24	99	3:27–31	113
2:25	99	3:28	12, 14, 113
2:25–26	114	3:29	114
2:25–29	99, 212	3:29–30	185, 196
2:26	100, 105	3:30	114
2:26–27	9	3:31	6, 12, 14, 16, 115, 130, 131
2:27	100, 105		156
2:28	100		
2:28–29	105	4:1	43, 138, 140

Romans (*cont.*)

4:1–8	42
4:1–25	9, 22, 31, 39
4:1—5:11	5, 9, 10, 12, 13, 15, 20
4:2	43, 93, 96
4:3	10, 44, 85, 104, 109, 114
4:4	44, 214
4:5	44
4:6	45
4:6–8	57, 107, 130
4:7–8	45, 89, 92, 106, 108, 112, 137
4:9	46
4:9–12	46, 102, 114
4:10	46
4:10–11	212
4:11	46, 47
4:12	12, 47, 138, 140
4:13	6, 48, 207
4:13–15	48, 115
4:14	48
4:15	6, 10, 11, 49, 57, 81, 83, 96, 108, 119, 139, 142, 155, 156
4:16	50, 54, 213
4:16–22	49
4:17	50, 85
4:17–22	207
4:18	51
4:18–21	195
4:19	65, 177
4:19–21	51
4:20	54
4:20–21	162
4:22	51
4:23	52
4:23–25	52, 138
4:24	53, 67, 110, 170
4:25	53
5:1	54, 119, 134
5:1–2	54, 214
5:1–11	10, 11, 22, 31, 54, 170//
5:2	62, 110, 213
5:3	58
5:3–4	55, 60, 94, 184
5:5	55, 101, 156
5:5–10	60, 177
5:5–11	55, 59
5:6	55, 65, 131, 177
5:6–8	15, 92, 167
5:6–10	146, 193, 208
5:7	56, 74
5:8	56, 64, 67, 89, 106, 110, 118, 131, 141, 144, 179, 182, 184, 205, 207
5:8–9	146
5:8–10	84, 111, 117, 127, 148, 183
5:9	57, 110, 140, 146, 204
5:9–10	111, 165
5:10	15, 57, 58, 67, 119, 145, 147, 169, 206
5:11	58
5:12	137, 138//
5:12–14	19
5:12–21	10
5:12—6:2	137
5:12—6:23	26, 137
5:12—8:30	10, 11, 12, 13, 14, 20
5:13	139
5:14	139
5:14–15	151
5:15	140
5:16	140, 213
5:17	141, 213
5:18	141, 151, 166
5:18–19	152
5:19	142
5:20	7, 142, 143, 157
5:21	143, 145, 213
6:1	143, 213
6:1–11	10
6:2	143, 144
6:3	144
6:3–4	16, 17
6:3–6	16, 172
6:3–11	144, 206
6:4	145

6:5	145, 147	7:18	162
6:6	146	7:19	162, 172, 187
6:7	146	7:20	163
6:8	147	7:21	163
6:8–11	153	7:21–25	163
6:9	147	7:22	166
6:10	148	7:22–23	164
6:11	148	7:23	225
6:12	149, 155, 160	7:24	164, 176
6:12–15	148	7:25	165, 170, 225
6:12–23	10	8:1	166
6:13	149, 171, 227	8:1–11	10
6:14	150	8:1–13	166
6:14–15	213	8:1–30	26, 137, 166
6:15	150	8:2	166
6:16	151	8:3	167
6:16–23	150	8:4	14, 168
6:17–18	151	8:5	168
6:19	152	8:6	168, 172
6:20	152	8:7	169
6:21	152	8:8	169
6:22	153	8:9	169, 179
6:23	153	8:10	170
7:1	154/	8:10–14	172
7:1–6	154	8:11	170
7:1–25	10, 26, 137, 154	8:12	171, 181
7:2	154	8:12–30	10
7:3	155	8:13	171
7:4	155	8:14	172
7:5	7, 155, 158	8:14–23	172
7:6	156, 166, 168	8:15	172
7:7	7, 156, 157	8:16	173
7:7–8	227	8:17	173
7:7–13	156	8:18	174
7:8	157, 158, 205	8:18–30	12
7:8–10	182	8:19:	174
7:8–12	14	8:20	174
7:9	158	8:21	175
7:10	158	8:22	175
7:11	158	8:22–23	177
7:12	11, 12, 159, 160, 204	8:23	175
		8:24	176, 186
7:13	159	8:24–30	176
7:14	160, 204	8:25	177
7:14–20	160	8:26	177
7:15	161	8:27	178, 193
7:16	161	8:28	179, 187, 220
7:17	162	8:29	179, 180, 182

Romans (cont.)

8:29–30	204
8:30	180
8:31	59
8:31–39	11, 12, 13, 15, 20, 22, 31, 54, 58
8:32	59
8:33	59
8:34	12, 59, 60, 97, 164, 178, 205
8:35	60, 116, 182
8:36	60
8:37	61
8:38–39	61
8:39	64, 131, 182
9:1	19, 192
9:1–5	27, 192
9:1—12:2	12, 13, 15, 17, 20
9:2	193
9:3	193, 203
9:4	12, 225
9:4–5	193
9:5	232
9:6	194, 206
9:6–7	195
9:6–13	194
9:6–29	27, 192, 194
9:8	195
9:9	195
9:10–11	196
9:12	196
9:13	196
9:14	197
9:14–18	197
9:15	197
9:16	197
9:17	198
9:18	198
9:19	199
9:19–29	199
9:20	199
9:21	199
9:22–23	199
9:24	200
9:25	200
9:26	200
9:27	225
9:27–28	200
9:28	14
9:29	201
9:30	202
9:30–33	202, 207
9:30–31	202
9:30—10:21	27, 192, 201
9:31	12, 102
9:33	202, 207
10:1	203, 212, 225
10:1–7	203
10:2	203, 228
10:3	203
10:4	7, 12, 204
10:4–5	12
10:5	204
10:6	205
10:6–7	205
10:8	206
10:8–13	206
10:9	206, 208
10:9–10	226
10:10	207
10:11	207
10:12	207, 208
10:13	208, 226
10:14–15	209
10:14–21	208
10:15	209
10:16	209
10:17	210
10:18	210
10:19	210, 215, 223
10:20–21	210
11:1	211
11:1–12	211
11:1—12:2	27, 192, 211
11:2	212
11:2–3	212
11:4	213
11:5	213
11:6	213
11:7	214
11:8	214
11:9–10	215
11:11	215, 225
11:12	215
11:13	216

11:13–24	216	12:14—13:7	13, 14, 15, 16, 20, 25, 82, 115
11:14	216, 222, 225	12:15	117, 120
11:15	216	12:16	117
11:16	217, 220	12:17	13, 118, 120, 162
11:17	217	12:17–21	129
11:18	218	12:18	118, 128, 133
11:19	218	12:19	13, 119
11:20	219	12:19–20	118, 119
11:21	219	12:20	16
11:22	219	12:21	118, 120, 122, 162
11:23	219	13:1	121
11:24	220	13:1–7	13, 14, 121
11:25	15, 19, 220, 223	13:2	121
11:25–36	221	13:3	13, 122
11:26	221, 225	13:3–4	129, 162
11:27	221	13:4	13, 122, 123
11:28	221, 224	13:5	123
11:29	222	13:6	124
11:30	222	13:7	125
11:30–31	224	13:8	181, 204
11:30–32	224	13:8–10	14, 15, 20, 26, 137, 181
11:31	222	13:9	182
11:32	222	13:10	14, 182, 183, 204
11:33	19, 223, 228, 232	13:11	15, 225, 226
11:34	225	13:11–14	14, 15, 16, 21, 27, 190, 225
11:34–35	223	13:12	226
11:35	223	13:13	227
11:36	19, 232	13:14	227
12:1	13, 224	14:1	64, 125, 177, 183
12:1–2	13, 17, 224, 229	14:1–3	130
12:2	225	4:1–4	68, 125
12:3	13, 62, 117, 126	14:1–12	15, 16, 21, 22, 31, 62, 64, 125
12:3–13	13, 14, 15, 22, 31, 62	14:1—15:21	17, 20
12:3—13:14	15, 17, 20	14:2	126
12:3—15:13	13	14:2–3	65, 126
12:4	13	14:3	127, 129
12:4–5	63	14:3–4	90
12:5	65, 125	14:4	65
12:6	13, 63	14:5	66
12:7–8	63	14:5–6	126
12:9	64, 94, 104, 117, 118, 120, 183	14:6	66
12:9–13	64	14:7	66
12:10	14, 68, 127, 181	14:8	15, 67
12:14	116, 118, 193	14:9	15, 67
12:14–21	13, 14, 16, 123		

Romans (*cont.*)

14:10	67, 90, 91
14:11	68
14:12	68
14:13	125
14:13–23	16, 21, 25, 82, 115, 125
14:14	125, 130
14:15	126, 127
14:16	127, 129, 183
14:17	16, 127, 133, 156, 162
14:18	17, 128, 169
14:19	128, 183
14:20	128
14:21	129
14:22	129
14:23	16, 130, 131
15:1	183
15:1–13	16, 17, 20, 26, 137, 181, 182
15:2	183, 187
15:3	183
15:4	184
15:5–6	184
15:5–7	17
15:7	184
15:8–9	17, 184, 212
15:9–12	185, 190, 198, 207, 209
15:13	16, 186
15:14	228
15:14–21	17, 21, 27, 192, 228
15:15	228
15:16	17, 229
15:17	229
15:18	229
15:19	23, 80, 230
15:20	230
15:21	231
15:22	69
15:22–24	69, 133
15:22–29	17, 18, 21, 22, 31, 68
15:22—16:27	17, 20
15:23	69
15:24	69, 125
15:25	70, 116, 132
15:25–26	23
15:25–29	70
15:26	70, 132
15:27	71, 171, 181, 218
15:28	71, 106
15:29	71
15:30	131
15:30–33	18, 21, 25, 82, 132
15:31	116, 132, 133
15:32	133, 179
15:33	133, 188
16:1	23, 72
16:1–2	18, 22, 72
16:1–16	2, 21
16:2	72
16:3	10, 24, 73
16:3–16	18, 19, 22, 31, 73, 104
16:4	74
16:5	74, 75
16:6	74
16:7	75, 76
16:8	75
16:9	75
16:10	75
16:11	76
16:12	76
16:13	76, 149
16:14	76
16:15	77
16:16	77
16:17	186
16:17–20	2, 19, 21, 26, 137, 186
16:18	187
16:19	187
16:20	19, 188
16:21	77
16:21–24	3, 19, 21, 22, 31, 77
16:22	19, 78
16:23	23, 78
16:24	19, 78, 133, 188
16:25	232
16:25–27	19, 21, 27, 192, 228, 231

16:26	19, 232
16:27	19, 232

1 Corinthians

1:1	8, 31, 216
1:2	34, 35
1:3	35
1:7	63
1:11	63
1:12	33, 116, 133, 212
1:14	23, 78
1:18–23	57
1:20	225
1:22–24	38, 41
1:30	111, 176
1:31	229
2:4	230
2:8	225
2:11	178
3:1–3	160, 161, 168, 169
3:10–15	230
3:22–23	61
4:1	221
6:9–10	88
6:11	180
6:14	53, 170
7:7	63
7:17–19	100
7:18	101
7:18–19	46
7:21–22	31
7:22–23	151
7:29	226
7:39	154
8:1	128
8:1–13	126
8:6	121, 203, 223
8:10–11	65
8:11	127
8:11–12	65, 67
8:13	129
9:1	216
9:6	80
10:23	128
10:23—11:1	126
10:30	127
11:24	59
12:3	193, 206
12:4	37, 63
12:7–10	63
12:8–11	37
12:9	63
12:10	63
12:12	63
12:14	63
12:20	63
12:28	63
12:30–31	63
13:2	203
13:8	203
14:5–5	128
14:12	128
14:17	128
14:26	128
15:1–2	41
15:1–5	40, 97, 145
15:3	55, 56, 75, 118
15:3–4	32, 33, 56
15:3–5	32, 40, 41, 53
15:5–7	74, 75
15:12	67, 170
15:20	170
15:21	138
15:21–22	141
15:22	58, 139
15:23	175
15:24	61, 121
15:25	141
15:44	170
15:45	140, 168
15:54	61
15:56	147
16:1	70
16:1–4	132
16:5	78
16:5–7	37
16:7	23, 69
16:8	30, 73
16:10–11	72
16:15	74
16:17	71
16:19	24, 30, 33, 80
16:21	78
16:22	193

2 Corinthians

1:1	8, 31, 34, 216
1:9	170
1:11	63
1:12	123
1:22	36
2:14	61
3:6	102
5:15–19	57
8:1	70
8:2–4	132
8:4	70
8:14	71
9:1	70, 133
9:2	70
9:6	71
11:6	187
11:13	132
11:13–15	133
11:15	188
11:22–23	133, 212
11:30	229
11:31	192
12:14	23, 37
12:19	128
13:1	23
13:2	37

Galatians

1:1	8, 31, 53, 67, 170, 216
1:2	34, 35
1:3	35
1:4	36, 56, 118, 164, 225
1:6–9	40
1:7	32
1:8–9	193
1:10	31, 170
1:15	32
1:15–16	229
1:16	33, 39, 216
1:16–17	40
1:17–18	80
1:18	40
1:20	192
1:21	80
2:1	80
2:1–10	70, 80
2:1–14	132
2:5	91
2:6	95
2:7–8	33, 100
2:10	71, 132
2:11–14	18, 40, 80, 133
2:14	91
2:16	34, 41, 43, 84, 114
2:17	144
2:19	144, 148
2:20	53, 56, 59, 60, 67, 118, 146, 161
2:21	44
3:1–5	210
3:2	113
3:3	169
3:5	42, 113
3:6	34, 42, 44, 51
3:6–18	25, 43
3:6–27	41
3:8	32, 51, 185
3:9	52
3:12	204
3:13	193
3:13–22	195
3:14–29	48
3:16	185, 195
3:16–18	25, 50
3:19	26, 49, 83, 142
3:20	60
3:22	34
3:24	98
3:27	144, 145, 227
3:29	173
4:1–9	48
4:4–5	107, 167
4:4–6	35
4:6	173
4:6–7	151
4:10	66
4:15	78
4:17	133
4:19	179
4:21—5:1	195
4:25	116

4:29	116, 169
5:3	99
5:4	44
5:6	101
5:7	84
5:10	59, 187
5:11	116
5:12	186
5:13	181
5:14	181
5:16	160
5:16–18	168, 171
5:16–21	162
5:16–24	168, 169
5:19–21	88
5:19–23	93
6:8	168
6:11	78, 228
6:14	229

Philippians

1:1	34
1:2	35
1:13	28, 133
2:15	225
3:2	116
3:2–3	133
3:9	34, 41
4:15	216
4:22	28

1 Thessalonians

1:1	34
1:9	86
1:10	49, 57, 67
2:7	8, 216
2:17–18	37
2:18	38, 69
3:5	116, 133
5:2	226
5:10	53
5:11	128
5:17	36
5:23	170
5:25	132

Philemon

1:1	133
1:2	74
1:3	35